C000259912

Restructuring and Workouts

Strategies for Maximising Value, Second Edition

Consulting Editor **Ben Larkin**

Consulting editor
Ben Larkin

Managing director
Sian O'Neill

Editorial services director
Carolyn Boyle

Production manager
Paul Stoneham

Group publishing director
Tony Harriss

Restructuring and Workouts: Strategies for Maximising Value, Second Edition
is published by
Globe Law and Business
Globe Business Publishing Ltd
New Hibernia House
Winchester Walk
London SE1 9AG
United Kingdom
Tel +44 20 7234 0606
Fax +44 20 7234 0808
Web www.globelawandbusiness.com

Printed and bound by CPI Group (UK) Ltd, Croydon, CR0 4YY

ISBN 9781909416147

Restructuring and Workouts: Strategies for Maximising Value, Second Edition
© 2013 Globe Business Publishing Ltd

DISCLAIMER
This publication is intended as a general guide only. The information and opinions which it contains are not intended to be a comprehensive study, nor to provide legal advice, and should not be treated as a substitute for legal advice concerning particular situations. Legal advice should always be sought before taking any action based on the information provided. The publishers bear no responsibility for any errors or omissions contained herein.

Table of contents

Foreword

Ben Larkin
Berwin Leighton Paisner LLP

The first edition of *Restructuring and Workouts: Strategies for Maximising Value* was published just after the collapse of Lehman Brothers. The years following its publication have seen unprecedented turmoil within the financial markets utilised by the western economies. The new skills and applications developed by the restructuring community have been tested and retested many times. Five years on, the UK economy is skirting a 'triple-dip' recession and, despite significant recent rises in the leading share indices, a stable recovery remains elusive. Against such an economic backdrop, it is perhaps unsurprising that there has been demand for a second edition of this book.

I am extremely grateful to the authors of each of the chapters that follow. They are leaders in their field and have taken time from their busy practices to share not just their intellectual knowledge, but also their hands-on experience of dealing with the challenges of this deep recession.

Once again, the chapters aim to provide a broad spectrum of analysis and assistance across the restructuring discipline. Formal insolvencies have remained at lower levels than most commentators would have predicted and, in their place, schemes of arrangement and holdco pre-packaged administrations have become ubiquitous. Both of these UK-driven restructuring tools have proved popular in the lender community. Their certainty of outcome and flexibility have led to them being used within the European Union and beyond. It remains to be seen whether the recent decision in *Rubin v Eurofinance* will lead to the UK restructuring community losing its goodwill among its international colleagues, with a consequent reduction in judicial appetite for accepting jurisdiction on these UK legal exports.

I am delighted that the excellent team of contributors has somehow found the time to update and, in some cases, completely rewrite their chapters, given the current time pressures on their respective practices. I would also like to thank my colleagues Ben Jones and Sophie Taylor for their assistance with this second edition.

I hope that if this book moves into a third edition, I will finally have the opportunity to write a foreword which looks forward to an economic boom and a time when the contributing authors can look forward to leaving the office before midnight at least a couple of times each year. Sadly, at the time of publication of this second edition, my suspicion is that both contributors and readers will be busy in their work for some time to come.

Ben Larkin is head of the restructuring and insolvency department of Berwin Leighton

Paisner LLP. He has specialised in restructuring and insolvency since qualifying as a solicitor in 1993 and has a significant reputation as an expert in workouts related to structured finance and real estate.

Notable recent assignments include advising the administrators of the White Tower conduit, one of the largest UK securitisation administrations to date; the administration of the Readers Digest group of companies; the restructuring of Marken Limited; the restructuring of the Q Hotels group; advising the Robert Dyas group on the sale of the group's parent company; the restructuring of the European Directories group; and the real estate restructuring of Westferry Circus.

Mr Larkin is recognised as a leader in his field in both Chambers *and* Legal 500 *and is a regular speaker at industry events.*

The restructuring and workout environment in Europe

Martin R Gudgeon
Shirish A Joshi
Blackstone

The current restructuring and workout environment in Europe is characterised by diversity and complexity, and has witnessed several transformative trends. While steps have been taken to make workouts easier and to limit value destruction from financial distress – particularly in the form of revisions to local insolvency laws to make them more reorganisation-friendly – several trends in the financing markets mean that financial restructurings in Europe will get progressively more complicated. Specific trends include:

- increased complexity in debt instruments, security packages and corporate capital structures;
- a growing secondary market in loans and other credit instruments;
- the still prevalent after-effects of an abundant expansion of credit over the last credit cycle;
- continued volatility and challenged prospects on a macroeconomic level;
- stresses on the capital markets and banking system; and
- an increasing number and variety of credit investors.

In general, the course and outcome of any restructuring process are principally dependent on factors such as:

- the prevalent insolvency regime, not just in the debtor's jurisdiction of incorporation or where its financial liabilities exist, but also in each and every jurisdiction where the debtor has material business operations;
- size and complexity of a debtor's capital structure;
- number of stakeholders in the company;
- composition of the company's creditor/lender base;
- degree of effectiveness of the contractual rights that creditors have against the company, as negotiated in the credit documentation; and
- macroeconomic volatility, the availability of alternative financing sources and general health of capital markets – in particular, the banking system.

The European markets have seen a transformation in each of those factors that will continue to have a long-lasting impact on the restructuring environment going forward.

1.   Legal environment

Relative to the United States where Chapter 11 of the Bankruptcy Code is more debtor-friendly, European jurisdictions tend to be creditor-focused. Often, control is ceded to creditors or the courts, either directly or through an appointee. Over the past several years many jurisdictions have attempted to move away from regimes that almost seemed to encourage liquidation in any bankruptcy and towards regimes that encourage business rehabilitation (where justified), which can be viewed as an attempt to emulate the Chapter 11 framework that has prevailed in the United States for over two decades. The intent has been to make restructurings and workouts easier to execute by allowing elements such as super-priority financings and classic debt-for-equity swaps.

Germany was one of the first nations in Europe to implement a new insolvency regime, the *Insolvenzordung*, in January 1999. Italy has had the Prodi *bis* Law since 1999 and the Marzano Decree, which was highlighted during the Parmalat restructuring, since December 2003. The United Kingdom reformed its insolvency law with the Enterprise Act that came into effect in September 2004. And France has implemented the *Procedure de sauvegarde*. Incremental revisions to local insolvency and restructuring laws continue to take place, including the German Bondholder Act 2009 and modifications to the Italian regime in 2010 and the German regime in 2012. While many of these new regimes have been used on an *ad hoc* basis, few of them have been tested to the extent that they are sufficiently well understood in terms of how they will cater to the range of specific situations and outcomes typically seen in restructurings.

Further, the approach and mindset of the relevant courts and of the various participants (particularly banks and other creditors) in the workout process have not changed sufficiently to make the European workout process through insolvency more efficient, from both a time and value perspective. The European markets are still going through a learning process, which should take a few more years to complete. Advances continue to be made in terms of recognising restructuring and insolvency procedures prevalent in one EU jurisdiction in another EU jurisdiction, but the lack of a pan-European insolvency protocol is proving detrimental to achieving a European multi-jurisdictional restructuring within a formal coordinated legal framework. The inflexibility and inherent uncertainty have resulted in a majority of European restructurings being accomplished on an out-of-court or consensual basis.

Consensual out-of-court restructurings add several layers of complexity to the restructuring process. In general, they require the unanimity of all stakeholders in order to be successfully implemented. The absence of court-imposed binding decisions or an alternative means to 'cram down' dissenting creditors results in individual stakeholders having disproportionate levels of influence in the negotiating process. The 'holdout' value extracted by out-of-the-money creditors and existing shareholders, which in theory hold investments of no value and should have no voice in the restructuring process, can be material.

The holdout problem is exacerbated when there are holdouts within a specific class of creditors, be they in the money or otherwise, as even creditors with a small holding theoretically have the same power as creditors with much larger holdings. Further, the requirement for unanimity also results in a protracted workout process. A compromise between the flexibility offered by out-of-court restructurings and the legal power of insolvency law has resulted in many transactions being negotiated, structured and agreed on an out-of-court basis, but formally implemented through a court process. While relatively rare in general, such pre-packaged procedures are being seen more often in the United Kingdom, which has a creditor-friendly insolvency regime and a court system that tends to be more commercial in its approach. Additionally, certain insolvency procedures, particularly in the United Kingdom, allow for a limited cram-down of dissenting creditors.

In contrast to the implied extraterritoriality of the US Chapter 11 process, individual jurisdictional analysis is an important part of European restructurings. For instance, a company may:

- be headquartered in one jurisdiction, with the parent company incorporated in another;
- conduct business operations, own key assets and owe financial debt in a further half-dozen jurisdictions; and
- have its primary credit documentation governed by English law.

In that example, while the overall relationship between the company and its creditors and among creditors themselves will be governed by English law, the efficacy and economic rationality of any enforcement of security or court procedure will be a function of each individual jurisdiction where the company operates. For instance, certain jurisdictions allow a lender to take security and derive benefit from guarantees granted by other members of the corporate group, but the quantum of any such guarantee is limited to the amount of direct corporate benefit derived by that particular entity as a result of the provision of credit by the lenders.

Further, the test of insolvency or prospective insolvency differs from jurisdiction to jurisdiction, ranging from solely a mechanical balance-sheet test to a cash-flow test, either in isolation or in conjunction with a balance-sheet test. Further, the cost and time intensity of enforcement action in certain European jurisdictions is quite high, making the threat of enforcement less effective in forcing a borrower or other creditors to negotiate a consensual transaction. Implementing cross-border insolvency may also prove challenging, given local insolvency, corporate and tax laws. The vast differences in insolvency laws across Europe have led to an increase in jurisdiction shopping, where companies in distress relocate either their jurisdiction of incorporation or their 'centre of main interests' to more favourable jurisdictions solely to implement restructurings that may not be possible in their home jurisdictions.

2.   Financial innovation

The European credit markets have seen an unprecedented level of financial innovation over the past few years. Credit markets have been characterised by the increasing complexity of capital structures and new classes of lenders and investors.

2.1 Complexity of corporate, capital and financial structures

Historically, European companies were funded by loans from traditional commercial banks. These loans were generally senior in nature and secured by substantially all of the borrower's assets. Large, well-established corporations had access to the public bond markets. Increasing leveraged buyout activity in Europe has led to innovative financing structures and instruments such as second-lien and mezzanine debt structures and payment-in-kind loans. Second-lien and mezzanine instruments may be structured as either loans or tradable notes, similar to bonds. These are junior instruments that are usually held not by traditional banks, but by alternative investors such as hedge funds, dedicated mezzanine funds, collateralised loan obligation (CLO) and collateralised debt obligation (CDO) funds and other 'special situations' investors. The number of layers in a company's financial structure makes workouts particularly problematic, as it increases the number of stakeholders that need to consent to a restructuring.

For instance, as the term suggests, second lien loans are debt instruments that share the same security package as a first-lien loan, but are second in priority of payment from any value realised through the disposal of collateral. Conflicts often arise between the senior and junior-lien holders with respect to the collateral, especially in the event that the immediate disposal of the collateral is value-maximising for the first-lien claim, but not for all the claims on the security package. The first-lien lenders would be incentivised to dispose of the collateral, to the extent that the value generated at least covers their claim. Certain transactions have featured instruments that have third and fourth liens on the same security package, which makes inter-creditor negotiations significantly more complex.

In addition to traditional corporate restructurings, Europe has seen a number of financial restructurings of non-corporate vehicles, such as securitisations. The growth of very highly structured transactions as a financing tool, such as mortgage-backed securities (both residential and commercial) and 'opco-propco' financing structures and the subsequent closure of the securitisation markets has resulted in a number of such vehicles having to be restructured on a standalone basis. Further, many of these structures were long term in nature and have correspondingly long-term hedging instruments, such as interest rate, inflation and currency swaps. Coupled with the current low interest rate environment, the associated hedging swaps have become a substantial part of the total liabilities of the borrower – which was hitherto not the case. These vehicles are complex and not well understood among the wider investment community because they are set up very differently from traditional corporate entities. In addition, they have original governing documentation that might well have not contemplated a refinancing or restructuring involving existing stakeholders and investors. Accordingly, existing corporate type restructuring constructs have had to be modified or new paradigms created to accommodate these situations.

2.2 Rise of loan trading and alternative investors

Traditionally, corporate loans were syndicated to a limited number of commercial banks that generally held the debt on their balance sheets until final maturity (the 'originate and hold' model). The borrower had a close relationship with the lead bank; and the lead bank – by virtue of its larger holding – was heavily incentivised to monitor the borrower closely. Over the past several years, banks have begun to syndicate the loans that they originate much more widely, even to the extent that the originating bank might not keep any of the loan on its books.

Under the original model, in the event of financial distress, any problem would have been flagged up to the banks at an early juncture, and the borrower would have had to negotiate with only a limited number of banks, which made it easier to execute the workout process and to maintain a relatively high level of confidentiality. During the negotiation process, the banks would act in close coordination with each other and would agree to provide the debtor with the liquidity and financial support necessary as it moved towards completion of an agreed restructuring programme – which usually involved a disciplined sale of individual assets or entire divisions of the debtor or, in certain cases, the sale of the debtor in its entirety. Banks did not want to be active shareholders in the business. During this time the debtor could operate free from the stresses and distractions that would be imposed in any formal insolvency procedure. This senior bank-centric, consensual out-of-court workout process came be known as the 'London approach'.

The London approach to the workout process has been rendered more or less obsolete by the rise of loan trading and the number of non-bank institutions in the credit markets. Traditional lending banks have shown an increasing appetite for selling their exposure in the secondary markets immediately upon the onset of financial distress rather than enduring a protracted workout process. The pro-cyclical nature of the Basel capital adequacy requirements has encouraged this trend as banks have to commit increasing levels of reserve capital against stressed or non-performing loans. The willingness of banks to offload their exposure has resulted in a number of alternative investors taking an active role in the bank debt markets. Loan trading has made the restructuring processes more complex as the number of debt holders has increased and alternative investors can have a more aggressive negotiating stance than traditional banks. The larger number of lenders means that confidentiality is much harder to maintain. As news of financial distress circulates in the wider arena, the debtor faces increasing pressure from suppliers, customers and employees, which delays the operational recovery of the business.

Alternative investors, such as special situations funds, are generally:
- more experienced in distressed situations;
- not burdened by the same regulatory and capital adequacy constraints as traditional banks;
- more willing to become equity holders in the restructured business; and
- more amenable to injecting new capital into the company as part of the restructuring process.

However, dedicated special situations investors may not have the same patience, incentives or return expectations as traditional banks, making negotiations more complicated. Further, bank debt markets are inherently opaque and loan trading adds an additional layer of complexity, in that it makes lender identification much more convoluted. Most existing credit documentation does not allow non-bank parties to become lenders. Consequently, hedge funds and alternative investors invest in loans through 'sub-participation' agreements, where a commercial bank fronts the investment on behalf of the hedge fund, while the underlying hedge fund controls the votes and benefits from the economics of the exposure. Loan trading also has the potential to increase inter-lender conflicts during restructuring negotiations as the incentives for par lenders are not the same as those for secondary market participants. For instance, a given restructuring proposal may be acceptable to a lender that purchased the debt at substantially below par value, but unacceptable to a primary lender that provided the original loan at par.

3.   **Negotiating leverage in the context of macroeconomic and credit market turmoil**

The timing, form and nature of corporate financial restructurings are often a function of the relative negotiating leverage among a borrower's key stakeholders, particularly the company, creditors and equity. Financings completed before the beginning of the current crisis in 2007-2008 typically had weak covenant packages and a general dilution of creditor rights via the negotiated documentation. While this dilution of creditor rights has been somewhat reversed in recent financings, the exercise of such creditor rights has been tempered by a weak and volatile macroeconomic and operating environment, continued stresses in the financing markets and weaknesses within the overall European banking system.

Any restructuring transaction will be based on an operating business plan that is agreed by all relevant stakeholders and forms the basis of developing a sustainable capital structure. Continued macroeconomic challenges mean that what was considered a reasonable and achievable business plan at the time of the initial restructuring transaction may cease to be viable. In a number of situations, the operating environment continues to be sufficiently volatile that no credible medium to long-term operational business plan can be prepared. Accordingly, stakeholders in such a situation must of necessity adopt a wait-and-see approach. In many instances, banks have been reluctant to force a transaction or enforce on their security so long as the company can afford to keep banks or bondholders current on interest payments. Continued volatility has also resulted in a number of restructuring transactions that were completed a few years ago being revisited more than once.

The prolonged turmoil in the credit markets has made refinancing difficult. Even healthy companies are finding it problematic to refinance maturing loans. In theory, one would expect a greater number of stressed companies and restructurings as a result of the closure of credit markets. However, one of the characteristics of the credit cycle pre-2007 has been the prevalence of loan packages with delayed amortising or non-amortising financial structures. Delayed amortising structures have given borrowers greater flexibility to avoid engaging with creditors as no material principal payments are due for the first several years of a loan package. Further, there have been a number of financing packages that have significant availability under revolving credit lines and other alternative sources of funding, such as capital expenditure, restructuring and acquisition facilities. The requirements under these alternative facilities are weak, which allows the borrower to draw down on these lines when distress-related liquidity needs arise.

The closure of credit markets implies that traditional sources of refinancing are limited and the borrower is forced to deal with existing stakeholders to provide a solution to maturity issues. Part of this maturity wall has been refinanced through the public high-yield capital markets; however, public markets tend to have short windows of opportunity to complete such transactions. This has resulted in a number of 'amend and extend' transactions, where the terms of the existing credit documentation are amended to extend the final maturity of the debt. While initial amend and extend transactions were short term in nature and seen as a bridge to a better day, with the expectation that refinancing would eventually be achieved through a new money bank or capital markets transaction, the continued turmoil in the capital markets has resulted in more long-term amend and extend transactions. The market has seen a few of the initial amend and extend transactions being extended for a second time.

The prevalence of financial restructurings in Europe has also been limited by the nature of financial borrowing in that region. A significant number of companies, particularly in Germany and Spain, have borrowed from state-owned or state-backed banks and financial institutions – mainly local savings banks. Local savings banks are motivated by more than just profitability and their remit encompasses additional considerations such as economic development and local or even regional employment creation. Additionally, many of these state-backed institutions are not bound by the mark-to-market and capital adequacy requirements to which traditional, publicly traded, lending institutions are subject, and tend to take a longer-term approach to lending. Such institutions are, to a degree, immune to the shareholder pressures faced by publicly traded financial institutions. The recent sovereign issues faced by a number of countries in the peripheral eurozone, particularly the inability of these national governments to continue to support state-owned financial institutions, may result in an increasing number of restructurings. However, whether such institutions will be able to raise the equity capital over a reasonable period of time necessary to absorb such restructuring-related losses remains a question.

4.   Summary and conclusions

In summary, restructurings in Europe are characterised by several layers of complexity arising from a multitude of jurisdictions and types of debt, varied investor classes and general macro economic uncertainty. Several recent developments have increased the complexity of the workout process, but others have attempted to make the restructuring process more efficient and less value-destructive. This level of complexity leads to a greater level of uncertainty and execution risk that requires higher levels of specialist financial and legal analysis.

Insolvency, restructuring and economic development: the World Bank Group and insolvency systems

Andres F Martinez
Antonia Menezes
Mahesh Uttamchandani
World Bank

1. Introduction

The myth that the Mandarin character weiji (roughly translated as 'crisis') is a combination of two words that, in English, translate as 'danger' and 'opportunity' has invaded popular culture and is a mainstay of mediocre corporate presentations and business school projects around the world.[1] Perhaps one of the reasons why this myth continues to flourish is that its basic message – that a crisis can have both positive and negative impacts – is intuitively appealing and resonates with one's own experiences. In light of the latest global financial crisis, it is worth revisiting the importance of insolvency reform both in the context of financial sector stability and in creating an optimal investment climate for private sector growth. Indeed, many countries have recently begun to undertake critical insolvency reforms that have been, at least in part, inspired by the recent global financial crisis.

1.1 Recent trends in insolvency reform

(a) Pace of reforms picking up globally

Bankruptcy reform is usually unattractive for policy makers. Building consensus among the many stakeholders involved (banks, tax authorities, labour unions, etc) requires a huge investment of time and effort before a bill can go to Parliament. And even in case of a successful legislative treatment of a suggested reform, the political gain for advocates can be limited, since bankruptcy is an unappealing topic to the general public. Therefore, it is unsurprising that bankruptcy reform had been at the bottom of the list in the policy makers' agenda before 2008.

Until 2008 an average of 13 countries per year had undertaken major reforms in the insolvency field, in the pool of 183 economies listed by the "Resolving

---

[1] For a complete debunking of this myth, see "Crisis Does NOT Equal 'Danger' Plus 'Opportunity': How a misunderstanding about Chinese characters has led many astray" at http://pinyin.info/chinese/crisis.html.

Insolvency" chapter of the World Bank – International Finance Corporation (IFC) annual report *Doing Business*, which dedicates an indicator to measuring what happens when firms are in financial distress and have multiple creditors.[2]

But things started to change with the beginning of the crisis. *Doing Business* has recorded a total of 60 reforms in insolvency systems worldwide in the years between 2008 and 2011, increasing gradually year-on-year. In *Doing Business 2012* "Resolving Insolvency" had risen to fourth place in the most active indicator count, with 29 countries then in the process of reforming their insolvency systems.

Figure 1 shows the number of reforms per region.

Figure 1: *Doing Business 2012* **"Doing Business in a more transparent world";** **www.doingbusiness.org**

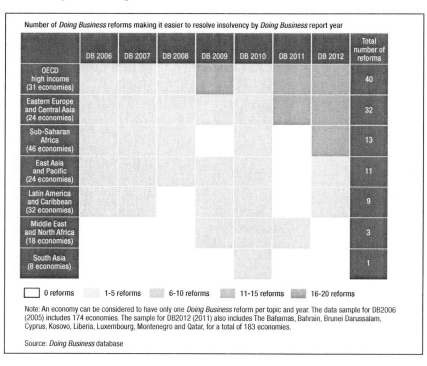

Countries that have engaged in insolvency reforms within the past four years include many European nations such as Germany, the United Kingdom and Spain,

---

2   Countries were reforming more actively in most of the other indicators reported on in *Doing Business*, including in procedure for incorporating companies ("Starting a business"), in tax systems and even in relation to formalities to extend construction permits or to register property. The resolving insolvency indicators measure the time, cost and outcome of insolvency proceedings involving domestic entities. This chapter tracks reforms taking place in the insolvency field in 183 countries. In reports previous to *Doing Business 2012* this indicator set was referred to as "closing a business", but this was changed in the last report in order better to reflect the outcomes measured. All *Doing Business* publications since the first year (2004), plus an explanation of the indicator's methodology, are at www.doingbusiness.org.

and also countries as disparate as Samoa, Malawi and Uruguay, just to mention a few examples. Some of the reforms have not only been legislative, but also institutional and regulatory and vary greatly in their objectives and content, depending on the particularities of each country and region.

It is possible to identify some common patterns across the varying reform initiatives. In countries that have frequent recourse to their insolvency systems, the emphasis seems to have been on mitigating the post-crisis increase in number of filings. In order to do that, a large number of countries promoted the use of out-of-court workouts and pre-packaged reorganisations.

Spain provides an example of this type of reform. After an increase in the number of filings by 263% in the third quarter of 2008 as compared with the same period in 2007,[3] Spain passed Decree 3/2009, which came into force on April 1 2009, introducing a framework for out-of-court workouts, which imposed:

- a four-month stay for bankruptcy claims initiated against debtors under this proceeding; and
- increasing substantially the monetary threshold for abbreviated procedures.

Along similar lines, the Ministry of Justice of Romania, together with the Romanian Central Bank, adopted a series of directives similar to the London Approach and the INSOL Principles in order to encourage banks and debtors to restructure out of court within a predictable framework. This was done with technical assistance by the World Bank Group.

Countries without a wide restructuring practice decided to put more emphasis on heavier legislative reform, such as enacting laws that contemplate a comprehensive reorganisation proceeding where none existed previously, or to strengthen the existing one when it proved to be insufficient or inadequate. The main aim of these reforms was to save viable companies that were facing temporary financial distress. A few examples of these types of reform were seen in particular in Eastern Europe (eg, Estonia and Hungary).

A third group was formed by countries that had in common the fact that they recognised that legislative reform was going to be insufficient without adequate implementation, so they focused on the regulatory framework for the profession: making it more difficult to obtain licences and to pass examinations to become an insolvency practitioner, or modifying fee structures (eg, Belarus and the United Kingdom).

It will be interesting to track the long-term impact of this wave of recent reforms, especially on policy makers and practitioners.

(b) Review of insolvency regimes in the Middle East and North Africa

Bankruptcy reforms are quite rare in the Middle East and North Africa (MENA).[4] This is true in spite of low recovery rates across the region – which makes the use of collective proceedings very uncommon. The regional average for 2012 was of 33.4%.

---

3   "The Restructuring Review", editor Christopher Mallon, *Law Business Research*, 2008, p254.
4   *Doing Business 2011*, "Making a difference for Entrepreneurs".

In any case, a study undertaken in 2009 by Hawkamah, The World Bank, OECD and INSOL International[5] showed that the insolvency systems across the MENA region are largely inconsistent with best practice. Some countries have no standalone law, and others keep old, punitive approaches towards honest debtors that fail in their businesses or are affected by market downturns. Almost no law in the MENA region encourages entrepreneurship. In contrast with, for example, a recent reform of Germany's insolvency law that suspended temporarily the obligation of directors to file for insolvency (in specific cases) to prevent a wave of filings, it can be considerably difficult in countries like Lebanon, Egypt or Jordan to gain access to any in-court restructuring proceeding and is therefore rarely sought in practice.[6]

In the past two years, the authorities in many MENA countries have been stressing (in different fora such as the FIRM[7]) the urgent need to adapt the suitability of their current insolvency systems to improve their investment climate. Committees in charge of analysing these pieces of legislation have already been formed in countries like Lebanon, Egypt and Jordan. Many of those systems were modelled after the old French law. However, unlike France, ulterior reforms such as the introduction of the *sauvegarde,* or the conciliation, the *mandat ad hoc* are absent in the current texts of such laws, making restructurings more difficult to achieve (see further part 3.3 below).

In light of the work that these committees are undertaking – sometimes with the assistance of international organisations – and the underlying political decision to start revisiting the insolvency regimes in the region, it is expected that MENA will start catching up with some of the modern restructuring techniques already adopted in many other jurisdictions.

1.2 Why is insolvency important?

Effective debt resolution and insolvency regimes form the backbone of sound credit markets and establish the rules by which market expectations and risks are set. This is important in today's global environment, with increased competition and heightened commercial risk, where investors are more keenly aware of the problems of recovery and have become more selective in where they invest or lend. While many factors drive investment choices, in volatile or tight credit markets decisions often favour markets with less risk and more reliable structures to support recovery. Effective legal systems enhance credit access and protection – an ingredient of growth in all markets – and enable stakeholders to act swiftly to mitigate loss when a debtor defaults on its obligations. As such, they are pivotal in the maintainance of confidence in daily commercial transactions and are vital to a prompt response strategy in the context of deepening insolvency, periods of economic decline or stagnation, or more systemic financial distress within a market.[8]

---

5   Available at www.oecd.org/dataoecd/51/30/44375185.pdf.
6   In the case of Egypt, for example, it has been said that "[d]espite the social and economic advantages that derive from the 'rescue' option known as restructuring or reorganisation (as opposed to liquidation), there is presently no restructuring law per se in Egypt", *Restructuring and Insolvency 2012, Getting the Deal Through,* editor Bruce Leonard, "Egypt" chapter by Motaz el Dreni.
7   Forum for Insolvency Reform in MENA, composed by World Bank Group, Hawkamah, the OECD and INSOL International.

As businesses become increasingly global in nature, investors, lenders and other stakeholders are seeking greater efficiency, predictability and transparency in commercial law systems in an effort to minimise or better manage performance risks. The existence of a more modern legal system can be a draw to investment, while its absence may lead to capital flight in times of recession or crisis. The notion of 'preparing for a rainy day' in order to stave off the domino effect of a financial crisis is equally important in emerging markets. Of course, most investors do not plan on failure or crisis, which is perhaps why the repercussions of these events have a bigger impact on market confidence when they occur. Effective frameworks for insolvency and creditor right systems:

- foster greater access to credit at more affordable prices;
- establish the legal framework within which corporate restructuring takes place;
- operate as a safety valve for corporate distress by enabling parties to salvage viable businesses or transfer assets efficiently to better uses; and
- promote good corporate governance.[9]

Competing in global markets requires that domestic businesses have maximum access to the fuel that drives modern commerce: credit and investment. Credit depends on willing lenders, which requires laws that facilitate lending on flexible terms and ensure reasonable and timely enforcement of remedies in the event of default. In mature markets, credit comes in all forms: secured, unsecured, trade, leasing, purchase money, securitisations, inventory and receivables financing, factoring and other forms – each of which carries different risks and affords different legal rights for stakeholders.

1.3   Reforming insolvency systems

In countries where lenders generally experience poor loan recoveries, a weak insolvency regulatory framework is often in place. Underdeveloped institutional capacities targeting commercial dispute resolution and insolvency proceedings also contribute. Successful debt resolution and insolvency systems need to address financial distress through formal and out-of-court tools, including mediation, arbitration and informal workout guidelines.

In many economies, enforcement tools are rigid with outdated insolvency frameworks. Traditional courts in many cases do not have the capacity to deal with creditors' recovery claims and business distress in a timely manner. This negatively impacts on entrepreneurship, access to credit, bank loan recovery and jobs.

The World Bank Group works with governments in emerging markets and transition countries to improve the quality of insolvency regimes. Through a variety of technical assistance programmes, the World Bank Group has assisted numerous countries in achieving these improvements. While each country's challenges and

---

8   Gordon W Johnson, "Impact of Global Market Developments in Latin America: Re-examining the Foundations of Trust", World Bank, http://siteresources.worldbank.org/GILD/ConferenceMaterial/20168306/LA%20Corporate%20Insolvency%20(Johnson).pdf.
9   *Ibid.*

opportunities are different, broad lessons can be drawn from years of reform experience.

2. Seven lessons from experience in developing and transition countries

2.1 The insolvency system is a key part of firm 'ecology'

The efficient entry and exit of firms is critical to the healthy functioning of a market economy. As new firms enter an economy, older and less efficient ones should be pushed out, with their productive assets 'recycled' into more efficient firms. This facilitates market dynamism and allows overall productivity in an economy to be maximised. The link between efficient exit and the redeployment of assets is well established. But what about other parts of the firm lifecycle? Practitioners have long extolled the impact of sound insolvency regimes on the availability and cost of credit, but this link has not been well documented in academic literature. Recently, however, this link has been looked at more carefully in two rigorous academic papers that focus on economic conditions for credit pre and post-insolvency reform and control for other exogenous factors that may influence credit. Both papers find that improving the overall insolvency regime of a country can have a measurable and positive impact on the availability and cost of credit.[10]

2.2 Outcomes are much more important than formalities

Much has been written on the subject of legal origin and the enabling environment for credit. A widely held view on this subject is that common law systems are more conducive to creditor rights and, therefore, to lending. Even within countries with a common law legal heritage, there is increasing pressure to ensure that laws conform with a perceived normative standard that 'increases access to finance'. While that debate is beyond the scope of this discussion, it is worth noting that the debate itself misses the critical point that insolvency law is much more about function than form.

This can be seen more clearly by looking at the example of the United Kingdom and continental creditor rights regimes. The conventional view is that the United Kingdom has a much more creditor-friendly system, while the French and German regimes are seen as overly protective of debtors. This view would appear to be borne out by Figure 2, which suggests a significantly higher recovery rate in UK liquidations than in France and Germany.

However, a more nuanced view provided by Figure 3 suggests that these recovery rates are driven by the low values (in all countries) of piecemeal liquidations. The difference in recovery rate drops dramatically when one looks at either going-concern sales or informal workouts. Indeed, the French creditors even tend to do slightly better than their English counterparts when it comes to recovering through informal workouts. This suggests that the designations of 'debtor friendly' or 'creditor friendly', while potentially useful in the broad sense of understanding a

---

10   The two articles are: B Funchal 2008. "The effects of the 2005 Bankruptcy Reform in Brazil", Economic Letters. 101: 84–86. and N Serrano-Velarde, G Rodano,E Tarantino "The Causal Effect of Bankruptcy Law on the Cost of Finance", Oxford University, October 2011 http://denning.law.ox.ac.uk/news/events_files/SERRANOVEL ARDE_15_Nov_2011.pdf.

Figure 2: Mean recovery rates across all firms

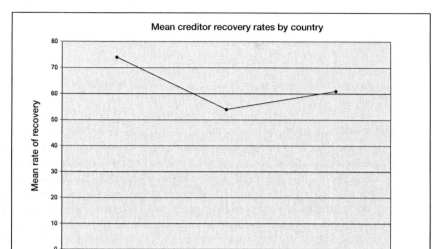

Figure 3: Mean recovery rates by recovery method[11]

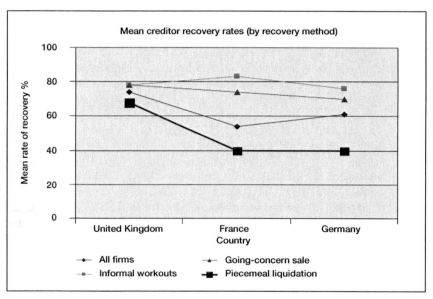

---

11   Figures 2 and 3 were created from data published in Sergei A Davydenko and Julian R Franks, "Do Bankruptcy Codes Matter? A Study of Defaults in France, Germany, and the UK", Rotman School of Business, University of Toronto, April 10 2005. The data involved a sampling of over 2,600 insolvencies across three jurisdictions.

system, obscure the importance of a system that provides stakeholders with the tools and incentives to achieve a variety of outcomes that are appropriate within the specific regulatory and institutional environment of that country.

2.3   **Ineffectual implementation of laws due to weak or lax institutional and regulatory frameworks**

Weak implementation mechanisms for enforcement and insolvency procedures in some countries hinder achieving observance of a principle even though the laws are essentially sound. Experience shows that a country with stronger and more effective institutional and regulatory frameworks will generally have more effective and efficient insolvency and creditors' rights systems, even where the laws have not been modernised. The most common institutional problems are the result of:

- inadequate training of judges and administrators;
- inefficient case administration practices and procedures;
- lack of transparency and inconsistency in decision-making; and
- ineffective regulation to redress problems of corruption and the risk that interested parties may unduly influence the courts, administrators, trustees or other stakeholders.

Problems in regulation often point to weakness or absence of procedures and institutions to license, qualify and supervise practitioners and professionals, such as insolvency administrators, enforcement and collection agents, and other specialised professionals.

2.4   **Insolvency systems: inefficient, outmoded and unsupportive of modern business needs**

Although the concept of corporate rescue as a means of maximising enterprise value and preserving jobs is gaining support among industrial countries and in developing countries, many jurisdictions continue to rely on outmoded laws to address the problems of modern corporate financial distress and insolvency. Many of these laws are relics from the past that were created for a more tranquil and sedate environment for smaller businesses and merchants, and where credit fell into several narrow categories. Today's environment requires statutes that can flexibly accommodate a wide range of business solutions that make economic sense and rationalise debt to actual enterprise value. Moreover, the spreading of constituent elements of an insolvency system across numerous laws, rather than in a single code, inhibits certainty and transparency.

2.5   **Countries frequently ignore the effects of their tax regime on business competition and corporate rescue**

Out-of-court workouts are frequently hampered by tax laws that penalise parties for engaging in a debt rationalisation process. For example, creditors may want to write off (or rationalise) debt or convert their debt into an equity interest in the debtor company. However, tax laws frequently impose heavier tax burdens on such transactions, forcing the creditors to adopt alternative measures that are tax safe, but which lead to unnecessary litigation, execution or liquidation of the debts and business. Alternatively, parties may be forced to carry artificially inflated asset values on their books to avoid the incurrence of taxes or the burden of provisioning for losses. Such laws create disincentives to restructuring. In other instances, the tax regime unfairly saddles the buyer of an insolvent debtor's assets with tax liabilities previously due and owing by the debtor. Thus, in addition to paying a fair market value for the assets, a buyer may be forced to assume a tax liability of an uncertain amount. These kinds of rule are generally designed to protect the state in the event of an insolvency, but unfairly shift the risk of loss to other market participants in a manner that stifles competition and efficient recycling of assets and businesses. While no empirical studies exist, common sense would suggest that the impact of adverse tax policies far outweighs any gains to the state in trying to recover taxes from a very small minority of insolvent enterprises.

2.6 Weak social protection mechanisms stifle corporate recovery by burdening the enterprise or successor with legacy costs of debtor's employees

The treatment of employee rights and social protection of labour is particularly weak in many emerging markets and is often the greatest obstacle to successful corporate restructuring. It is extremely difficult to establish a healthy balance sheet without reducing costs and this often means laying off employees. This can be difficult to accomplish and can result in excessive hardship in the absence of effective rules to enforce a fair process and to provide protection for redundant workers. Rampant layoffs are not always the best solution, as we saw in Indonesia during the early stages of its financial crisis. In many developing countries, such as India, although social protections for employees are weak, the *de facto* leverage of labour is often high. One approach to protecting workers is to establish a protection fund or a guarantee payment fund that sets priorities for access by employees laid off during corporate restructuring. These techniques have been used in many countries, in particular throughout the European Union, with positive results.

2.7 Delay inhibits choice and success

Although possibly an obvious point, it needs to be restated that delays negatively impact on both recovery levels and limit the choice of outcome (ie, going-concern sale versus piecemeal liquidation). The reasons for this are numerous: the longer a business is in distress, the more likely valuable human capital will flee, the greater the damage to brand and the harder to negotiate with suppliers. All of this leads to a cumulative level of market devaluation of the distressed entity. At some point, this devaluation makes going-concern sale impossible and piecemeal liquidation becomes the only option. Recovery values in piecemeal liquidation are, on a macro level, lower than those in going-concern sales, and the longer the liquidation period drags on, the older the assets become, which typically leads to a decline in value. A survey of practitioners in over 175 countries, as displayed in Figure 4 (overleaf),[12]

---

12   "Private Credit in 129 Countries", Revised, January 2006, Simeon Djankov, Caralee McLiesh, and Andrei Shleifer, *Doing Business*.

Figure 4: Average rate of recovery

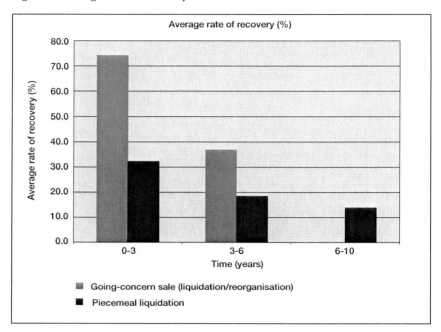

shows that while going-concern sales yield higher recoveries than liquidations, both yield lower recoveries over time and, eventually, liquidations become the only option. This leads to the conclusion that while processes must be sped up, this must be done in a way that results in increased preference for liquidation. Higher recoveries mean greater distributions, particularly to unsecured creditors (eg, employees and trade creditors), and more going-concern sales result in lower job losses.

3. Emerging issues

3.1 Regional harmonisation of insolvency laws is of increasing interest to many states

As access to markets is increased, numerous states are exploring economic and trade cooperation across borders in order to enhance competition and investment. Regional integration is considered an effective tool here.[13] Although such integration can take many guises, a common trend in Africa is developing regional harmonised commercial laws, including insolvency, to improve uniformity, transparency and coordination across states. *L'Organisation pour l'Harmonisation en Afrique du Droit des Affaires* (OHADA) is a regional international organisation, first established by treaty in 1993, which focuses on harmonising the business laws of its 17 member states.[14]

13　Schiff and Winters, "Regional Integration and Development", The World Bank Group, Washington DC.

Accordingly, it has a number of 'uniform acts' that have direct effect in its member states, including an insolvency law.[15]

Analysis of existing insolvency practices in the OHADA region suggests that improvements could be considered, as set out in Table 1 below.

Table 1: Regional comparisons of closing a business

Region	Time (years)	Cost (% of estate)	Recovery rate (cents on the dollar)
OHADA	3.8	22.5	14.7
Common Market for Eastern and Southern Africa (COMESA)	3.3	20.0	14.1
East Asia and Pacific (EAP)	2.7	23.2	28.6
European Union (EU)	1.9	10.6	59.3
Latin America	3.2	13.9	30.4
Southern African Development Community (SADC)	3.0	17.0	22.9

Source: Doing Business 2011

OHADA is accordingly reforming many of these uniform acts in line with best practices and to reflect current developments in the region, including its insolvency law. The reforms envisaged for the Insolvency Law, which is expected to be adopted in 2013, aim to:

- strengthen the business rescue culture across the region to save viable businesses;
- streamline procedures; and
- encourage cooperation.

Although the OHADA member states of will ultimately decide what reforms are

---

14   Benin, Burkina Faso, Cameroon, Central African Republic, Chad, Comoros, Cote d'Ivoire, Democratic Republic of Congo, Equatorial Guinea, Gabon, Guinea, Guinea-Bissau, Niger, Mali, Republic of Congo, Togo and Senegal. See www.ohadalegis.com/anglais/presohadagb.htm.
15   These acts are, General Commercial Law, Secured Transactions, Commercial Companies and Economic Group Partnerships, Debt Collection Procedures and Measures of Execution, Insolvency, Arbitration, Company Accounting, Carriage of Goods by Road and Cooperative Credit by Banks.

viable, it is hoped that the revised insolvency law will help strengthen the regional credit environment and promote business rescue.

Harmonisation of insolvency laws can have powerful effects, enabling countries to benefit from a similar legal regime, as well as physical proximity. Different regional blocs are considering adopting uniform insolvency laws or principles – for instance, in the Caribbean,[16] the East Africa Community[17] and the Middle East. It should be appreciated, however, that a choice of different models is available. For instance, whereas OHADA's model allows direct applicability of the law in its member states, other countries are considering non-binding model laws or principles. Ultimately, the effectiveness of either model will depend upon its implementation and the efforts of the respective states to share knowledge, experiences and training.

3.2   Insolvency regimes for micro and small and medium enterprises

The majority of businesses in most countries are small and medium enterprises (MSMEs)[18] which are commonly referred to as the 'engines of growth'.[19] For instance, MSMEs account for almost 45% of total manufacturing output, 95% of the number of industrial units and 40% of the export sector in India.[20] Because of this dominance, MSMEs are particularly vulnerable to weaknesses in the credit environment as they experience small economies of scale and are exposed to extensive risk. However, when their entrepreneurship potential is appropriately harnessed, they can make a significant contribution to overall economic growth.

From a legal form standpoint, MSMEs can be divided into two broad categories: corporate and non-corporate entities.

Corporate entities under most legal systems enjoy the protection of limited liability for shareholders.[21] In common law jurisdictions, however, non-corporate entities[22] possess no distinct legal identity from their shareholders and, as such, if a sole proprietorship goes out of business, the debts accrue to the individual.[23] The MSMEs have to be regulated under the personal bankruptcy frameworks, which are often time-consuming and costly for small businesses.[24] In many countries those regimes are out-dated, even anachronistic,[25] often with some stigma attached (see further below at 3.3). Unless debt forgiveness is entrenched in the system, the businesses become mired in debt, with no way out.

Governments are beginning to appreciate the importance of efficient exit

---

16   www.jamaicaobserver.com/business/Caricom-story_7517389.
17   http://news.eac.int/index.php?option=com_content&view=article&id=182:meeting-on-approximation-of-national-laws-nairobi&catid=48:eac-latest&Itemid=69.
18   Note that the term 'MSME' varies across jurisdictions and institutions, and is often defined in terms of employees and/or turnover.
19   www.ifc.org/ifcext/sme.nsf/AttachmentsByTitle/OutcomesOctDec2008/$FILE/Outcomes_Oct_Dec_2008.pdf.
20   SME Policy: Bank of India.
21   These include limited liability companies or limited liability partnerships.
22   These include sole traders, sole proprietorships and partnerships.
23   Mahesh Uttamchandani and Antonia Menezes, "The Freedom to Fail; Why Small Business Insolvency Regimes are Critical for Emerging Markets", *International Corporate Rescue*.
24   IMF Staff Position Note, "Principles of Household Debt Restructuring", June 26 2009, at p6.
25   For instance, in India, SMEs are largely subject to the Presidency-Towns Insolvency Act 1909 and the Provincial Insolvency Act 1920. In Malawi, the Bankruptcy Act was promulgated in 1928.

mechanisms in reallocating productive assets to viable assets, reducing credit risk and promoting entrepreneurship. Different and varied concepts are being promoted in legislation to reflect these concerns, including an increased variety of preventive procedures, simplified processes and support for a fresh start. In some civil law countries, they are widening the scope of collective proceedings provisions to include commercial entrepreneurs, farmers or self-employed professionals. They are also adopting expedited, fast-track restructuring and liquidation processes, which are less document and process-heavy. Studies have shown that forgiving bankruptcy regimes can have an effect on levels of entrepreneurship.[26] Although acceptance is slow, discharge is becoming an important concept in some countries, as they start to perceive entrepreneurship as a learning experience and make efforts to distinguish between honest versus fraudulent bankrupts.

Nonetheless, in many jurisdictions where non-corporate MSMEs are subject to personal bankruptcy regimes, these frameworks will need to be updated and a concerted effort made to cater for MSME business debt compared with household consumer debt.

3.3 Complementing workouts with innovative out-of-court tools

Much has been written on the importance of out-of-court workout regimes in an effort to encourage flexible and timely debt restructuring. As with rehabilitation measures, there is a variety of ways to encourage out-of-court workouts and many emerging markets are developing innovative tools to encourage preventive pre-insolvency measures.

(a) France

France has developed a conciliation procedure that is a confidential pre-insolvency procedure, and that offers the benefit of beginning and ending in court. The judge appoints a conciliator, who seeks to reach an agreement between the parties as to the restructuring terms, and the final plan is court approved. This is a very light-touch procedure, and leaves the power very much in the parties' hands to reach a restructuring plan (within a four-month period, as set out in the law). France has also developed a special mediation regime, which is also pre-insolvency, called *mandat ad hoc*. As with conciliation, this is a confidential procedure, although the *mandataire* plays a more proactive role in helping the parties reach a restructuring agreement, and reports to the court regarding the financial situation of the company. Unlike conciliation, there is no fixed timeframe in place within which to reach an agreement.

These procedures are particularly important in jurisdictions where the force of law is seen as fundamental to create a binding restructuring plan, as opposed to a mere contractually negotiated agreement. They are also useful tools in countries where the negotiation culture between banks and businesses is weak, as these procedures are judge-approved and have the benefit of a third-party neutral to ensure that ethical conduct and good-faith negotiations take place.

---

26 John Armour and Douglas Cumming, "Bankruptcy Law and Entrepreneurship", *American Law and Economics Review*, Oxford University Press, vol 10(2), 303–350.

Lastly, in many emerging markets, a significant problem is the stigma attached to any type of bankruptcy proceeding. As a result, debtors often wait until they are in severe financial distress before seeking a solution, by which time it is too late to put any preventive measure in place. The confidentiality of these two proceedings is appealing, and it is possible to ensure that the law provides for the terms of the restructuring plan to remain confidential, despite being court approved.

(b) ***Specialised commercial courts and debt tribunals***

One method being used to encourage debt recovery, particularly in countries where court proceedings are extremely lengthy, is having specialised commercial courts or debt tribunals. Some countries are starting to go even further to introduce mandatory mediation in these fora. Debt tribunals – for instance, in South Asia – were established with the goal of creating a special forum in which to hear debt recovery claims and improve stakeholder recovery. Despite this specialisation, the backlog of debt cases remains significant, with the result that stakeholders' loans remain non-performing and recovery is a lengthy process. Bangladesh, for instance, has tried to address this by developing specific out-of-court dispute resolution frameworks to resolve debt claims and incentivise banks to lend to smaller business entities.[27] This in turn is expected to reduce credit risk and improve business opportunities and performance of businesses by reducing value destruction of distressed businesses and preserving viable entities. As countries continue to look for innovative ways to improve debt recovery, a possible emerging space is the use of such informal, flexible tools that promote negotiation and early action.

---

27   Artha Rin Adalat Court Act 2003 with mandatory mediation provisions in 2012.

Debt-for-equity swaps

Karl Clowry
Paul Hastings LLP

1. Introduction

The principal element of any debt-for-equity swap is a restructuring of the balance sheet of a corporate debtor so that the relevant participating creditors (often, only financial creditors) receive equity interests in a reorganised capital structure in consideration for reducing their debt claims against the company. In its simplest form, it may be a route by which a company can avoid an imminent or prospective insolvent liquidation caused by prolonged negative cash flows and/or balance-sheet solvency issues. In either case this may be due to the company's inability to service a relatively high level of debt, a situation that may have arisen because of the debtor's poor operational and financial performance. Alternatively, such conversions have been used opportunistically by creditors that purposefully acquire sub-performing debt for the sole intention of gaining corporate control of a debtor (a so-called 'loan to own' strategy).

From a debtor's corporate perspective, such balance-sheet restructurings can have a positive impact by enabling it to continue to trade and compete more effectively on the basis of a significantly reduced debt burden. A debt-for-equity swap may be the stimulus for effecting a corporate and/or operational restructuring that may provide further benefits for the restructured debtor and its stakeholders. While the time and resources invested in a formal procedure-based debt-for-equity restructuring can be considerable, the resulting benefits can create a valuable business in the medium to longer term for the resultant equity holders. The traditional alternative for over-indebted debtors is to cease trading and accept the onset of a formal insolvency or enforcement procedure. Such alternatives may realise some value for certain creditor classes, but often destroy an opportunity to rescue a business that otherwise might create new value in the longer term.

In the UK lending market, by the early 1990s many bank lenders had become more willing to continue to fund stressed borrowers rather than pursue enforcement strategies if they were given an opportunity to increase their returns on a turnaround of the borrower by receiving equity or equity-like rights (usually in the form of convertible warrants or via synthetic instruments). Consequently, when economic conditions deteriorated across a number of sectors in the early years of this century and lenders were presented with numerous borrowers whose balance sheets required a reduction in debt, many lenders already understood the practical implications of holding equity in such enterprises. This created an environment in which lenders were reasonably receptive to the reality of needing to write down debt for an equity stake in borrowers' groups as the only alternative to insolvency. A simultaneous catalyst for this trend was provided by an increasingly liquid secondary market in the expanding European leverage loan and high-yield bond markets. Many secondary creditors had purchased debt exposures at deeply discounted prices and so could profitably afford to accept substantial write-offs on the ostensible face value of that debt, while gaining an opportunity to acquire substantial equity-like returns in restructured debtor companies. This trend was repeated in more recent years since the 2008–2009 downturn, although at lower rates than many in the European market anticipated due to financial institutions being unwilling or unable to take further debt writedowns on their own balance sheets.

Certain other markets have been less receptive to lenders taking shareholder or quasi-shareholder roles due to the doctrine of equitable subordination, whereby on any subsequent insolvency the equitised lenders' remaining debt claims may be regarded as a loan made by a shareholder that should be accorded treatment as equity and so be repayable only once all debts to 'true' creditors are discharged.

A number of common factors need to be considered with any debt-to-equity swap. This chapter examines these, looking at how they are typically addressed by debtors, the converting creditors and other stakeholders. In particular, they include whether:

- the swap can be effected on a purely consensual contractual basis;
- a statutory cram-down mechanism needs to be utilised so that the will of a majority or super-majority of relevant creditors can bind a dissenting creditor minority; and
- a formal enforcement needs to occur to enable a class of creditors to gain equity control.

The key elements in any debt-to-equity swap may be categorised as follows:

- agreeing the basis for, and ascertaining, the valuation of the debtor's group;
- assessing how much debt (and of what classes) is/are sustainable and/or might be converted to equity;
- agreeing the type and terms of equity or quasi-equity to be issued to the converting creditors;
- quantifying the allocation of the final equity value between converting creditors, existing equity holders and any other relevant stakeholders; and
- choosing a suitable mechanism that delivers the necessary debt-to-equity conversion in view of the respective rights of relevant stakeholders, tax considerations and the jurisdiction of the debtor.

2.   Impetus for debt-to-equity swaps

The board of directors, being the executive manifestation of a company, should in theory be the first constituency to identify the need to restructure the company's balance sheet. In reality, it may be the company's financial advisers that identify a likely need for such a financial restructuring, and they may need to convince the board that such a restructuring should be pursued. It will be less fortuitous for the debtor's board if the proposal comes from a disgruntled creditor group once the pricing of the debt or other indicia trigger market interest in what may be a debtor in incipient distress (with rapidly plunging equity value). As with any other form of restructuring, the necessity might arise unexpectedly – for example, if a sector suffers a crisis of investor confidence with lenders and purchasers of debt securities becoming unwilling to refinance companies. Equally, a business that has pursued an aggressive expansive phase, incurring relatively high levels of debt, may find that on a sudden slowing in the pace of expansion or indeed a contraction of its market and earnings, it struggles to service that debt burden.

Very often, the difficulty in servicing such debt is due to the underperforming nature of the business, which may focus the board of a company on undertaking an operational restructuring. If a limited operational restructuring fails to yield the necessary free cash flow available to service – and indeed discharge – excess debt, the company may consider making a proposal to its financial creditors. However, where directors have been incentivised either directly by receiving equity or indirectly by reference to the company's value, there may be some reluctance to initiate a process that will ultimately result in such apparent value being greatly diluted or ablated completely. The unenviable reality for directors in such a position is that the longer the process is forestalled, the fewer options are available for the debtor and the less control they may personally have in the outcome of the process. Although recent English case law has questioned whether a company – at a given moment in time where the value of its assets are exceeded by the amount of its liabilities (present, future and contingent) – is susceptible to being deemed insolvent and so liable to being wound up, directors and counterparties aware of such a balance-sheet position would need to consider carefully how they proceed with such a company.[1]

The wealth of financial information now available to trade creditors and credit insurers means that these stakeholders may be a further constituency that applies pressure to the cash flow of a company by altering their terms of business due to a perceived deterioration in creditworthiness. In some instances these creditor groups may unintentionally be the trigger for a restructuring that ultimately results in a debt-to-equity conversion.

3.   Recent European backdrop

For a number of years, a key feature of the European debt markets had been the relative ease with which private equity sponsors obtained sizeable advances of keenly priced leverage finance. In certain cases this debt was provided on the basis of apparently continuously improving businesses set against a benign economic backdrop. This enabled strong sponsors to obtain relatively high multiples of financial debt relative to the earnings of their acquired groups. Consequently, such sponsors could reduce the level of equity capital that they injected into such structures. As a result of the magnifying effects of such leverage on equity returns, any financial underperformance by such debtor groups means that the shareholder sponsors quickly find their equity holdings to be rendered out of the money. Lenders may expect such private equity sponsors to inject more capital promptly into such structures or risk losing their investments entirely to the lenders (ie, where value

---

1   See *BNY Corporate Trustee Services Ltd v Eurosail UK 2007–3BL PLC* [2011] EWCA Civ 227.

breaks well into the debt capital). Where sponsors benefit from 'covenant-lite' terms in their finance documents, they may have more time in which to seek to turn around ailing businesses before having to decide whether to inject additional equity or otherwise cede control to the lenders. Another factor delaying the implementation of thorough debt-for-equity conversions resulting in 'pretend and extend' situations is the requirement for bank lenders to minimise losses on their balance sheets in the writedown of the relevant debt exposure while trying to characterise the new equity with as high a value as possible to minimise their overall loss.

As discussed elsewhere in this book, in the United Kingdom trustees of defined benefit pension schemes in funding deficit now play a much more active role in restructuring negotiations and, under the watchful eye of the Pensions Regulator, are expected to negotiate robustly in any debt-for-equity swap. Such trustees will typically seek enhanced payment schedules to accelerate elimination of such deficits and potential equity in the restructured company. In the 2011 instance of Uniq plc the pension deficit debt was converted into 90.2% of the ordinary equity of the restructured company, the first UK-based deficit-for-equity swap.

4. Valuation

A significant issue in any balance-sheet restructuring is the basis for assessing the value of the business. This determines how much debt it is likely to support, which financial creditor groups are in/out of the money and, crucially, the debt tranche in which the value breaks (ie, the creditor group/class that will suffer a partial loss on a formal insolvency). Creditors in that debt tranche will be the constituency expecting to receive the largest portion of equity in the restructuring. This constitutes one of the fundamental elements underpinning, and yet the most contentious issue challenging, any debt-for-equity swap.[2] The intense debate and litigation on this issue in the European arena are addressed elsewhere in this book.

In the numerous debt-to-equity conversions completed between 2002 and 2005, many unsecured bondholders, second-lien and mezzanine lenders saw all or substantially all of their debt holdings converted into 90% to 95% of the ordinary equity of the resultant restructured parent entity, with the remaining balance split between existing shareholders (by way of a consent fee) and/or new management incentive plans.

Since 2005, many European leverage finance transactions have been structured with relatively high multiples of debt to earnings and modest junior-debt-to-senior-debt ratios. This combination, together with a precipitous fall or even a stagnation in earnings experienced by many debtors since 2008, and a fall in the value of the relevant traded debt has meant that many of the debt-for-equity swaps completed more recently have involved senior secured lenders taking very high percentages of the restructured equity in such debtors, while junior creditors secured little or no recoveries.

---

2   See *Re Bluebrook Ltd* [2009] EWHC 2114 (Ch) for an examination of the court's reasoning in this area.

5. Competing aims

5.1 Company's aims

As noted above, a traditional corporate borrower/issuer with private shareholdings may initially seek to forestall a balance-sheet restructuring while it reconsiders its business model and other options to the alternative of yielding control to its financial creditors. For a number of years before mid-2007, such a delay could be achieved simply by refinancing with another creditor group with looser financial covenants at an increased margin. In the absence of a suitable refinancing proposal, debt may be reduced from the proceeds of new equity infusions. However, many shareholders prefer to see such injections being used within the debtor's business rather than for the direct benefit of financial creditors. In the absence of a refinancing or a further equity injection, the equitisation of debt may be the only realistic alternative for a company in order to restructure its balance sheet. A company's management team, if it remains in place, may well seek to negotiate some equity for itself if it retains the support of the converting creditors so that it can share in any eventual value appreciation after the restructuring. If a company is cash-flow negative, then over time the directors may become concerned about wrongful trading-type personal liabilities and subsequent risk of disqualification, in the event that the company were eventually to enter insolvent liquidation.[3] This is amplified in certain civil law jurisdictions such as Germany, where criminal liability[4] may arise for directors if they continue to permit a company to trade when either balance-sheet or cash-flow insolvent.[5]

5.2 Creditors' aims

The degree of scepticism with which a creditor may view a debtor group in need of a balance-sheet restructuring may in part depend on whether the creditor acquired the debt at par or at distressed prices. While traditional-par creditors may be relieved eventually to realise a par return on their exposure, distressed debt investors will be more likely to seek to engineer an opportunity to restructure the company so as to create returns well above their investment costs. This aim may be met by:

- extinguishing the current shareholders' interests;
- eliminating the debt interests of more out-of-the-money'junior creditors; and
- securing equity interests for themselves that may ultimately result in returns far higher than could ever be realised from a par-debt investment.

---

3   See Section 214 of the Insolvency Act 1986 and the Company Directors Disqualification Act 1986.
4   Under Section 15a para 1 of the Insolvency Code 2012 recently introduced in 2008 by the Law Modernising the GmbH and Combatting its Abuse, directors of limited liability companies may be criminally liable and punished by up to three years' imprisonment or a fine for failures under Section 15a, para 4.5 of the Insolvency Code 2012.
5   Section15a, para 1 of the Insolvency Code 2012 imposes a duty on directors of limited liability companies to file for insolvency without undue delay, and in any event no later than three weeks after the date on which they become aware of the over-indebtedness or illiquidity, although the filing requirement in respect of over-indebtedness has been suspended since 2008 under the Act on the Implementation of Measures to Stabilise the Financial Markets 2008, and is likely to continue to be disapplied for several more years.

In recent years many distressed credit opportunity funds have been founded that specifically target companies susceptible to a debt-to-equity conversion. Such 'loan-to-own' strategists identify overleveraged debtor groups, particularly in jurisdictions where a cram-down procedure can be utilised to bind out-of-the-money and/or fulcrum creditors in conjunction with the relevant inter-creditor documentation.

6. Equity and shareholders' agreement issues

The fundamental principle in issuing equity or equity-like instruments to the converting creditors is to enable them to realise increases in the value of the company, while ensuring that the company is not unduly burdened with potential payment obligations as it completes any operational turnaround. When the amount of debt to be converted to equity is relatively non-dilutive of the existing equity, the converted equity may be configured as non-voting redeemable preference shares so that the debtor/issuer can fund dividends and any redemption payments while conferring the converting creditors with the right to receive dividends in priority to the ordinary shareholders. Reflecting the recovering nature of most companies after implementation of a debt-for-equity swap, the dividend rights may be cumulative, variable or incremental in nature, and may be indexed against a number of performance and other quantifiable variables. This enables the debtor to be insulated for a time while it effects any necessary operational turnaround, yet provides comfort to the new equity holders that dividends will increase commensurate with the improved performance and cash flows of the debtor, so compensating them for lost debt interest income.

Conversion rights in equity warrants often permit the holders to convert (at a premium to the then price of the ordinary shares) to become holders of a fixed number of ordinary shares, enabling them to reap the benefits of any significant increase in the value of the debtor. The holders will expect the conversion rights to prevail for some time to capture delayed appreciation in the value of the debtor, while simultaneously restricting the debtor's ability to effect the conversion in an overly flexible manner. The holders of preference shares will seek to include redemption rights in the preference shares. Such rights may be exercised optionally (sometimes bilaterally) during a certain period or otherwise on the occurrence of particular events, on a future date or upon the breach of specific terms. In some situations it may not be feasible to incorporate such rights into the shares if the debtor's distributable reserves are likely to remain low for a protracted period after a debt-for-equity swap or otherwise if local accounting rules demand that such equities be treated as debt instruments. Additionally, where the shares of a debtor are listed on a regulated exchange, detailed technical consideration must be given to ensure that the general transparency principle that other shareholders are made aware of these potentially dilutive rights.

In circumstances where a significant dilution of equity will occur on conversion, ordinary shares may be attractive to converting lenders; this provides them (collectively) with control over the strategic corporate direction of the debtor, while enabling them to share in any value appreciation of the debtor. Issuing ordinary shares to the converting lenders is also likely to involve a swifter negotiation process than for preference shares, especially if the ordinary shares are confined to a single class.

Warrants enabling holders to exercise a call to subscribe for shares in the company at a fixed price have figured in a number of UK debt restructurings where the lenders acquiring the warrants acknowledged that the existing shareholders be permitted to continue to enjoy future increases in the debtor's value. Warrants may be issued in a variety of forms or series, enabling different classes of creditors *qua* warrant holders to subscribe for shares at different pricings on exercise or with varying maturities.

Most European debt restructurings have involved companies without public share listings. However, where applicable listing rules apply, an additional regulatory regime may require a super-majority of ordinary shareholders to vote in favour of the proposal, quite apart from the need to comply with applicable prospectus rules when circularising any proposal among equity and debt holders.[6]

Following a debt-to-equity conversion, lenders will likely want to be involved in the strategic direction of the company as it pursues any ongoing corporate turnaround strategy, so will typically seek representation or observation rights on the board of directors. If lenders have acquired the majority of the ordinary shares in a company, a new shareholders' agreement may prohibit them from transferring the shares to third parties for a period of up to two years. Similarly, the company may be restricted from undertaking certain activities by the adoption of new constitutive documentation.

7.   Elements and dynamics of transaction

The commencement of negotiations for a debt-for-equity swap may be initiated upon a prospective financial covenant default or a prospective interest/coupon payment default, necessitating the convening of a lender/bondholder call or meeting to explain the company's situation. Around this time, the company and its creditor groups may retain financial and legal advisers on the matter and appoint lender steering committees/*ad hoc* committees of bondholders to assist in liaising with the debtor and coordination among the relevant creditors.[7] There is likely to be considerable debate and disagreement on the valuation of the company and the amount and class(es) of fulcrum debt that need to be converted to result in a sustainable balance sheet for the debtor. A number of tactical weapons may be used by the different creditor groups in order to settle upon a valuation that is most advantageous to their interests. Many debtor companies retain the services of a highly skilled chief restructuring officer to assist in guiding the company through the most fraught phases of the restructuring negotiations, as well as using his or her sectoral knowledge and financial acumen to coordinate its operational turnaround.

The applicable jurisdiction of the borrower, the group obligors and the governing law of the documentation will affect the timing and direction of negotiations if

---

6   For example, in the United Kingdom a debt-for-equity swap and consequential cancellation in premium listing effected by a scheme of arrangement or an administration would otherwise typically require the prior consent of 75% of the ordinary shareholders to approve the transaction.

7   For examples of the contractual arrangements and operating protocols between a borrower, its lenders and a coordinating committee of lenders, see the Loan Market Association's suite of restructuring related documents.

conducted against a backdrop of a board of directors threatening to file for insolvency to protect their personal interest rather than risk working through a difficult phase to preserve value outside insolvency. Once it is apparent that a debt-for-equity swap will need be concluded, the company may seek to lock up the participating creditors on the basis of a term sheet or restructuring agreement. This is particularly so where the company needs to complete the balance-sheet restructuring via a formal procedure in which it may require a super-majority of creditors to agree to the conversion. By locking up a sizeable majority of creditors that agree to vote in favour of the substantive terms of the conversion, a nucleus is created that encourages other creditors to enjoin in a formal vote to implement the restructuring. There will be an intensive period of discussion while the company and proponent creditors of the proposal continue preparatory work, as well as fall-back planning in the event that the proposal is not accepted. The lock-up period for creditors may last for several months while further negotiations continue on elements of the proposal with outstanding financial creditors.

8. Principal methods of effecting conversion of debt to equity

8.1 Fully consensual/contractual basis

This option is likely to be available only where a debtor company and its shareholder(s) accept the need to reduce its debt burden and where that debt is held among a relatively discrete group of creditors with similar rights (eg, under a single syndicated loan agreement). Such situations may arise in debtor groups that have historically relied on bilateral debt funding, but which during an overly ambitious growth phase have tapped the syndicated loan or high-yield debt markets for more significant debt investors. A number of debt-for-equity swaps in the early 1990s involved such enterprises in the United Kingdom, many of which took the form of a debt writedown in exchange for the issuance of warrants rather than ordinary shares in the debtor. Where only a single class of financial creditors exists, this is likely to make for a less involved intercreditor discussion. The principal downside of pursuing this path is that the process may fail at any time until all converting creditors have irrevocably committed to the conversion process. In many relatively underdeveloped syndicated loan markets or in some jurisdictions where recently state-acquired banks operate, debtor companies are often faced with hold-out lenders that insist on being bought out by other lenders rather than agreeing any conversion of their debt. In such circumstances it may be crucial to have the guidance of a steering committee or coordinating financial institution to liaise with the company and coordinate advice and discussion among the creditor group. Conversely, if a group of creditors can be convinced to act positively in unison, the company may be more likely to avoid a formal insolvency and undue adverse publicity when brokered in the private context of a fully consensual transaction.

Tracking the evolution of debt capital structures in Europe, consensual restructurings have also progressed in terms of sophistication. However, in common with any restructuring process, a fully consensual arrangement is likely to have a higher probability of success if it is commenced as soon as a problem in the debtor group is identified. This may begin with the company, along with its financial advisers, convening an 'all-bank meeting' in order to explain the difficulties being faced by the company and its strategy to deal with such issues. However, in many instances a debtor's management may be unwilling initially to countenance the need to undertake a debt-for-equity swap until evidence about the unsustainability of its financial debt relative to its operational performance is presented, once due diligence is performed for the creditors' benefit. By that time the management may have lost the credibility of the creditor group. However, in a number of complex commercial mortage-backed securities restructurings a consensual approach has been pursued because of the perceived legal and business risks, potential value degradation and class hold-out rights that may have ensued from implementing more formal cram-down/enforcement processes.

While providing flexibility in terms of timing, unlike a formal court-based conversion, a consensual process that is allowed to continue for a protracted period will not only cost the debtor more in terms of fees, but may also require converting creditors to revisit the business assumptions and financial models. That may result in a higher portion of the equity going to them than might otherwise be the case if completed expeditiously before market speculation where straitening circumstances have weakened the company's hand in negotiations. The obvious challenge for any borrower/issuer in seeking to corral its lenders/creditors is the typical unanimity required under the relevant debt documentation to effect the debt conversion. If a small minority of financial creditors resist the will of an overwhelming majority, then absent a buyout of such a minority, the only alternative route to achieve a successful conversion is to cram down such a dissentient minority using an appropriate statutory scheme or arrangement.

8.2 Schemes of arrangement

A scheme of arrangement under English law is a compromise or arrangement made between a company and its creditors or members (or any class thereof), under Part 26 of the Companies Act 2006.[8] The detailed procedural aspects of schemes of arrangement are considered elsewhere in this book, so here we focus on some recent market developments and considerations when using schemes of arrangement to execute debt-for-equity swaps. All classes of creditors affected by the scheme must approve the scheme, requiring at least 75% in value and more than half in number of the creditors in each such class present and voting at the scheme meeting (in person or by proxy) to endorse it. Consequently, only a minority of up to 25% of each creditor class can be crammed down.

A 'class' of creditors/members is restricted to persons whose rights are not so divergent as to make it impossible for them to consult each other with a view to their common interest.[9] Hence, it is the rights of a party, and not its interests, that determine the class to which it belongs.[10]

It should be noted that schemes of arrangement have been used increasingly

---

8   Parts 26 and 27 of the Companies Act 2006 replace (and restate) the provisions of the Companies Act 1985 relating to schemes.
9   *Sovereign Life Assurance Company v Dunn* [1892] 2 QB 573.
10   *Re Telewest Communications Plc* [2004] EWHC 924.

frequently in the past few years to restructure the debt and equity of non-UK entities.[11] In such circumstances many European companies with substantial bank or bond debt governed by English law or with other sufficient connections with England can use schemes of arrangement to effect the reduction of such debt from their balance sheets without the need to enter a potentially less favourable insolvency regime in their jurisdiction of establishment/incorporation. In many cases the incumbent shareholders may be able to negotiate the retention of certain rights after the completion of a debt writedown, often at the expense of the relevant out-of-the-money classes of junior debt.

There are several advantages to using a scheme of arrangement:

- Once effective, the scheme binds all shareholders of the class that has approved the scheme;[12]
- Through a scheme of arrangement, almost any type of restructuring can be effected[13] (subject to approvals). It is possible to use such a scheme to restructure all of a company's share capital and indebtedness (including that of unsecured trade creditors) or upon releasing a primary debt claim to effect the release of other group members from their related guarantee obligations;
- It is possible to remove minority shareholders;
- A scheme can be structured to provide a lower threshold to acquire control over a target company;
- It may be possible to make a stamp duty saving when transferring shares; and
- It is likely to be recognised across most other EU jurisdictions under the Rome Convention or Rome I Regulation.[14]

Disadvantages include the following:

- the company must comply with all procedural requirements (including Part 26). Also, where applicable, the scheme 'circular'[15] must also comply with the procedural requirements of the Takeover Code, the Listing Rules and/or the Prospectus Rules;
- the court will not approve the scheme if it is *ultra vires*[16] or thought to be unnecessary;
- a scheme cannot be altered once approved without returning to court for the court's approval of a further scheme; and

---

11   See the court's consideration of these issues in *Re La Seda de Barcelona SA* [2010] EWHC 1364 (Ch), *Re Rodenstock GmbH* [2011] EWHC 1104 (Ch) and *Primacom Holding GmbH v Credit Agricole* [2012] EWHC 164 (Ch)
12   Section 899(3) of the Companies Act 2006.
13   For example, an acquisition, a reorganisation or a demerger.
14   The Rome Convention on the Law Applicable to Contractual Obligations 1980 applies to contracts concluded prior to December 17 2009, while the Rome I Regulation on the law applicable to contractual obligations (EU Regulation 593/2008) applies to contracts concluded after that date. There are doubts about the recognition in other EU jurisdictions of an English court's order made in the context of sanctioning even solvent schemes of arrangement under the EU Regulation (EU Regulation 44/2001) on Jurisdiction and the Recognition and Enforcement of Judgments in Civil and Commercial Matters (Judgments Regulation; also known as the 'Brussels Regulation'): see *Re Rodenstock GmbH* [2011] EWHC 1104 (Ch).
15   That is, the document submitted to the court that sets out the details of the scheme of arrangement.
16   *Re Oceanic Steam Navigation Company Limited* [1939] 1 Ch 41.

- if there are material changes to the scheme, the court may refuse to approve it unless the company notifies its members and creditors, on the basis that the members/creditors did not have enough information on which to base their decision.[17]

Lastly, a shareholder may appeal the decision to approve the scheme, provided that it has a justifiable grievance.[18] Otherwise, once agreed, the scheme will bind all creditors/members (or class thereof) whether or not they are in favour.

8.3 Company voluntary arrangements

Company voluntary arrangements (CVAs) are arrangements between a company and its creditors under Part I of the Insolvency Act 1986 and Part 1 of the Insolvency Rules 1986. The terms of the CVA are negotiated between the creditors and the company; however, they are subject to certain procedural requirements. A CVA may be proposed by a company director, administrator or liquidator, who will send a proposal and a statement of the company's affairs to the nominee (ie, a person qualified to act as an insolvency practitioner or a person authorised to act as a nominee under the voluntary arrangement).[19]

Once the proposal is received by the nominee (as long as he is not also acting as either the liquidator or administrator), he must, within 28 days, submit a report to the court.[20] This report may state that a meeting of the company and its creditors is necessary to consider the terms of the proposal.[21]

If such meetings are necessary, they must be held within 14 to 28 days of the date on which the nominee first filed his report with the court. It is important to ensure that all filings are lodged promptly with the court; otherwise you may run the risk of being statute-barred for failing to submit documentation in time.

Decisions will bind the company only if they are made by both the meeting of creditors and the meeting of members or, subject to any order under Section 4A of the Insolvency Act 1986,[22] by the creditors' meeting alone. If the decision is taken by the creditor's meeting alone and a member disagrees with it, then within 28 days of that creditor's meeting, the member may request that the court make an order for the decision of the members' meeting to prevail or to make such other order as the court deems fit.[23]

---

17 Following *Re Jessel Trust Limited* [1985] BCLC 119, a court may not approve a scheme if it believes that the creditors/members' vote would have been different had they known about a matter that was not disclosed.

18 If a minority shareholder, for example, raises a grievance at the court hearing to approve the scheme, the court may order, as a condition of its approval, certain modifications to the scheme or refuse the scheme altogether (eg, *Re Abbey National PLC* [2004] EWHC 2776 (Ch)).

19 The ability of individuals who are not licensed insolvency practitioners to act as nominees was introduced by Section 4 of the Insolvency Act 2000. This section inserted Section 398A into the Insolvency Act 1986, which gave the secretary of state power to declare that certain professional bodies were able to authorise their members to act as nominees.

20 If the nominee is either the administrator or liquidator, there is no requirement to submit a report.

21 Typically, the proposal will also set a time and date for the holding of such a meeting.

22 Section 4A was inserted into the Insolvency Act 1986 by the Insolvency Act 2000.

23 Alternatively, if a person was not given notice of the meeting, an appeal must be made within 28 days of it becoming aware that the meeting had taken place.

Once the CVA has been approved, the arrangement binds all persons that were entitled to vote at the meeting or that would have been entitled to vote had they had notice of it, as if they were a party to the CVA.[24] However, certain persons[25] may apply to the court to appeal a decision taken in a company meeting. Such an appeal may be made only if it can be shown that the CVA unfairly prejudices the interests of a creditor or member and/or that there was some material irregularity at or in relation to the meeting. On appeal the court may, for example, revoke or suspend the CVA or summon a further meeting to consider a revised proposal.

A foreign entity may also be subject to a CVA if it has its centre of main interests in the United Kingdom. This has proved useful when seeking to compromise dissentient minority unsecured creditors under bond instruments.

The advantages of using a CVA include the following:

- CVAs are binding on creditors if they are approved by a majority vote at appropriately convened creditors' and members' meetings;[26]
- it is an offence for a director to make a false statement or to omit to do or fraudulently do anything that induces creditors and members to approve the CVA;[27]
- small companies can avail of the protection afforded under a moratorium;
- creditors have the ability to approve the CVA without the approval of the members (however, this is subject to appeal);
- it is less costly than schemes of arrangement; and
- a CVA is a recognised main insolvency proceeding so has direct effect in most other EU jurisdictions.[28]

Disadvantages include the following:

- CVAs are not binding on secured or preferential creditors unless these parties expressly agree to the CVA;
- no proposal may be approved which affects the rights of a secured creditor to enforce its security, except with the consent of that creditor;[29]
- no proposal may be approved which permits other debts (which are not preferential) to be paid in preference to preferential debt, without the consent of the preferential creditor;[30] and
- the conduct of directors is under no formal scrutiny (ie, there are no formal checks or reports on directors' actions).

---

24   Section 5(2) of the Insolvency Act 1986, as amended by the Insolvency Act 2000.
25   That is, persons entitled to vote at either of the meetings; persons that would have been entitled to vote at the creditor's meeting had they had notice; the nominee; the liquidator; or the administrator.
26   The approval is also binding on those who did not have notice of the meeting but would have been entitled to vote if they had.
27   Section 6A of the Insolvency Act 1986.
28   See Article 3(1) of EU Regulation 1346/2000 on insolvency proceedings.
29   Section 4(3) of the Insolvency Act 1986.
30   Section 4(4) of the Insolvency Act 1986.
31   As defined in Schedule A1, paragraph 3 of the Insolvency Act 1986.
32   Larger companies and companies that do not meet the criteria to obtain a moratorium will continue to use a traditional CVA or may, prior to proposing a CVA, use the protection afforded under an administration moratorium.

Developments to the law governing CVAs mean that it is now possible for small companies[31] to use an optional moratorium before any CVA is put into place.[32]

8.4   Share enforcement and credit bids

In circumstances where a debt-for-equity swap cannot be effected via either a consensual agreement or statutory compromise procedure, the only realistic alternative may be to undertake a transfer of equity to participating creditors by an enforcement of share security. This route is often chosen by 'loan to own' strategists as, with suitable preparation, it can often be completed relatively quickly and privately and without the cooperation of more junior financial creditors or existing management/shareholders. Many intercreditor agreements grant junior creditors an option to purchase senior debt upon enforcement by the senior creditor group. In most restructurings this option remains unexercised as:

- the junior creditors often hold a significantly smaller amount of debt than the senior creditor group;
- the junior creditors must complete exercise of their purchase option within a relatively short period – typically, within 10 business days of notice of the senior creditors' enforcement; and
- most prohibitively, they need to pay the senior creditors the full par value of the latter's debt.

Equity interests in the debtor group are transferred not directly to the participating secured lenders, but to a BidCo newly established by them for that purpose in a suitable jurisdiction. If the shares/partnership interests in the existing debtor group's holding company/partnership are not subject to security in favour of the lenders, the share enforcement will usually take place at a level immediately below the holding company borrower level. In a typical corporate group structure, this may ideally require only the enforcement of one security interest over the equity interests in an intermediate holding entity, rather than lower down a group's equity capital structure when several security interests over shares in operating companies are involved. In the latter case this greatly increases the costs, time and effort required to complete simultaneously the debt-for-equity swap, particularly if several jurisdictions with differing enforcement criteria are involved.

As the BidCo will become the new holding company of the debtor group, the terms of its constitution and its shareholders' agreement must be agreed by the lenders in advance of any bid. The participation of existing lenders in the BidCo's debt and equity capitalisation will be a matter for negotiation.

Security granted by the relevant borrower(s) over the shares in its/their subsidiaries will become enforceable upon the acceleration of indebtedness if there is an inability to discharge the then due debt. In common law jurisdictions, such an enforcement will usually be undertaken by a receiver (appointed by the security trustee), which will transfer the shares to the BidCo under a sale and purchase agreement without the need for a public auction. The receiver will need to undertake a valuation of the shares to be transferred to the BidCo so that it can avoid any liability to junior creditors that the value obtained was not the best price reasonably obtainable in the circumstances. This may involve retaining a number of valuers depending on the complexity of the group and the terms of the release provisions in the finance documentation, which may require only that a fair market value opinion be obtained from an investment bank or firm of accountants. To preserve value and confidentiality, the BidCo may complete the acquisition on a pre-pack basis (ie, where the terms of the transaction are agreed well in advance of enforcement and sale of the relevant equity interests to the BidCo). This usually requires some assistance of the debtor's management, but can mean that the BidCo can announce that a successful restructuring of the balance sheet of the group has occurred together with the basis for any new funding provided to the BidCo.

One of the key issues for any BidCo structure will be whether the receiver/officeholder will require the receipt of cash from the BidCo or whether consideration in the form of a credit bid will be sufficient. In its simplest form, a credit bid involves creditors agreeing to release their claims against the chargor/borrower in consideration for the transfer of the secured shares to the BidCo. Consequently, the converting creditors do not have to provide new funding to make the bid. In certain jurisdictions, even if a credit bid is an acceptable form of consideration, local law may require the process to be undertaken via public auction. This can result in potentially adverse publicity, higher costs and a longer timeframe during which the chargor may be obliged to file for a formal insolvency procedure, which in turn may result in a stay on enforcement. However, financial creditors often have the largest claim against a debtor and can use that quantum to bid for the auctioned shares and be confident that their bid will be the one to be accepted by the receiver.

One increasingly complicating factor associated with groups having several layers of financial debt is the need to ensure that the intercreditor documentation permits the release of members of the debtor group from the primary borrowing claims of junior creditors that might otherwise have a veto on any such transfer. In many leverage finance transactions, where there may be three or more layers of bank and capital markets debt, the intercreditor documentation may permit the security trustee to release the relevant subsidiaries and their assets, which are to be transferred to the ownership of the BidCo from all security, intra-group claims, and all guarantee claims. If such release provisions do not enable the release of borrowers from their junior debt claims, the senior creditors will need to negotiate a release fee with the relevant junior creditors. Very often this may be a cash repayment on completion of the restructuring if further debt is to be provided. Otherwise the junior creditors may anticipate receiving a small percentage of the final equity allocation – possibly 5% to 10% of the ordinary share capital in consideration for releasing their junior debt claims. However, in the past few years courts in both the Netherlands and the United Kingdom have expressly approved a pre-pack sale in circumstances where junior creditors believed that they had implied rights to prevent such sales.[33]

---

33   See *Schoeller Arca Systems* (Amsterdam District Court, September 23 2009) and *HHY Luxembourg SARL v Barclays Bank plc* [2010] EWHC 2406 (Ch).

8.5 Other strategies

In certain jurisdictions the subordination of certain debts, particularly inter-company balances, to the debts of all other creditors may be sufficient to restore the balance-sheet solvency of certain group companies. This will be available only where such subordinated debt will be accounted for as equity (eg, under a German law subordination agreement). This became a feature in some telecommunications groups several years ago in which huge inter-company trading balances arose that often dwarfed the financial creditors' claims. However, this often led to inter-company creditors becoming insolvent more quickly than the inter-company debtors.

9. Tax issues

Debt-for-equity swaps raise a number of complex tax issues and, as with any similar restructuring alternative, such issues should be considered at the outset of any transaction (including whether to apply for a tax clearance). The discussion below relates to certain key tax issues and is confined to the relatively common scenario of a bank lender and a UK resident company borrower.

9.1 Debtor issues

The main issue for the debtor is to avoid a tax charge on the debt-for-equity swap. The starting point is that the UK tax treatment of corporate debt generally follows the accounting treatment,[34] so whenever a debt obligation is modified or extinguished, a tax charge may arise if a profit is recognised in the accounts of the debtor. In a debt-for-equity swap, a specific exemption is typically relied upon. This, broadly, provides for no tax charge where a debt is released in consideration for the receipt of ordinary shares[35] in the relevant borrower in an accounting period for which an amortised cost basis of accounting is used. HMRC, the UK tax office, has also indicated in published anti-avoidance guidance that this tax treatment should not be affected where banks sell on their equity shortly after having been issued with it. However, each case should be considered on its facts to ensure that the particular debt-for-equity swap is not susceptible to challenge from HMRC; for example, where shares issued to the lender are immediately sold to a party connected to the borrower, then the consideration for the debt may be the cash received on the on-sale.

A change in control of the debtor company can also affect the availability of tax losses and raise the sceptre of secondary tax liabilities and degrouping tax charges.

9.2 Creditor issues

The main issues for the creditor will be ensuring that tax relief is available in respect of the debt that is capitalised (ie, for its commercial loss), and that there are no tax charges on the borrower in connection with the debt-for-equity swap (for which, see above).

---

34   See the UK loan relationship rules in Part 5 of the Corporation Tax Act 2009.
35   'Ordinary share capital' means all of the issued share capital of the company apart from capital the holders of which have a right to a dividend at a fixed rate but have no other right to share in the profits of the company.

Where there is no prior connection between the debtor and creditor, relief should be available to the creditor. However, if the creditor and debtor are 'connected' (which is defined by reference to control) at any point in the accounting period in which the debt-for-equity swap occurs, loss relief is denied. Given the potential disincentive of this rule for corporate rescues, loss relief may not be denied to a creditor where the connection, broadly, arises solely as a result of a debt-for-ordinary equity swap. Furthermore, special rules apply to banks.

10. Conclusion

Debt-for-equity swaps are likely to prove to continue to be an integral part of the restructuring landscape when many overleveraged capital structures are threatened with insolvency or are otherwise in capable of being refinanced. Debt-for-equity swaps, while potentially contentious for some stakeholder groups, do provide a mechanism to enable enterprises to be rescued and for significant present value to be preserved while providing an opportunity for future value appreciation to be shared among participating stakeholders.

Table 1: Jurisdictional comparisons among certain statutory schemes/arrangements						
Jurisdiction	Procedure	Regulation	How/when/by whom	Timetable	Consents and approvals	Effect
Belgium	Voluntary reorganisation: judicial composition proceedings.	Act of January 31 2009 on Continuity of Enterprises Act 2009.	Any debtor can negotiate a reorganisation or debt restructuring with its creditors.	From the moment the company files its petition for a judicial reorganisation until the time the court takes a decision on whether or not to open such proceedings (which will be made within 10 days of the company filing its petition), it is protected from any of its creditors seeking enforcement and attachment measures. If the court decides to open judicial reorganisation proceedings, the court may grant a further suspension of payments for a period of up to six months (and it is possible for the court to extend this by a further three months). This applies to court-supervised judicial reorganisations only. Then the court may approve a final suspension of payments plan, which will suspend payments for up to 24 months (with a possible 12-month extension) for	Judicial confirmation or authorisation is not required for an out-of-court reorganisation, although it will be required for a court-supervised judicial reorganisation.	The Commercial Court has discretion to allow a moratorium for a period of six months. During this period, creditors cannot enforce judgments against the debtor. The stay does not affect, however, the status of receivables that have been pledged to a third party. During the preliminary suspension, the debtor may be restricted from entering into certain transactions and no enforcement proceedings may be taken against the debtor During the final suspension, the creditors will be bound by the recovery and payment plan. The suspension of payments and enforcement apply to all acts of enforcement against the debtor, including enforcement of any security, as well as any assertions of retention of title claim.

continued overleaf

Table 1: Jurisdictional comparisons among certain statutory schemes/arrangements						
Jurisdiction	Procedure	Regulation	How/when/by whom	Timetable	Consents and approvals	Effect
Belgium continued				creditors generally or 18 months in the case of secured creditors that have not consented to the plan.		
Belgium continued	Involuntary reorganisation.	Act of January 31 2009 on Continuity of Enterprises Act 2009.	A request may be filed only by the debtor itself or by the public prosecutor.			Creditors have no right to commence judicial composition proceedings, although they may lobby the public prosecutor to do so.
British Virgin Islands	Administration The administration procedure allows insolvent companies to be reorganised and refinanced.	Part III of the Insolvency Act 2003. The provisions have not yet been brought into force (and are not expected to be brought into force in the short term), but may be introduced at any time in the future by resolution of the Executive Council of the British Virgin Islands.	Application is made to the court that has ultimate discretion as to whether to grant an administration order.			The order restricts the rights of creditors to enforce security or take action against the company or its property while it is in force.

continued overleaf

Table 1: Jurisdictional comparisons among certain statutory schemes/arrangements						
Jurisdiction	Procedure	Regulation	How/when/by whom	Timetable	Consents and approvals	Effect
British Virgin Islands continued	Company creditor arrangement (CCA). The directors of a company may propose to the members and creditors of the company a composition in satisfaction of debts.	Part II of the Insolvency Act 2003.	The directors of a company can make a written proposal to an insolvency practitioner, who then decides whether to call a creditors' meeting to consider the proposal. When the company is in liquidation or administration, the arrangement can be proposed by the administrator or liquidator.	Seventy-five percent (in value) of the creditors of the company present and voting must vote in favour of the CCA.		The CCA binds every creditor that had notice of, and was entitled to vote at, the meeting. Preferential and secured creditors are not bound by the CCA unless they so agree. The CCA must be supervised by an insolvency practitioner. CCAs are modelled on the UK CVA, but there is no court involvement in the CCA procedure.
British Virgin Islands continued	Plan of Arrangement.	A plan of arrangement may be used to effect a reorganisation or reconstruction of the company.	Section 177 of the Business Companies Act 2004.	The directors of a BVI company must set out the details of the proposed plan of arrangement. An application is then made by the company to the court for approval of the proposed arrangement.	The plan of arrangement will be effective only when the articles of arrangement are filed with the British Virgin Islands Registrar of Corporate Affairs. The effective date may be either the date of the filing or a later date, not more than 30 days after the filing date, as stipulated in the articles of arrangement.	The court will make an interim or final order, giving directions as to the requisite approvals that must be obtained. The court has wide discretion to determine, among other matters: • any notice of the proposed arrangement that needs to be sent and to whom; • whether approval of the arrangement needs to be obtained and if so, from whom; and • whether shareholders, creditors or other security holders may dissent from the arrangement.

continued overleaf

Table 1: Jurisdictional comparisons among certain statutory schemes/arrangements						
Jurisdiction	Procedure	Regulation	How/when/by whom	Timetable	Consents and approvals	Effect
Cayman Islands	Scheme of arrangement.	A scheme of arrangement allows the company to enter into an agreement with its members or creditors (or both) to: • restructure its affairs while solvent so that it can continue to trade and avoid liquidation; or • reach a compromise with creditors after liquidation has begun.	Sections 86 to 89 of the Companies Law (2004 Revision). The procedure can be initiated by the company, any creditor or shareholder of the company or a liquidator applying to the court, where the company is already in liquidation or provisional liquidation. Accepted practice is to send out with the scheme document an explanatory memorandum detailing the proposals of the scheme to be considered by the company's members and creditors. The court usually orders a meeting of the creditors, a class of creditors or shareholders (as appropriate).	The company, as applicant, presents a petition commencing the court process and then makes an *ex parte* application to court for directions about the calling of shareholder and creditor meetings. From drafting the scheme document to this stage takes approximately four to six weeks.	A majority in number representing at least 75% in value of the creditors, a class of creditors or shareholders (as appropriate), present and voting either in person or by proxy at the meeting, must agree to the compromise or arrangement. It is typically necessary to call meetings of only those classes of shareholders whose existing rights will be directly affected by the scheme. An application to the court must then be made to approve it. The scheme of arrangement is binding on all parties and cannot subsequently be altered, even if the shareholders and creditors acquiesce to the alterations.	A scheme of arrangement includes a reorganisation of the share capital of the company by the consolidation of shares of different classes or by the division of shares into shares of different classes (or both). In practice, the scheme will come to an end once all terms of the compromise or arrangement to which it relates have been complied with. The scheme will be effective once a copy of the court order has been lodged with the Registrar of Companies.

continued overleaf

Table 1: Jurisdictional comparisons among certain statutory schemes/arrangements						
Jurisdiction	Procedure	Regulation	How/when/by whom	Timetable	Consents and approvals	Effect
France	*Mandat ad hoc* proceedings. Used to organise an informal negotiation between the company and its major creditors. Confidential and voluntary. The president of the court appoints an agent to carry out appropriate tasks.	Articles L 611-3 of the Commercial Code.	Petition to be filed to the president of the court by the company's management. Company must be solvent.	No statutory time limit for appointed agents completing their tasks. Usually lasts from one month to a year.	No approval by the board of directors unless otherwise stated by the articles of association.	The company's management and its major creditors should negotiate a solution to the company's financial difficulties. A debt rescheduling plan accepted by some creditors cannot be imposed on the other creditors. If an agreement is reached between the company and its creditors, the agent's duties end.

continued overleaf

Table 1: Jurisdictional comparisons among certain statutory schemes/arrangements						
Jurisdiction	Procedure	Regulation	How/when/by whom	Timetable	Consents and approvals	Effect
France continued	Conciliation proceedings. Voluntary proceedings aiming to reach a workout agreement between the company and its creditors under the supervision of a court-appointed agent.	Articles L 611-4 and following of the Commercial Code.	Petition to be filed by the company chairman with the president of the court. The company must face financial or legal difficulties, but must not have been insolvent for more than 45 days.	Agent appointed by the court for a maximum period of four months, which can be extended by up to a month at the agent's request.	None required. A company has two options: • request formal court approval of the workout agreement – this is a public judgment and subject to challenge by a third party; or • obtain the president of the court's approval. This involves no publicity but implies that the creditors waive their right to priority of payment.	This procedure does not involve an automatic stay of proceedings. However, the court can force creditors that attempt to enforce their rights during conciliation to accept a moratorium for up to two years (Article L 611-7 of the Commercial Code.)

continued overleaf

Table 1: Jurisdictional comparisons among certain statutory schemes/arrangements						
Jurisdiction	Procedure	Regulation	How/when/by whom	Timetable	Consents and approvals	Effect
France continued	Safeguard proceedings.	These allow solvent companies to be restructured under court supervision. Petition to be filed by the company with the president of the court. The company must face financial difficulties that cannot be overcome, without yet being insolvent.	Articles L 620-1 and following of the Commercial Code.	Observation period of up to six months to assess the company's situation, which can be extended once for six months and, in exceptional circumstances, for a further six months at the public prosecutor's request.	No specific consent is required unless expressly specified in the articles of association. If classes of creditors are created, the plan is deemed approved by the classes if the requisite percentages vote in favour of the plan. The court must then approve the plan. If there are no classes of creditors, the plan must be negotiated on a one-to-one basis with each creditor.	Automatic stay of all actions against the company and individuals acting as guarantors and joint debtors. There are exceptions to the automatic stay, such as: • set off between connected claims; or • claims secured by a security interest conferring a retention right. All creditors must file proof of their claim within two months of publication of the judgment opening safeguard proceedings (four months for creditors outside France). Once approved by the court, the plan is enforceable against all members of the creditors' committee.

continued overleaf

Table 1: Jurisdictional comparisons among certain statutory schemes/arrangements						
Jurisdiction	Procedure	Regulation	How/when/by whom	Timetable	Consents and approvals	Effect
France continued	Accelerated financial safeguard procedure.	Article L.628-1 of the Commercial Code.	Petition to be filed by the company with the president of the court. The company must face financial difficulties that cannot be overcome, without yet being insolvent. In addition, the debtor must have been under conciliation proceedings prior to the opening of the accelerated financial safeguard.	Observation period of up to one month, which can be extended once for one month.	The debtor must reach a 'pre-pack restructuring' agreement that will ensure the continuation of its business, and that is likely to gain the support of the holders of at least two-third of the amount of the financial debt that will be affected by the restructuring.	Same effects as the safeguard proceeding above.
Germany	Voluntary out-of-court/out-of-insolvency restructuring.		Negotiated between the company and its creditors. Management of the company has to file for insolvency (maximum three weeks), if the company is illiquid, or over-indebtedness (eg, due to a calling of loans in the absence of a standstill agreement)	Typically, three to six months (in more complex situations: up to nine months).	All affected creditors must approve. Consent of shareholders required to the extent that their rights are affected.	This is an out-of-court, informal procedure.

continued overleaf

Table 1: Jurisdictional comparisons among certain statutory schemes/arrangements						
Jurisdiction	Procedure	Regulation	How/when/by whom	Timetable	Consents and approvals	Effect
Germany continued	Restructuring by way of insolvency plan proceedings. The German Insolvency Code gives a company the ability to initiate reorganisation proceedings by way of insolvency plan proceedings (comparable to a scheme of arrangement). According to the revised German Insolvency Code, the management of the company can use the so-called 'protective shield mechanism' in combination with debtor in possession proceedings when filing for insolvency due to imminent illiquidity or over-indebtedness in order to be granted a period of up to three months to prepare a reorganisation plan.	Insolvency Code 2012.	An individual creditor cannot submit a reorganisation plan; only the debtor and the insolvency administrator have that authority. The creditors at the creditors' meeting can instruct the insolvency administrator to produce a reorganisation plan.	Under the revised German Insolvency Code, presumably three to six months (formerly up to nine months)	The required consents depend on the forming of the groups in the reorganisation plan. In each group, the majority of both creditors and total claims is required. It is now possible under German insolvency law to form a group for the shareholders of the debtor. Dissenting groups (including, but not limited to, shareholders) can be crammed down if evidence can be provided that the respective group is put economically in a situation not worse than in comparison with a liquidation scenario. The obstruction potential of dissenting voters can furthermore be mitigated by already inserting potential settlement amounts in the reorganisation plan.	The reorganisation plan has to be confirmed by the insolvency court to come into force and effect. The reorganisation plan is a very flexible tool that can be used for various measures of restructuring, including the restructuring of the debt side of the company (also by way of debt-to-equity swap). In the reorganisation plan, any and all corporate actions can be taken, including share transfers and capital reductions combined with subsequent increases.

continued overleaf

Table 1: Jurisdictional comparisons among certain statutory schemes/arrangements						
Jurisdiction	Procedure	Regulation	How/when/by whom	Timetable	Consents and approvals	Effect
Italy	Restructuring Plan.	Article 67 (III)(d) of the Bankruptcy Law (RD 267/ 1942).	The company proposes a restructuring plan, the feasibility of which and the veracity of the underlying company's data must be assessed by an independent expert. The plan usually (but not necessarily) involves negotiations between the company and certain of its creditors.	Typically, three to six months, but will vary depending on the circumstances.	No specific consents are required. If the plan provides for a specific agreement with certain creditors, the consent of all such creditors is required.	This is an out-of-court procedure that provides protection from clawback actions for the acts and payments made pursuant to the plan approved by the expert, in case of a subsequent bankruptcy of the debtor.

continued overleaf

Table 1: Jurisdictional comparisons among certain statutory schemes/arrangements						
Jurisdiction	Procedure	Regulation	How/when/by whom	Timetable	Consents and approvals	Effect
Italy continued	Debt restructuring agreement(s). The most frequently used procedure in recent Italian restructurings.	Article 182*bis* of the Bankruptcy Law	A company in financial difficulties with the agreement of its creditors holding 60% of the total outstanding claims may, among other things, reduce the debts of the participating creditors, subject to (i) an independent 'expert' certifying that the debt restructuring agreement allows the debtor to repay all non-adherent creditors and the veracity of the company's underlying data, and (ii) the court's approval.	Usually several months – with possibility (in the very first steps of the proceeding) to switch from *concordato preventivo* procedure to Article 182*bis* procedure.	The agreement must be approved by creditors representing no less than 60% of the outstanding claims. Non-adherent creditors must be repaid within 120 days of: (i) the court's approval, for claims already due at the time of the filing; or (ii) the day when the claim was originally due, for claims that were not yet due at the date of the filing. Court approval is required for the debt restructuring agreement to become effective.	Non-adherent creditors may oppose the agreement. Protects acts and payments made under Article 182*bis* from clawback risks. Protection of bridge financing.

continued overleaf

Table 1: Jurisdictional comparisons among certain statutory schemes/arrangements						
Jurisdiction	Procedure	Regulation	How/when/by whom	Timetable	Consents and approvals	Effect
Italy continued	Composition agreement.	Article 160 of the Bankruptcy Law.	A debtor may file in court a proposal for a composition with creditors. If approved by the court, such proposal has to be voted by creditors (which may be divided into classes with different treatment). The proposal is approved by the majority of the creditors (and the majority of the classes of creditors). If approved, it binds also dissenting creditors.	First stage of the proceeding takes 60 to 120 days (extendable for up to 180 days). The duration of the overall proceeding cannot exceed eight months.	Majority in value of creditors and majority of creditor classes.	Protects acts and payments made under from clawback risks. Protection of bridge financing.
Jersey	Scheme of arrangement between the company and its creditors or a class of them, or between the company and its members or a class of them.	Article 125 of the Companies (Jersey) Law 1991.	Application to court to convene a meeting to approve such compromise may be made by a company, a creditor, a member or a liquidator.	No predetermined timeframe, but may take several months to implement.	Three-quarters by value of the creditors, class of creditors, members or class of members present and voting must approve the compromise or arrangement. Court approval is also required.	The court may order a moratorium for a period against proceedings when approving a reconstruction, however, there is no automatic stay.

continued overleaf

Table 1: Jurisdictional comparisons among certain statutory schemes/arrangements						
Jurisdiction	Procedure	Regulation	How/when/by whom	Timetable	Consents and approvals	Effect
Luxembourg	Controlled management. This is a voluntary procedure to reorganise a company's business or to realise its.	Grand-Ducal Decree, May 24 1935.	The request must be given by the company to the commercial court together with the list of creditors.	There is no set time limit for a controlled management. The court sets a schedule that depends on the particular circumstances.	The court must approve the procedure. The plan of reorganisation must be approved by a majority of creditors in number and in value and then be ratified by the court.	The company will be placed under the control of a commissioner, who will plan the reorganisation of the company's debts. The company cannot transfer any of its rights or assets in the course of the reorganisation without the approval of the commissioner.

continued overleaf

Table 1: Jurisdictional comparisons among certain statutory schemes/arrangements						
Jurisdiction	Procedure	Regulation	How/when/by whom	Timetable	Consents and approvals	Effect
United States	Reorganisation under Chapter 11 of the Bankruptcy Code, which allows a company in financial difficulties to continue its business while preparing a reorganisation plan with its creditors.	Title 11 of the US Code, Sections 101 and following (Bankruptcy Code 1978)	A company can file a voluntary petition for relief with the bankruptcy court or a creditor can file an involuntary Chapter 11 petition with the bankruptcy court.	No limit on duration of Chapter 11 proceedings, except for the reorganisation of railway companies, which is limited to five years.	Creditors and shareholders are divided into different classes for the purpose of voting. All creditors and shareholders whose rights are deemed impaired by the plan receive ballots by which they are given the opportunity to vote for or against the plan. With the ballot, creditors and shareholders receive a disclosure statement. A plan can be confirmed if the bankruptcy court has approved a disclosure statement and holders of two-third in amount and more than half the number of allowed claims of each affected class have voted to approve the plan.	The filing of a petition triggers an automatic stay that prevents creditors from taking further action against the company. However, relief from the automatic stay can be obtained for cause. The existing management can continue to manage the company's affairs and finances. A confirmed and effective plan of reorganisation acts as a contract binding on the company and all creditors and all shareholders, including those that do not vote to accept the plan.

Workouts and restructuring: pre-packs at an operational level

Mark Shaw
BDO LLP

1.   What are pre-packs and why do they remain a topical issue?

The expression 'pre-pack' has become near ubiquitous in modern insolvency and restructuring practice. It covers a multitude of transactions – from the sale of assets to directors of very small companies, which can attract concern and sometimes even derision among commentators – to highly sophisticated and considered transactions worth billions of pounds. The public concern over pre-packs largely stems from a perceived lack of transparency, especially around valuation of the business sold.

This chapter concentrates on operational or trading companies in the context of mid-market and upwards transactions. It does not deal specifically with the issues that arise in private equity-backed structures, involving only holding companies and more limited numbers of financial stakeholders. However, the issues and thought processes are likely to apply to virtually all pre-packs, to one degree or another.

Pre-pack sales of operational or trading companies tend to have a greater impact on the underlying business in a group than, for example, pre-packs that take place only at the holding company level.

Some years ago, it was relatively common for even quite large and complex insolvency appointments, such as administrative receivers or administrators, to be made with little warning or planning. The appointed insolvency practitioner would then need to decide whether the business should be traded on with a view to it being marketed and, hopefully, sold as a going concern. This meant that any business sale would be executed some time after appointment.

However, over the past decade or so, stakeholders – especially lenders – have become adept at identifying potential problem exposures early on, which has meant that there is normally a period of time between the identification of a problem and the likelihood of an insolvency process. This in turn means that the business can often be marketed for sale prior to, rather than after, an insolvency process has commenced. While a detailed discussion of distressed M&A and accelerated M&A processes is beyond the scope of this chapter, such processes are nonetheless relevant, as their proliferation has caused a consequent growth in the use of pre-packs.

Distressed M&A and accelerated M&A processes market a business for sale using a variant of more traditional M&A techniques. The timeframe is usually much shorter than for a traditional M&A process and information/due diligence is limited, but the focus remains the sale of a bundle of underlying cash flows to a purchaser in as seamless a manner possible, as opposed to the historically more common sale of a bundle of assets. The aim of this approach should be to preserve and maximise value.

Once the sales process has been run and the price maximised through such competitive tension as it has been possible to create within an expedited timeframe, the sale is commonly executed using a pre-pack.

Another factor which is likely to have contributed to the use of pre-packs is the risk of litigation for loss-making trading against insolvency practitioners following appointment. There have been various cases of this and the use of the pre-pack mitigates much of this risk – although, as discussed below, it does create other risks instead.

Therefore, a pre-pack is usually a sale of a business from within a company to a new owner, which has been arranged and documented prior to the commencement of an insolvency process. In a pre-pack, the first transaction which the appointed insolvency practitioner enters into is to sign a pre-arranged and pre-negotiated sale agreement.

Pre-packs also tend to reduce costs, as the work must be carried out within a limited timeframe. In some circumstances, very much less work needs to be carried out to arrange a sale compared to that required to trade on post-insolvency.

This chapter is a high-level discussion of some of the practical issues that affect pre-pack sales at an operational level. It is not intended to be a complete guide or checklist of all issues to which an insolvency practitioner should have regard. Each situation will be different and insolvency practitioners will need to use their own judgement and seek appropriate advice as needed.

2.   The decision to pre-pack

In broad terms, any appointed insolvency practitioner has a duty to maximise realisations and distribute those realisations among creditors in the right manner. Overall, this duty means that returns to creditors must be maximised.

If a pre-pack sale is arranged, there is always a risk that the insolvency practitioner could be criticised or even sued for not properly marketing a business for sale.

The prudent insolvency practitioner will therefore wish to consider carefully any decision to execute a pre-pack sale, given the potential for such criticism or litigation.

Some factors that may be taken into account in deciding whether to execute a pre-pack sale are discussed below. This list is not intended to be exhaustive.

However, the essence of the decision to pre-pack is the answer to the following question: is it likely that a pre-pack sale will, overall, be better than any realistically achievable next best option? In some cases, the answer to this will be clear. In others, the insolvency practitioner will need to undertake careful analysis and risk management processes in exercising his judgement.

The following illustrative factors are all likely to be supportive, if not determinative, of a decision to pre-pack.

2.1 The position of senior debt

If a bank is owed a significant sum of money which is secured on all assets of the company, this can make a decision to pre-pack more straightforward in certain circumstances.

An example could be a highly geared business that has underperformed significantly at an operational level and now needs additional funds, which the current lenders are unwilling to provide and which cannot be obtained from an alternative lender.

Let us assume that, over time, £70 million of debt has built up in the business. Its assets on a break-up are worth less than £10 million. The enterprise value of the business is currently, say, £35 million – as determined by market testing, independent valuation or both.

Therefore, the business would need to be worth £35 million more before the insolvency practitioner would be at risk of a justifiable claim of undervalue, on the assumption that the holder of the £70 million of debt agreed with the strategy. For simplicity, it is assumed that all of the company's assets fell to fixed charge realisations and hence the prescribed part is not a consideration.

Put another way, the lender can decide for itself whether a given level of loss is acceptable to it and the outcome does not affect other stakeholders, in practical terms.

The closer the value gets to the next level of debt down – say, unsecured creditors – the greater the risk becomes.

An important factor surrounding senior debt is the ability to deliver the assets to a buyer. If a senior lender has security over the assets, a deed of release will likely be needed to deliver the assets unencumbered to a buyer. Therefore, in most circumstances, the lender needs to be in agreement with the strategy to be able to do this. Similar issues can arise in relation to lower-ranking creditors, such as bond holders, where a change of control consent is required in the indenture. This can give rise to complex contractual positions, making proper legal advice essential.

2.2 Loss of customers in insolvency

Some businesses will have customers that dissipate quickly once the prospect of formal insolvency is scented. This is not necessarily the same as the situation in which contracts for sale of a debtor's goods or services are determined on insolvency, but is more a commercial issue about being able to rely on a debtor for continued supply.

A pre-pack sale is still a sale out of insolvency and hence contracts which determine automatically on insolvency will still do so.

An example of such commercial customer risk could come from a supply of engineered goods where warranties are essential. In such cases, customers are likely to move to alternative suppliers rather than risk the potential loss of warranty or after-sales care. Trading by an insolvency practitioner after the commencement of insolvency would therefore be more difficult.

In a pre-pack sale, the message to customers could be: "X Ltd has bought the business, your past warranties will be honoured and X Ltd has ample resources to fund the business in the future." Revenues would thus be preserved and value maximised. If this were contrasted with an insolvency process, with post-appointment trading and a subsequent sale, the value of the business would likely be lower due to loss of revenues. Debtor and stock realisations would likely be suppressed as well.

2.3   Loss of key people

This can happen where there are highly mobile people whose retention is key to preserving business value. An example would be a professional services firm. Again, the issue would arise not so much from determination of employment contracts as from rivals calling directly to poach key staff and to exploit the debtor's distressed position.

2.4   Regulated businesses

Some businesses are regulated such that a formal insolvency process would destroy value in them, through withdrawal of that regulated status. A pre-pack may avoid this as the formal insolvency process happens only at the instant of sale.

Financial services and legal businesses are good examples of such situations.

2.5   Post-insolvency trading would be loss-making or require significant funding

This is commonly the case, as suppliers can hold a debtor to ransom for ongoing supplies – not just in terms of, say, *pro forma* supplies for new deliveries, but also for past debts and/or retention of title claims.

An example is useful to illustrate the issues. An insolvency practitioner has identified that a prudent post-appointment marketing period to execute a sale would be four weeks. In that time, the debtor would make an accounting loss of approximately £5 million, on the assumption that no customers would be lost. Further, the insolvency practitioner has formed the view that he would need to borrow £3 million to achieve that £5 million loss. On the assumption of no customer losses, the £3 million of borrowings would likely be repaid at the end of the four-week trading period. It is far from certain that the value of the underlying assets would be increased from such trading.

Meanwhile, current lenders have stated that they see that the debtor is over-borrowed already and therefore would lend money to the insolvency practitioner only if he were to accept personal liability for the loans. There is no logical argument for an insolvency practitioner having to borrow money personally in such circumstances, when the underlying stakeholders themselves do not see the economic sense in it.

In these circumstances, overall, it could well be better to consider the use of a pre-pack sale. This example also begins to highlight some of the potential conflicts and risks which pre-packs create. If the business is to lose money and require funding, surely some of that would happen under the directors' trading during, say, an accelerated M&A process? Who, then, provides funding or bears the effects of these losses? This issue is important and is considered in further detail below.

2.6 A good business, but with historical liabilities

A good example of this would be a manufacturer which is operationally profitable, but has a legacy environmental or health and safety liability which renders the business unsustainable for the future.

In certain circumstances, a pre-pack can be used to clean up a business, passing it to new owners but without liabilities which would otherwise render it unviable. This can carry significant reputational risk and hence careful consideration of other alternative options is needed, especially around value. For example, a more collective process (eg, a company voluntary arrangement or scheme of arrangement) may be worthy of consideration. The purposes of administration require that these be considered before a pre-pack sale of assets is used.

Defined benefit pension schemes are another example of such situations.

2.7 Other issues

It could be said that an accelerated M&A/distressed M&A process followed by a pre-pack is intended to facilitate a seamless sale of a business, with minimal taint from insolvency.

While it is true that the taint from insolvency would be less than in, say, an insolvency appointment followed by a marketing period and a sale, not all of the problems would disappear.

For example, property leases cannot just be 'sold' to a buyer. They need to be assigned by tripartite agreement between landlord, tenant (ie, seller) and buyer. Therefore, the solution is usually to grant a licence to occupy in the pre-pack sale agreement to the buyer. This will normally be in breach of the lease and can give rise to applications for forfeiture. Therefore, this will need to be considered and the risks mitigated in advance.

The same can be true for certain other types of rights being sold.

Trade creditors, to the extent that they are not paid or otherwise taken over the buyer, may well refuse to supply the buyer without their debts being settled. Any information memorandum for an accelerated M&A/distressed M&A process would need to consider carefully the likely extent of supplier ransom to ensure that the effect on value was understood and minimised. The position is similar for retention of title claims.

Generally, a review of contracts should be undertaken to ascertain which of these determine automatically in an insolvency process and which may be determined by the counterparty on an insolvency process. If key contracts vanish, this can go to value. It is not ideal to hope that a buyer will not notice; it is better to know about and deal with such issues in advance of a sale.

Generally, insofar as possible, with an accelerated M&A/distressed M&A process for a trading business, it makes sense to identify and deal upfront with potential problems that could go to value which the insolvency process might cause, so that potential buyers can be comfortable and value can thus be maximised. Suggestions for post-sale communications processes are also important to this.

3.   **Documenting the decision**

Having set out the position where criticism could be levelled at an insolvency practitioner for failing to achieve proper value before executing a pre-pack sale, it follows that having a detailed written justification of why that decision was made would be sound risk management.

This justification should be an answer to the potential questions that, for example, an unsecured creditor which is left out of the money on such a sale could ask of the insolvency practitioner.

It is vital, in making and documenting the decision to execute a pre-pack sale, that the insolvency practitioner thinks objectively about the sorts of criticism he would level at another insolvency practitioner if he were engaged by, say, an unsecured creditor to assess the appropriateness of a pre-pack sale. This is a 'poacher turned gamekeeper' thought process.

Robust internal procedures are vital. In making the decision and preparing the consequent file note to evidence this decision, it should always be borne in mind that there is the potential for litigation around value, and that the note being prepared could be adduced in evidence in legal proceedings. It is far better to consider and document such issues at the time, to deal with any likely questions in advance of litigation occurring.

The file note documenting the decision must be carefully structured and fully worked. It should include an assessment of the following at a high level.

Evidence of insolvency	• What evidence do you have that the debtor is insolvent? • How did you come to that conclusion? • From which source(s) did you draw information?
Why the business cannot trade post-insolvency	• Explain why such trading would not be appropriate (eg, lack of funding, supply difficulties, people difficulties, nature of business). • Explain why even limited trading cannot be conducted post-insolvency. • Comment on post-appointment trading profitability. • Comment on post-appointment funding needs and likely sources.

continued on next page

Why the offer in the pre-pack is better than the next best alternative	• Prepare an outcome statement for all classes of creditor for the pre-pack, contrasting with the next best alternative. • Comment on valuations and marketing exercises undertaken. If one or more of these has not been undertaken, explain why not. • Explain why a break-up would not be more appropriate. • Explain why it would not be possible or as effective to market the business post-insolvency. • Consider the impact of costs in each alternative.
Who will lose money?	• Which creditors/shareholders will be adversely affected by the pre-pack sale and what is their likely reaction? • How will you be able to defend your decision against such reactions? • Are there any management or shareholder disputes which could affect the decision?
Other matters	• Consider any other matters which a person who does not fully understand the pre-pack sale decision at hand would need in order to understand the issues and the conclusions reached. • What would an investigative journalist make of the transaction? How would you hypothetically answer his criticisms? • Take account of insolvency process issues (discussed further below). • Consider the use of a scorecard to aid decision making. • Prepare the letter to creditors required under Statement of Insolvency Practice (SIP) 16 and Dear IP 42. Can you adequately deal with all matters set out in those documents?
Conclusion	• Include a summary and clear conclusion as to why this pre-pack sale is justifiable and the best course of action in the circumstances.

The file note should be signed off by its originator, the insolvency practitioners who are to be appointed and any internal risk controllers. All documents referred to in the file note should be appended to it in a clear, structured manner. The disciplined process of doing this will usually mean that most, if not all, relevant issues are considered before final sign-off is given.

There will naturally be a cost/benefit analysis in the amount of detail and justification that is provided in the file note – a matter for the insolvency practitioner's judgement in each case.

4. Choice of insolvency process

Readers will note that, so far, this chapter has referred to the terms 'insolvency practitioner' and 'insolvency process' in generic terms.

In reality, more than one process could well be available. These are discussed below, together with some relevant issues which would need to be considered. However, the majority of pre-packs will likely be executed using administration. Not all of the issues relating to these processes are discussed – just some key ones which may be relevant to pre-pack sales.

4.1 Administrative receivership

Administrative receivership is usually initiated by a lender holding appropriate security. In effect, administrative receivership is a dying process, as it can be initiated only by holders of certain security which, other than certain exceptions, it has not been possible to create after September 15 2003.

The key point about administrative receivership in the context of a pre-pack is that the lender can make, demand and appoint on just a few hours' notice. There is no need for the involvement of the courts in any way. It is entirely a private remedy.

Of further relevance to pre-packs is that the administrative receiver's duties are relatively limited: in commercial terms, they are to maximise the repayment to the appointer without undue disadvantage to preferential creditors and, by implication, unsecured creditors. In situations where there is a clear shortfall to a secured lender, an administrative receiver has a great deal of latitude.

An administrative receiver has few tax issues to deal with, as the majority fall to be dealt with by the company in a subsequent liquidation. Other than in situations where the secured lender would be repaid in full, an administrative receiver can largely ignore tax issues, especially those relating to chargeable gains.

Administrative receivership does not, however, provide a moratorium against legal proceedings in the same way as administration. Practically, where administrative receivership is available, the trade-off between tax and moratorium issues will be key to the choice between administrative receivership and administration.

Technically, the disclosure obligations of SIP 16 and Dear IP 42 do not apply to administrative receiverships, but it remains best practice to apply them in such situations.

4.2   Administration

This is likely to cover the majority of pre-pack sales. The process can be initiated by the directors of a company directly, by application to the court or by the holder of a qualifying floating charge. For most pre-pack sales, it is likely that the director route or qualifying floating charge route will be used, as these require no court decision, only filing.

Except for certain types of company, the appointed administrator has a so-called 'waterfall' of objectives to meet. These objectives are, in commercial terms:

- to rescue the company;
- to achieve a better result for creditors than in a winding-up; and
- to realise property in order to make a distribution to one or more secured or preferential creditors.

The administrator may cascade down the waterfall only in the event that an objective cannot be met.

It is likely that the Insolvency Act as currently amended intended that the administrator would consider these duties only once in office. However, in a pre-pack the prospective administrator must consider these issues before accepting the appointment. Therefore, to the extent that the first or, where relevant, the second objective cannot be achieved, the administrator will need to be able to show he has considered in appropriate detail why that is the case. As set out above, this should be documented in the file note justifying the pre-pack sale. The author is unaware of any claim against an administrator in this regard, but it is arguably only a matter of time before one is made.

An administrator is an officer of the court and under its ultimate control, and administration is a collective procedure. However, the decision of whether and how to exercise the power to execute a pre-pack sale is one for the administrator, not the court. Therefore, despite the court-supervised nature of administration, in practice the administrator gets on with the job, using his commercial judgement, unless and until a creditor or other stakeholder applies to the court to argue otherwise. Any attempt by the administrator himself to get the court to sanction the exercise of his commercial judgement is unlikely to be successful.

The administrator's status as an officer of the court obliges him to be fair and balanced to all interested parties in his decisions; this can add extra considerations in certain pre-pack sales.

Recognition in many European states may be helpful in the aftermath of a pre-pack. Administration allows this as a collective procedure.

Tax planning in contemplation of a pre-pack is touched upon below, as this is much more relevant in the context of an administration.

Another issue of relevance to administrations relates to costs of advisers in the run-up to the pre-pack. If these are not settled before the administration is started, they must meet certain criteria to be paid as expenses of the administration.

4.3   Other types of receivership

Receivers may also be appointed under certain fixed charges and under the Law of

Property Act. They are not discussed further in this chapter as they have practical limitations for pre-pack sales, because they do not provide the ability to sell assets which are subject to floating charges – just those subject to some fixed charges or mortgages.

4.4 Liquidations

Liquidation is not discussed in detail as, in practice, it is rarely seen in the context of pre-pack sales. This is because of the time delays which legislation and practical matters impose on a liquidator.

However, there are certain situations and types of corporate body for which administration is not possible; liquidation or provisional liquidation may provide the solution – although such situations will be rare.

4.5 Company voluntary arrangements and schemes of arrangement

These tend to establish arrangements to compromise claims, as opposed to providing a framework for the sale of assets from a debtor in satisfaction of claims. They therefore tend to be an alternative to pre-packs, as opposed to a means of achieving them. There could well be specific circumstances in which this is not the case, but the scope of this chapter is on more usual practice.

An example of such specific circumstances would be the use of company voluntary arrangements to restructure retail and similar businesses over the last few years. As such, in practice, the consideration of company voluntary arrangements and schemes of arrangements is more likely to be an alternative to a pre-pack than a means of executing one. These are particularly important in considering the cascade of the three administration purposes above, especially the first.

5. Risk

Certain risk issues warrant further discussion.

5.1 Advisers/insolvency practitioners

For the sake of simplicity, it is assumed for these purposes that the adviser is the insolvency practitioner in waiting.

The most significant likely risk for an insolvency practitioner is the allegation of not achieving proper value. This can be mitigated to some extent by ensuring that the guidelines outlined above on making and documenting the decision to execute a pre-pack sale are followed.

It is usually important to obtain professional valuations for physical assets (eg, real estate, plant and machinery) on a break-up basis, an existing use basis and – especially for real estate – an alternative use basis. The latter could include development potential, for example.

The insolvency practitioner will need to provide estimates of the values of monetary assets, such as debtors, stock and work in progress. The judgement and experience of the insolvency practitioner and the nature of the relevant business will be important here.

Goodwill and intellectual property are much harder to value, especially in distress situations. It is particularly in respect of these types of asset that market exposure is useful in reducing risk.

For this reason, it is always best that some form of market exposure be used wherever possible. This is likely to be through accelerated M&A/distressed M&A processes. The insolvency practitioner will need to ensure that any such process is run properly, especially if (as is likely) his own firm runs the process.

In some circumstances, it can be appropriate to obtain a range of likely valuations from a third-party valuer on business value, whether that be in conjunction with exposure to the market or in place of it. Current practice dictates that market exposure is the normal starting point. Sometimes, such market exposure may be only to financial buyers and not to trade buyers as well. Although this is not the best means of market exposure, it may be a pragmatic compromise where the business is at risk from a sales process being made public by competitors for their own commercial advantage.

There is reputational risk for the insolvency practitioner. For example, if a case is likely to attract press attention due to the fact that, although a pre-pack may be commercially desirable, a high-profile group of creditors or shareholders will lose money, steps must be taken to manage this. This will involve a combination of robust internal risk management processes and ensuring that appropriate communications are in place for the firm when the pre-pack is made public, such that the insolvency practitioner's position is explained before concerns are raised in the press. Considering likely public reaction can often be a good way of assessing the risks of a pre-pack sale in itself.

Conflicts can arise (eg, between the insolvency practitioner advising the directors in respect of their duties and a lender, which may be perceived to desire a continuation of trade) in achieving a pre-pack sale following an accelerated M&A/distressed M&A process. This is commented on in more detail below, but the insolvency practitioner will need to be sure that he does not find himself in a position of unmanageable conflict.

If the pre-pack sale is to directors, there is nothing to stop the insolvency practitioner from requesting warranties from them personally to minimise its risk. This would be on the basis that the directors would effectively be on both sides of the transaction, with the insolvency practitioner in the middle, standing to benefit only from its fees, not the value in the business in the future – which in part could depend on the sale price being reduced.

It is helpful to have internal risk management policies which require an independent senior partner or a similar committee to approve a pre-pack sale to make sure that there is proper consultation on the decision. This protects not only the firm, but also the individuals within it as, once approved, the decision becomes a collective one.

The insolvency practitioner cannot seek to limit his liability contractually against claims from creditors or other stakeholders.

5.2 Directors

In a pre-pack sale, the directors will not be executing the sale and so are unlikely to be at risk of breach of duty claims that they did not achieve a proper price. All the same, they need to do all they can to maximise value and returns to creditors, and to ensure that the decisions that they take are defensible after the event. This usually suggests that directors should take expert advice from someone who is clear of unmanageable conflicts.

Commonly, a lender will want trading to continue during an accelerated M&A or distressed M&A process where further funds cannot be provided. If the business is loss making, this gives rise to the question of who should bear that loss. If the directors allow the position of, for example, trade creditors to worsen by such continued trading when the likely benefits of so doing will accrue to a senior lender, this could be a *prima facie* case of wrongful trading. This exposes the directors to the risk of personal liability for restitution, as well as disqualification from acting as a director in the future.

The language of the wrongful trading provisions can be summarised in commercial terms as: directors should not do anything or suffer anything to be done, including allowing a company to trade on, which reduces the return to creditors as a class or to any individual creditor, once insolvency is inevitable.

This is not the same as the legal wording, but it conveys the commercial reality in straightforward terms.

In a pre-pack sale, directors are in the unusual position of generally knowing that insolvency will happen and roughly at what point in the future. Therefore, they cannot use the defence that insolvency was not inevitable. In the case of a pre-pack sale, the directors need to ensure that creditors are held in the same position at the time of the pre-pack sale as they were when the pre-pack sale or insolvency became inevitable. This is not just in terms of the amount of debt owed to a class of creditors; it should be applied to the creditors as between themselves and also to the return they would likely receive in an insolvency process. This requires careful consideration and advice from advisers who are used to thinking in this way.

Creditors' positions can be preserved by managing their respective exposures or using creditor payment trusts. In the latter instance, funds are declared to be held on trust for creditors whose claims arose after a certain date, with the aim of protecting their positions. Apart from the need for free funds to place on trust in this manner, legal challenges to the validity of such trusts have increased in recent years.

Directors will wish to avoid these types of risk, and careful, reasoned, well-advised and well-documented decisions are thus essential.

A further complication for directors can arise if they are contemplating a pre-pack sale to themselves – in effect, a management buy-out from a pre-pack. In such circumstances, they will wish to ensure that the marketing or valuation process is robust to prevent accusations of breach of duty. Such conflicts of interest need to be managed, based on professional advice.

5.3 Valuations

Any professional providing a valuation for use in support of a pre-pack sale will seek to minimise his risk. Unlike the insolvency practitioner, such advisers can (and usually do) seek to limit their liability.

For example, an insolvency practitioner could seek to rely on the opinion of a third-party valuer on the value of a business (as opposed to its assets) when executing a pre-pack sale. If the sale were attacked, the claim would likely be against the insolvency practitioner for breach of duty. He might then seek to join in the valuer who provided the valuation, although the extent of that adviser's liability would be limited.

A similar position could be seen with asset (as opposed to business) valuers.

The insolvency practitioner will wish to ensure that any instructions to such valuers are clear, including recording that the advice will be relied upon for the execution of a pre-pack sale.

The insolvency practitioner will also want to understand fully all provisions which relate to limitation of liability in such engagement terms, such as proportional liability clauses.

5.4 Stakeholders

This section concentrates on lenders, as they are most likely to be involved in a pre-pack transaction in this context. Other stakeholders can also have exposure to risk in pre-packs.

Lenders will be alive to reputational risks, especially in situations where a management buy-out is likely and trade creditors or shareholders could lose money. The same is also true where there is a loss of employment or a defined benefit pension scheme. Steps to mitigate would include well-planned communications and public relations. This has become more acute in recent years.

Lenders will also wish to make sure that they do not engage in behaviour which could be argued in favour of a claim that they somehow took part in the management of a debtor company. In extreme circumstances, this could give rise to claims against a lender for loss to creditors or disqualification.

5.5 Pensions

The Pensions Act 2004 includes various 'moral hazard' provisions concerning certain persons connected to debtors where there is a deficit on a defined benefit pension scheme.

These moral hazard rules can allow the Pensions Regulator to pierce the corporate veil in significant ways. Given the amounts of money which are often at stake, as well as the public attention which they often generate, pensions can be a significant issue.

Although a detailed discussion of pension issues is beyond the scope of this chapter, if there is a defined benefit pension scheme in any company for which a pre-pack sale is contemplated, specialist advice should be sought as to whether there should be a clearance application or other protective steps.

6. Tax planning

A detailed discussion of tax issues is also beyond the scope of a relatively short chapter such as this. However, it would not be complete without some mention of the potential significance of tax planning in pre-pack sales.

The issues which can arise in relation to tax in pre-packs include:

- whether gains on the sale of goodwill or other relevant assets can be sheltered by losses when administration triggers a new accounting period;
- that tax on gains which are triggered post-administration is usually an expense of the administration, as opposed to an unsecured claim;
- other considerations relating to group relief shelters where only part of the group goes into insolvency; and
- the tax advantages which administrative receivership, where the charge allows it, has over administration. For example, it does not trigger a new accounting period or impact on group relationships and the resulting liability is not an expense of the administrative receivership.

The above, particularly in relation to administrations, may well make it more tax efficient for sales to take place immediately before the commencement of the formal insolvency process (eg, administration). However, this would not, strictly speaking, be a pre-pack, but rather a sale prior to an insolvency appointment. There are often practical and legal difficulties in achieving such sales.

For example, directors may be concerned about their own positions in executing a sale prior to insolvency and a well-advised buyer may also have concerns about the risk of being pursued by an insolvency practitioner for additional value on the basis that the price was not high enough (ie, a transaction at an under-value claim). These issues do not arise in a sale executed by an insolvency practitioner.

Also, if the directors sell the business before the insolvency process, it is arguable that administration may not be an appropriate procedure, due to difficulties in achieving the relevant statutory purpose of administrations.

The author is unaware of any insolvency practitioner being sued for negligence relating to tax planning on a pre-pack, but it would be prudent to assume that it is only a matter of time before such a claim is made.

7. Legal documents

These need to be negotiated in advance so that they are ready to be signed at the instant of appointment.

A practical point is that the insolvency practitioner will want to ensure that the buyer will go through with the agreed purchase once the company is in insolvency. If not, the buyer could seek to reduce the price and the insolvency practitioner might have no other strategy to preserve value.

Conversely, the proposed buyer may want to ensure that the time and cost that it has invested in the process up to that point will not be lost if the insolvency practitioner decides to market the business in any way.

The logical answer is to have pre-negotiated and signed documents which are held on solicitors' undertakings, pending the appointment being made – a kind of lock-up agreement.

The key documents are likely to include the following.

7.1 Sale and purchase agreement

A sale and purchase agreement should include any ancillary documents, such as property licences and IP assignments. It will likely take the same form as a normal insolvency practitioner sale agreement.

Although insolvency practitioners do not give warranties, directors sometimes do in pre-pack sales and these will need to be negotiated and agreed before appointment.

It is important that confidentiality clauses in sale and purchase agreements do not prevent the insolvency practitioner from issuing the reports/disclosures required under SIP 13, SIP 16 or Dear IP 42, nor in general statutory reports to creditors. SIPs are issued by the bodies which grant insolvency licences.

The specific SIPs deal with certain disclosures necessary where sales are made to directors and in pre-packs generally. These disclosure requirements are not listed here; suffice to say that insolvency practitioners need to ensure that they comply with their provisions where needed. Such compliance needs to be in spirit as well as letter.

Compliance with SIP 16 has become an important issue for insolvency practitioners. It is closely monitored by the Insolvency Service and breaches are reported as a matter of course to the bodies which grant insolvency licences.

SIP 16 was introduced in response to concerns about public confidence in the pre-pack process. As an aside, there have been various attempts by governments to provide for express notice to be given to certain stakeholders in pre-packs, but these consultations have been ended, for the time being.

Where the sale is to a mortgagee (see below for more issues relating to this) or to directors, it is important that they have separate legal advice to prevent conflicts of interest.

7.2 Deeds of release

These are usually needed to sell assets which are the subject of a lender's security. The buyer will want to see deeds of release to be sure that it is buying the assets free of such security interests. From a practical perspective, this means that the insolvency practitioner will have to organise this in advance. This is usually achieved by his lawyers holding the documents to the lender's order pending completion.

7.3 Appointment documents

These will need to be ready to effect an appointment at the desired time, remembering that this could be outside normal business hours. This means that the relevant logistical arrangements will need to be made to effect the appointment when needed. There may be limitations on who can effect an administration appointment outside normal business hours.

There has been an increasing trend recently for buyers' lawyers to look at appointment documentation to ensure that the insolvency practitioner has been validly appointed and hence can execute the sale.

In the last year or so, there have been several cases where the validity of an administrator's appointment has been challenged, so this is a topical issue.

8. Substantial property transactions with directors

Until recently, a conflict existed between the significant powers given to an insolvency practitioner under the Insolvency Act 1986 to dispose of a company's assets and other provisions in the Companies Acts which related to directors' fiduciary duties.

The Companies Act 1985 (as amended) stated that shareholder approval was needed where a substantial amount of a company's property was sold to directors of a company or another company controlled by them. This makes sense from a fiduciary duty perspective in relation to solvent companies, to prevent directors dealing with themselves. However, it was somewhat strange that an insolvency practitioner appointed under statute with a power to sell an insolvent company's assets, when the shareholders have no economic interest, should be restricted in the same manner.

That was nonetheless the effect in *Demite*. Since then, the Companies Act 2006 has replaced the earlier act in this respect so that this is no longer an issue in administrations. However, it remains something to be dealt with in administrative receiverships. Therefore, in the context of administrative receivership pre-pack sales where the buyer and seller have some common directors, it will need to be dealt with at or before sale by obtaining shareholder approval or by ensuring that none of the directors in the seller has a financial interest in the buyer at the point of sale.

9.   Sales to mortgagees

There is a restriction on sales to a mortgagee or self-dealing in administrative receiverships known as the rule in *Farrar's Case*. This is, in essence, that neither a mortgagee nor its receiver can sell to the mortgagee. The simple solution here is for a new special purpose vehicle to be created, which may even be a subsidiary of the mortgagee. It is unclear whether this applies to an administrator in analogous circumstances, but it would make sense to use a similar structure.

The economics of an insolvency practitioner selling to a mortgagee are similar to a debt-for-equity swap in favour of a mortgagee.

10.   'Post-packs'

This is one of a number of terms used to describe a situation in which a pre-pack sale is executed, but with some form of buy-back option for a limited period. The buy-back is usually at the original price, but with some allowance for costs.

There has been much market commentary on such arrangements, but very few practical uses are known.

An example of a potential use would be a business where even accelerated M&A or distressed M&A processes would be fatal to value – for example, due to customer loss, a run on working capital which could not be funded or regulatory issues. Therefore, a sale is executed with market exposure to take place afterwards.

The economics of such arrangements are similar to asset hive-downs. This is where the business is hived down in clean form to a new company and that company is sold.

Such arrangements can arguably have useful applications, but they are most likely to be limited to situations in which they are no more than a 'belt and braces' on value risk. An example could be where a business is sold to its lenders and there is no reasonable belief that anyone else would pay more for it than the lender has done.

Put another way, it is designed to be a defence to the possible assertion from a potential buyer of, "Had I known it was for sale, I would have paid more for it than you did". This is an easy assertion to make when you know that you will not have to go through with it. However, post-pack provisions can neutralise this.

Use in any other situations would usually be limited due to the risks of the deal being undone. It is much easier for an existing lender or similar to make a calculated risk assessment than a trade buyer. This is not always the case and each situation inevitably has its own facts.

Valuation of distressed businesses

Alastair Beveridge
Paul Hemming
Graeme Smith
Zolfo Cooper

The valuation of distressed businesses is a key element of many restructuring and workout situations. It is a decision-making tool that can help to shape the exit strategy and guide planning in terms of seeking to sell the business or assets, or follow a restructuring process. Within a restructuring process, valuation is a central theme in negotiations to determine the ownership levels and level of required finance provision of the various stakeholder groups, which often have differing views and perspectives.

Where possible, distressed valuation follows the same principles and techniques as those used to value a healthy business, but the process needs to be more rigorous and reflect the realities of a distressed situation.

This chapter sets out the principles of valuing a business and then considers the specific challenges and nuances that need to be addressed when performing this exercise in a distressed environment. Each situation has its own individual characteristics and raises different issues, but with a structured approach a sensible result can be achieved.

1. Valuation techniques

When considering the appropriate valuation approach, one needs to decide whether the business is a going concern or whether best value will be generated from a break-up sale of the assets. A going-concern valuation implies that the business will generate profit in the future on the assumption of sound management, suitable future investment and an appropriate funding structure.

Three basic valuation techniques are commonly applied to valuing a business:

- discounted cash flow (DCF);
- comparable multiples; and
- asset-based value.

Each technique has challenges that are amplified in a distressed situation. DCF, the purest valuation technique, depends on management's ability to produce reliable cash-flow forecasts. This is often extremely challenging in a distressed situation. The comparable multiples valuation methodology is applicable only if the business is generating a sensible level of pre-financing cost profit (earnings before interest and tax (EBIT)); earnings before interest, tax, depreciation and amortisation (EBITDA)), and asset-based values are likely to vary considerably between a going-concern value and a break-up value.

As many of these techniques as possible should be used in order to build a valuation range for the business in question. A summary of the three valuation techniques is set out in the table below.

Table 1: Summary of valuation techniques

	DCF	Comparable multiples	Asset-based value
Basis	Values free cash-flow potential by discounting these back to a present value using a relevant cost of capital.	Applies the market valuation multiples of similar companies that either are quoted or have recently been acquired to the subject company's relevant financial metric.	Asset value in current use for a going concern, which often equates to book value or the current realisable market value of the assets in a liquidation scenario.
Rationale	The value of a company is the potential future cash flows discounted to reflect the opportunity cost of the total capital investment.	The assumption is that the market applies fair valuations to companies. The value of the subject company can be considered comparable to companies in the same sector with similar economics.	For a going-concern valuation in an asset-intensive business, single year profitability may not be an appropriate guide to value. In a liquidation, realisable asset value gives the best guide to value as there is no going-concern premium.
Requirements	Mid to long-term reliable cash-flow forecasts. Reasonable assessment of the relevant cost of capital.	Positive EBIT or EBITDA. Suitable comparable companies and transactions with similar economics to the subject company.	Market values for the assets.

continued overleaf

	DCF	Comparable multiples	Asset-based value
Applicable companies	All companies with future cash-flow visibility.	All companies with comparable data points.	Asset-intensive businesses.
Impact of distress	Cash-flow forecasts need to be rigorously challenged to assess deliverability. Discount rate needs to reflect increased risk. Potential for failure should be factored in.	Comparable data points must be thoroughly examined to assess level of comparability. Discount should be applied to reflect distress and risk.	Even in a going-concern sale, realisable value will be an important metric as it represents the buyer's downside position. Quality and level of continued investment in assets will impact on value. Important to assess whether third-party claims exist on each asset.

These techniques can all be used to generate either equity or enterprise valuations (ie, the combined value of both equity and net debt). When valuing a distressed business, it is more appropriate to consider the enterprise valuation, as it is unlikely that the current capital structure will remain in place and if the business is distressed then the equity is often of nil value. For this reason, all of the valuation approaches we consider are for enterprise value.

2. **Valuation process**

The process for valuing a distressed business can be broken down into four steps:
- understand and evaluate the business and the impact of the current and potential level of distress;
- review and adjust historic and forecast financial data;
- perform valuation analysis; and
- consider other items that can impact on value.

This four-step process should enable all relevant aspects of the business and its current situation to be factored into the valuation. Distressed valuation is often required in an accelerated timetable, so the use of this structure can help to ensure that key points are not missed.

2.1 Understand and evaluate business and impact of distress

When performing a valuation of any business, it is important to understand the quality and competitive positioning of the business in question. This reflects the importance of relativity in valuation. A business that holds a dominant position in its markets with high barriers to entry would typically carry a valuation premium to a weaker competitor that faces a high risk of substitution.

It is unusual to find a distressed business that holds such a dominant position and a review of its competitive position would be expected to highlight a number of risk areas that pose threats to future growth and prosperity.

Another key area when performing the initial review of the business is to assess the management team in terms of stability and quality. Distressed situations are often characterised by a great deal of management change and by management teams that have been unable to deliver on strategic goals. When a business is in distress, the ability of the management team to turn the business around and deliver on the business plan is critical. Without this, the achievability of a business plan can be highly questionable.

(a) Balance-sheet v operational distress

Companies become distressed for many reasons and understanding the underlying causes is essential in order to arrive at a sensible valuation.

In some cases the company being considered is a well-run and viable business, but is overleveraged. The most common cause of overleveraging is major acquisitions – whether from the business's own leveraged buyout or from the acquisition of other businesses. In the years up to 2007, a large number of companies built up high levels of leverage with little headroom for underperformance.

Despite a sound underlying business, the leverage structure, repayment profile or refinancing requirements left many companies unable to service their debts as they fell due, making them technically insolvent. This scenario will be referred to as 'balance-sheet distress'.

Failure to tackle balance-sheet distress at an early stage through reset covenants, rescheduled debt repayments or some debt restructuring to reduce the current interest burden often leads to more significant operational issues because of lack of funds for investment in the development of the business.

The valuation of a business in early stage balance-sheet distress should not differ greatly from that of a healthy company, as alterations to the capital structure should eliminate the cause of distress rather than requiring changes to the operations of the business.

At the other end of the spectrum, some businesses are facing a marked decline in revenue or an unsupportable cost base due to changes in their market. Without significant operational restructuring, these businesses may not be viable as going concerns in the short or medium term. This scenario will be referred to as 'operational distress'. A good example of this is the UK high-street retail market. This market grew its property footprint to meet continually rising consumer demand. It has since been hit not only by declining consumer spending, but also by the switch to online purchasing. This has left many companies with leasehold estates with a significant number of loss-making sites. Companies in this market that are unable to take advantage of the switch to online and exit from loss-making sites are facing major operational distress often resulting in restructuring events.

Businesses in operational distress typically require significant investment to deliver their turnaround plans and present different valuation challenges from a healthy business. The valuation approach should be modified accordingly to reflect the cost and additional risk associated with the turnaround.

In the real world, of course, a distressed business will lie somewhere between the two extremes. It is a matter of judgement how detrimental an impact that distress has had on a business and the level of discount that should apply as a result.

(b)   *Distress and value*
Before considering how to value a distressed business, it is worth understanding why distress has an impact on value.

Figure 1 demonstrates the type of relationship that can typically be seen between the level of distress that a business is facing and its potential valuation.

Figure 1: Relationship between level of distress and valuation

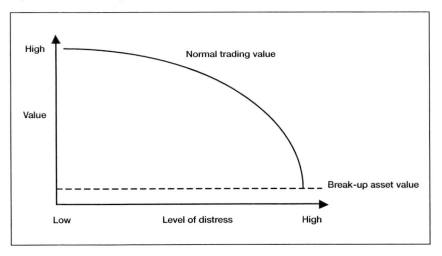

As the level of distress increases, the value of a business can be expected to fall rapidly as the risk of failure becomes a realistic possibility. This relationship can be explained by considering the following definition of the 'enterprise value of a business':

Real enterprise value = enterprise value – PV of costs of financial distress

This equation recognises that there are real costs associated with financial distress and the risk of business failure. The risk of business failure grows rapidly with increasing distress and, as such, the costs of financial distress can also significantly reduce the real enterprise value.

The costs of financial distress are numerous and exist both when the business is at risk of insolvency and during a formal process itself.

Table 2: Examples of costs of financial distress

Operational and financial	Strategic and management
• Detrimental credit terms • Reduced access to lines of credit for overseas supply • Higher incremental financing costs • Fire-sale asset values • Investment required for business recovery • Professional fees	• Restraints on capital investment • Project decision making focused on short-term rather than long-term value • Distraction from running the business • Conflicts of interest between stakeholders

For these reasons, financial distress has a direct impact on valuation.

2.2 Review and adjust historic and forecast financial data

(a) Lies, damn lies and business plans

The one certainty of a company's business plan is that actual trading will always be different from the financial forecasts. This means that before the valuation analysis has started, a source of error has already been introduced.

When considering a distressed business, it is likely that the financial forecasts will have been prepared some time ago – potentially, before the business had fully appreciated its true circumstances. It may even be the case that the person who prepared the forecasts is no longer with the company. It is therefore essential that the current management re-forecast based on current macro market issues and the company's own position. Any underperforming business with significant leverage is likely to have had an independent business review. This is an independent review of the deliverability of the financial forecast that highlights appropriate sensitivities and vulnerabilities to the management's forecasts.

It is also possible that the results from the last financial year may no longer be an appropriate basis for a valuation, as they may no longer represent the new realities facing the business.

These facts mean that the financial forecasts and historic results need to be analysed more thoroughly than may usually be necessary for a healthy business. The analysis needs to drill down into the underlying assumptions to challenge them in order to check that they still hold, given the current conditions facing the business. This is especially important in the absence of an independent business review.

(b) Future net maintainable earnings

It is vital, as part of any distressed valuation, to review fully the financial forecasts and historic results to consider what adjustments need to be made to ensure that both the comparable multiples and DCF analysis use the appropriate financial data. These adjustments are all made with the objective of determining the company's future net maintainable earnings. The future net maintainable earnings reflect the earning capacity of the business when the impact of distress has been eliminated through either a refinancing or a formal insolvency process.

When considering the appropriate adjustments for the financial forecasts, only items that are ongoing in nature should be included. Any items that are considered situational, caused only by the current level of distress, should be excluded. Typical ongoing adjustments include:

- step reductions in sales – for example, due to changing market conditions or contract losses (eg, service companies supplying the public sector, construction companies following the credit crunch and music and DVD retailers following the switch to digital distribution);
- increased costs due to input cost inflation (eg, utility prices and metal commodity prices such as copper and platinum); and
- increased capital, maintenance or research and development (R&D) expenditure where these costs have been cut to preserve cash.

These ongoing adjustments also need to be taken into account for the historic results. When reviewing the historic results, additional consideration needs to be given to assess whether there are any one-off or non-recurring costs that can be eradicated once the company emerges from distress which need to be removed. Examples include:

- less favourable credit terms and discounts from suppliers;
- professional fees associated with restructuring or other corporate activity;
- above-market salaries and other distributions made to related parties in anticipation of distress; and
- profits or losses from asset sales.

Once these adjustments have been quantified and an assessment of the future net maintainable earnings has been made, the financials are in a position to be analysed for valuation purposes. Care should always be taken to ensure that any adjustments are supportable under scrutiny by third parties.

(c)   *Continued investment?*
A tool used by management in distressed situations to conserve cash is to cut back on investment in the business. This may be through a reduction in capital expenditure, repairs and maintenance or R&D expenditure. No matter what category of cost is cut, this will almost certainly have a detrimental impact on the business if these cuts have been in place for any significant period of time.

Business plans typically underestimate the impact of lack of investment on the future profitability of the business. New investment takes time to implement and even longer to impact on profitability, and should be carefully considered as a sensitivity for the valuation.

To assess the impact on value, it is necessary to understand the extent to which the business is underinvested. This can be achieved by comparing the current investment levels in the management accounts with those of prior periods and by benchmarking the investment levels with comparable companies.

This catch-up investment should be included in the cash flows used for the DCF analysis and its discounted value deducted from the comparable multiples valuations.

This approach takes into account the physical shortfall in investment and the cash impact of rectifying this. What it does not consider is the long-term damage that lack of investment causes to the business and its brands.

(d) Is goodwill now badwill?

Building and maintaining goodwill and brand value is crucial to the success of many businesses. This is normally an expensive and long-term process that can be undone in a much shorter time period by mismanagement and underinvestment.

Even in non-brand led businesses, successful performance is often directly linked to strong relationships with customers, suppliers and even finance providers. This goodwill generates customer loyalty, enables favourable terms to be negotiated and allows flexibility to cope with business fluctuations.

In times of distress, however, new priorities appear for management. Conserving cash, either through aggressive working capital management or through cutting investment, has the potential to damage the goodwill and brand value built by the business.

Typically, the damage caused by a limited period of distress is short-lived and can quickly be repaired. However, where these measures are in place for any substantial period of time, the damage can be more serious. Stock shortages are a classic consequence of distress. Short-term shortages can lead to long-term reputation issues associated with a lack of reliability, which can have a lasting impact on the business.

The assessment of the level of damage, if any, that has been caused to the goodwill and brand value of a business is important in assessing the deliverability of its financial forecasts. Market-leading growth rates and profitability indicate that management believes that the company's goodwill has been maintained and has not suffered a material impairment. If it is apparent that this is not the case, then either the growth and profitability rates need to be reduced or additional investment needs to be factored into the plan.

A practical point not to be overlooked in a distressed situation is the legal ownership of any intellectual property that is necessary for the business. When times are good, informal arrangements in place over important intellectual property may well be sufficient for the ongoing operation of the business. When the situation becomes distressed and the future of the business is uncertain, these informal relationships can break down.

If informal relationships exist and a formal insolvency process is undertaken, the holder of any business-critical intellectual property will often try to extract as much value as possible from this situation. It is better for a business to deal with such issues in advance when trading is still good and the spirit of a long-term partnership still exists with the owner of the intellectual property.

Table 3: Summary checklist for reviewing financial forecasts

- Check when they were prepared and by whom.
- Consider whether they reflect current market conditions.
- Make necessary future net maintainable earnings adjustments.
- Make any step changes to sales or costs.
- Eliminate any current distress costs.
- Assess whether the proposed adjustments are supportable.
- Make allowance for reversal of underinvestment.

2.3   Perform valuation analysis

The main techniques that are used to value a normal business – comparable multiples and DCF analysis – can be difficult to apply in a distressed situation.

The main reason for this is that these techniques start with the assumption that the business in question will continue into perpetuity. This is a bold assertion for any company, but for one already in distress it is a step too far, as the business has already demonstrated its capacity to be at risk of failure. Moody's data indicates that while the long-term average default rate for speculative grade debt issuers is around 4.6%, this rate rose to a peak of over 13% in 2009.[1] So when using these techniques, this risk of failure needs to be factored into the analysis.

(a)   Comparable multiples analysis

Comparable multiples analysis looks at the valuation multiples that apply to comparable companies quoted on the public markets and comparable (or precedent) transactions that have taken place. This analysis is based on the assumption that similar valuation multiples apply for businesses with similar economics. It can be applied only to businesses that are profitable at least at the EBITDA level.

The quoted companies that are considered to be comparable will likely be in much stronger financial shape than the distressed business being valued, and as such their enterprise value as a multiple of EBIT or EBITDA will be higher. The degree of comparability and the number of comparable companies can vary greatly, and the appropriate discount will be a matter of judgement based on the individual circumstances. However, value is likely to be at the bottom of the multiple range suggested by the comparable company analysis or even at a further discount, given the risk associated with the specific distressed business.

When valuing a healthy business, it is common practice to consider the level of control premium that should be applied to the comparable company data. This premium for control is applied to take account of the fact that the share price of a quoted company reflects the valuation of a minority shareholding. To acquire the company, a party will generally need to pay a premium over the current share price in order to acquire control of the company. In a restructuring, the restructured company often has a wide shareholder base, which would mean that a control

---

1   Moody's Investors Service, Global Credit Research, March 22 2012.

premium would not be applicable, and in general it is unlikely that a premium for control will be appropriate in a distressed valuation as it is likely to be offset by the risk factors in the business.

The publicly available data for comparable transactions can often be misleading when used for valuation purposes, as there is generally a lack of information about the future prospects of the target company for all but the larger public company transactions. The dynamics and drivers for each transaction will vary widely. Most deals are driven by current and future prospects rather than historic profitability and therefore the implied historic multiple can be a particularly unreliable comparator. Additionally, with a corporate acquisition, the valuation may have assumed that significant synergies would be available when the businesses are merged which would not be applicable to a standalone business valuation.

Comparable transaction data therefore needs to be analysed fully to try to eliminate these distorting factors. As with the comparable company analysis, the comparative health and growth prospects of the subject company should be considered when assessing the most appropriate multiple and the most comparable deals weighted accordingly.

However, precedent transactions may provide the most applicable guide to valuation multiples in the situation where companies have previously been acquired out of distress, as the value paid will have reflected the distressed situation and is likely to have focused more heavily on current recovery prospects. Again, it is important to try to analyse the publicly available information to ensure that the most applicable underlying financial data is considered.

With either comparable company or transaction analysis, care needs to be taken to apply the resultant multiple to the most appropriate underlying financials. The multiples should be applied to the future net maintainable earnings of the business.

An example of the importance of this would be the valuation of a drug company with its main drug coming off-patent. At the point where manufacturers can launch generic versions of the drug, the profitability of the patented product is likely to drop significantly. If this change happened towards the end of an accounting period, the full-year impact of this would not be evident in the year-end results. Applying a historical multiple to unadjusted results would overvalue the business by being based on unsustainable profit levels.

Normalised working capital: When a business becomes distressed, one of the first operational areas to suffer is working capital. As cash becomes short, management tends to seek ways to preserve it through stretching creditors and chasing debtors more aggressively. However, as a situation becomes more distressed and this becomes apparent to suppliers, they may seek to protect their positions by moving to more adverse credit terms and, in extreme cases, cash on delivery.

These factors mean that in a distressed situation, the working capital levels are unlikely to be representative of normal conditions. Following an acquisition and a return to normal trading conditions, these working capital balances will return to normal levels with an associated inflow or outflow of cash.

If the business is to be acquired out of administration, then all non-essential creditors will remain with the administrators and the purchaser will benefit from a buildup of these creditor balances post-acquisition, which will improve the cash flow of the business in the short term.

These working capital effects need to be taken into account in a valuation. When considering a DCF analysis, these effects will be accounted for by the inflow or outflow of cash in the post-acquisition period. Comparable company and transaction analysis assumes that the business is being acquired with a normal level of working capital. For these methodologies the short-term cash impact of working capital returning to normal levels should be an adjustment to the valuation. This adjustment would be the discounted value of these short-term cash flows.

In assessing the normal level of working capital, it may be necessary to consider the business performance in previous financial periods before the effects of trading in distress became apparent.

Figure 2: Impact of working capital stretch on completion amount

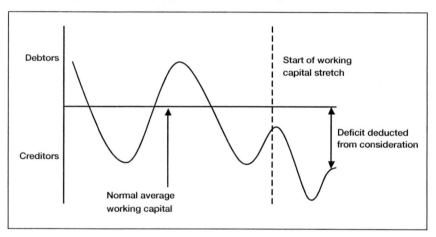

(b)   *DCF*

DCF analysis is a flexible valuation methodology that can be tailored to the outlook of the subject company. Whereas comparable multiples attempt to apply the economics of similar businesses, a DCF approach analyses the specific cash flows of the business in question. This enables the impact of specific issues facing the company to be factored into the cash-flow forecasts and the valuation impact assessed.

As this analysis is based on medium-term financial forecasts, it is dependent on the reasonableness of these forecasts to provide a sensible estimate of value. For this reason, it becomes vital that the financial forecasts have been subjected to the rigorous review that we have discussed, and that they have been adjusted to reflect future net maintainable earnings of the business.

DCF analysis provides an estimate of value by considering the net present value (NPV) of the future cash flows implied by the financial forecasts of a business. They include a terminal value to take account of cash flows into perpetuity beyond the forecast period at the point where the cash flows have reached a stable growth state. When considering enterprise value, this analysis is performed on the cash flows of the business before taking into account any financing costs.

These cash flows are discounted at a rate that reflects the required rate of return of the company's equity and debt providers, weighted according to the proportion of funding provided. This discount rate is known as the weighted average cost of capital (WACC) and is defined below:

$WACC = rd (1 - tc) D / (D + E) + re E / (D + E)$

rd = cost of debt

tc = marginal tax rate

re = return on equity

D = level of debt

E = level of equity

These rates of return compensate the finance providers for the level of risk that they are accepting by making an investment in the company. The returns required for equity providers are much higher than those of the debt providers. This is to reflect the security that debt providers enjoy primarily from holding specific security on a company's assets or structural priority in the event of insolvency.

In the case of a distressed business, this perceived risk level will be higher than that of a healthy business. As a result, equity and debt finance providers will likely require higher rates of return to compensate for the increased risk. This in turn will require that a higher discount rate be applied to the future cash flows.

A higher discount rate will partially reflect the impact of distress in a DCF, but will not be sufficient on its own. This is because a real risk facing a distressed business is that it will eventually fail and there will be no further cash flows beyond those of an insolvency process. By using a higher discount rate, the present value of the future cash flows is reduced, but value is still attributed to cash flows into perpetuity.

The area where ignoring this risk has the most material impact on valuation is the terminal value. The terminal value often accounts for the majority of the DCF valuation and represents the value of the company beyond the financial forecast period. The terminal value is typically calculated in one of two ways:

- Using a perpetuity formula: the terminal-year cash flow is divided by the delta of WACC and the terminal growth rate. This assumes that the business continues to trade into perpetuity; or
- Using the exit multiple methodology: this assumes that the business is sold in the terminal year and an appropriate valuation multiple is applied to the relevant financial metric in the terminal year to estimate a sale value. This assumes that the new owner derives value from the business into perpetuity.

The terminal value should be estimated using both methodologies in order to sense-check the results. This is important because the terminal growth value relies on an estimate for the growth of the cash flows of the business into perpetuity and this rate is difficult to predict.

A guideline for a healthy business is that the terminal growth rate should be roughly equal to the long-term forecast gross domestic product (GDP) growth rate for its country of operation. For a distressed business, the long-term prospects are likely to be more uncertain and a terminal growth rate between zero and GDP is more typical.

Both methodologies make the assumption that the cash flows continue into perpetuity. For a healthy business this is a reasonable assumption, but for a business in operational distress this is far more uncertain, given the risks associated with this kind of situation.

To take account of this risk, an estimate of the break-up asset value of the business in the terminal year should be used as a third terminal value data point in a distressed situation. The break-up asset value provides an estimate of the return that could be realised in an insolvent sale and would represent a floor value for the terminal year. In order to determine a reasonable range for the terminal value, it is necessary to assess the likelihood of the business recovering fully by the terminal year and the likelihood that its business model has longevity.

If there is a high probability of the business recovering fully with good long-term prospects, then a terminal value based on the growth and exit multiple methodologies would be appropriate. If it is highly uncertain whether the business will be secure in the long term, then a terminal value based on break-up asset value would be more appropriate.

(c)   *Pricing probability of failure*

The traditional method for performing a DCF does not take adequate account of the risk of corporate failure. One methodology that can be used to rectify this is to apply the basic principles of adjusting bond prices for the risk of default (this methodology does not claim to reflect all the complexities of bond pricing, only the basic principles).

In basic bond pricing, if a one-year bond with a face value of £1,000 carried an interest rate of 5%, it would be expected to pay out £1,050 at the end of one year. If this bond had no risk of default and the risk-free rate were 5%, then these bonds would be priced as follows:

$$\text{PV of bond} = \frac{£1,000 + 50}{1.05} = £1,000$$

However, if these bonds carried a 10% risk of default this risk would need to be factored into their price. In this example there would be a 10% chance that the bondholder received nothing and a 90% chance that the bondholder would receive full payment. The probability weighted expected return would therefore be (90% × £1,050) + (10% x 0) = £945.

$$\text{Probability-weighted PV of the bond} = \frac{£945}{1.05} = £900$$

This would make the implied yield of the bond £1,050/£900 = 17%.

This methodology can be applied to DCF analysis by replacing the risk-free rate by the calculated WACC (discount rate) and the break-up value of the business for the pay-out in the event of default (replacing the zero return to bondholders assumed in the previous example).

Shown below is a simple worked example using a three-year cash flow with free cash-flow and break-up value growing at a constant rate. The terminal value is calculated using an exit multiple and the probability of failure in any one year is assumed to be constant (in reality, the risk of failure may change from year to year).

This methodology considers the possible outcomes that can occur in each year:

- The company survives to generate free cash flow; or
- The company becomes insolvent so the break-up value is realised.

The present value of each of these potential outcomes is calculated and then multiplied by the probability that each outcome will occur. By adding these results together, a probability-weighted NPV can be calculated.

Table 4: DCF analysis including failure potential

Assumptions	
Annual growth rate of free cash flow and break-up value	2.0%
Discount rate	2.0%
Annual probability of failure	15.0%
Terminal year exit multiple (of free cash flow)	10.0×
Break-up value year 1	£20m

£m	Period			Terminal value
	1	2	3	
Free cash flow	10	10.2	10.4	106.1
Discount factor	0.89	0.80	0.71	0.71
Present value	8.9	8.1	7.4	75.5
Break-up value	20	20.4	20.8	21.2
Discount factor	0.89	0.80	0.71	0.71
Present value	17.9	16.3	14.8	15.1

Scenario	Present value by period (£m)				NPV (£m)
	1	2	3	TY*	
No failure	8.9	8.1	7.4	75.5	100.0
Failure in exit year	8.9	8.1	7.4	15.1	39.6
Failure in year 3	8.9	8.1	14.8		31.9
Failure in year 2	8.9	16.3			25.2
Failure in year 1	17.9				17.9

*TY = terminal year

Scenario	Probability by period				Probability (%)
	1	2	3	TY	
No failure	85%	85%	85%	85%	52
Failure in exit year	85%	85%	85%	15%	9
Failure in year 3	85%	85%	15%		11
Failure in year 2	85%	15%			13
Failure in year 1	15%				15
					100

Scenario	NPV (£m)	Probability	Probability-weighted NPV (£m)
No failure	100.0	52%	52.2
Failure in exit year	39.6	9%	3.6
Failure in year 3	31.9	11%	3.5
Failure in year 2	25.2	13%	3.2
Failure in year 1	17.9	15%	2.7
	Total	100%	65.2

This example shows that the DCF valuation with no risk of failure would be £100 million; when this is adjusted to take account of the estimate probability of failure, the NPV falls to £65 million. This implies a 35% discount to compensate the buyer for the additional risk of acquiring this distressed business.

This methodology enables the potential for failure to be factored into the DCF analysis and also forces the user to consider in more depth that potential for failure and the break-up value for the business that may be recovered in this scenario.

(d) ***Risk and return***

One area that is often overlooked when considering the valuation of distressed businesses is the requirements of the buyer. There are now more and more investment vehicles and funds specialising in investing in distressed assets. These funds often have a mandate from their limited partners to pursue specific types of investment and specific levels of risk. Funds allocated by limited partners to these investment vehicles will typically demand a higher level of return to compensate for the increased level of risk assumed when making distressed investments.

This requirement for increased rates of return has a direct impact on the price that the buyer is able to pay for the asset. When performing a returns analysis on a distressed asset, the typical private equity rule of thumb of a target increased rate of return of 20% to 25% needs to be revised upwards towards levels of 35% or more.

(e) ***Asset value***

When considering a seriously distressed business, there are often severe time constraints on the restructuring or sale. This makes preparation of reliable financial forecasts unrealistic, either because future prospects cannot be predicted with any level of certainty or because the existing forecasts do not reflect reality. In this circumstance a reliable DCF-based valuation is impossible.

In addition, the business may be loss making or generating only a relatively small profit. This undermines the use of the comparable multiple-based valuation methods, leaving an asset-based valuation as the most appropriate, and sometimes only, valuation basis.

Asset-based valuations are therefore core to many distressed valuations. As outlined at the start of this chapter, there are two asset valuations: the going-concern value and the realisable value.

If a business is being sold as a going concern – that is, if the operations of the business will be kept together and the business will continue to trade – then the appropriate asset value will represent the value in use of the assets being considered. A good proxy for this value will often be the depreciated book value of the assets in the accounts. A review should be made of the depreciation policy adopted by the company to check that the depreciation rate reflects the useful economic life of the assets, to ensure that the value of the assets is representative.

Asset valuations are particularly useful for capital-intensive businesses where investment in equipment and tooling is made to support long-term cash-flow generation, typically against supply contracts. Examples of this would be the automotive supply industry, where heavy capital investment against multiple-year supply contracts provides the majority of value when a business becomes distressed.

In asset-light businesses, however, the future value of the business is tied into intangible assets such as supply contracts, brand names and human capital. In these businesses, value is better assessed through the consideration of future cash-flow potential using DCF or comparable multiples analysis.

In a going-concern situation, the net asset value of a business should be considered taking into account the liabilities of the business.

(f)   *Realising asset value in insolvency*

If the subject business does not represent a going concern, then the assets should be valued on a realisable value basis, often referred to as a 'break-up basis'. This represents the value that can be realised from selling individual assets or collections of assets with the business ceasing to trade.

This method of valuing a business is typically the base valuation that is considered when estimating recoveries from an insolvent situation. When estimating recoveries in this manner, it is important to consider the realisation costs associated with asset sales (eg, intermediaries' fees and distribution costs).

The realisable value of assets is very much dependent on the specific assets in question, particularly their condition, portability, flexibility of use and the presence of a secondary market for the assets in question. In addition, when realising asset value in an insolvent situation, the risk of successful retention of title claims needs to be considered. If third parties are well placed to enforce retention of title, the assets to which this applies should be considered of nil realisable value.

In addition to these general issues, Table 5 outlines some of the key factors to be taken into consideration when assessing realisable value for the major asset classes.

Table 5: Key considerations for assessing realisable value for different asset classes

Asset class	Key factors impacting on value
Fixed assets	
Freehold property	Alternative use potential, planning permissions, environmental liabilities, tenants
Leasehold property	In addition to the freehold points above, remaining lease term, assignment provisions, Landlord and Tenant Act 1954 protection, ability to assign
Leasehold improvements	Limited value on a break-up basis

continued overleaf

Asset class	Key factors impacting on value
Plant and machinery	Age, ownership of associated tooling, risk of property damage on removal, decommissioning to installation costs
Fixtures and fittings	Limited value on a break-up basis
Intellectual property	Documented legal ownership, ability to assign, associated litigation
Current assets	
Stock	Ownership (third-party stock held on site), recoverability (stock held by third parties), age, obsolescence
Debtors	Age, ability to collect, foreign exchange exposure, legal documentation, offsetting creditor balances

When acquiring a distressed business, break-up value is used as the contingency value to determine the level of financial risk being assumed at a given purchase price. The delta between break-up value and consideration is the initial value at risk for the buyer in the acquisition.

When assessing the level of net realisation from an insolvency, it is important to seek specific tax advice to understand how the timing of certain actions, such as the sale of freehold property, can impact on the priority of payment of any resultant tax charges.

2.4 Consider other items that can impact on value

(a) Partial business sale – solvent

When considering the valuation of a distressed business, careful analysis should be performed to understand whether value can be maximised by selling parts of a business rather than the whole.

In a solvent situation, this may be driven by the potential to divest part of the business which offers no synergies with the rest of the group, but which would be attractive to third parties. Selling this business may realise more value than the ongoing value of that business to the group.

In this situation the whole business should be valued on a sum-of-the-parts basis. A sum-of-the-parts valuation considers each part of the business separately and applies different valuation metrics to reflect the different economics of each business.

It is important when performing a sum-of-the-parts valuation to make sure that the costs of any business support functions carried out by the business being sold are reflected in the remaining business' financials, and that any cross-selling benefits should be excluded.

(b)   *Partial business sale – insolvent*

When a business has reached a more advanced level of distress, maximum value may be achieved by leaving behind loss-making or value-impairing elements of the business through the use of an insolvency procedure.

This situation can occur for a number of reasons, but common examples include the presence of onerous leases or contracts, loss-making locations or potentially high exposure to past legal liabilities. An example of this would be the restructuring of a retail business with a number of loss-making sites. The profitable sites could be sold as a group in a trade and assets sale out of insolvency, with the loss-making units remaining with the administrator.

If value for a business is to be realised through an insolvent sale, careful analysis needs to be undertaken to determine which assets and liabilities will transfer as part of the sale.

In a theoretical insolvent transaction, only the assets necessary to continue the operations of the business would transfer and the valuation would be based only on these, with all liabilities excluded. In reality, a number of historic creditor balances and liabilities need to be taken into account.

Some of the most common liabilities that need to be taken into account in an insolvent sale are the employee costs associated with the Transfer of Undertakings (Protection of Employment) Regulations 2006 (TUPE). This provides protection to employees when all or substantially all of the business is sold. This will impact on value because the buyer will often stipulate as a condition of the deal that an amount be held back from consideration to cover the potential TUPE liability. The eventual TUPE cost that is suffered varies from case to case, but the range of cost should be assessed upfront so that the potential impact on value can be understood.

Examples of other typical items to be considered are set out in Table 6.

Table 6: Main creditor balances/liabilities to be considered in insolvent sales

Creditor or liability	Considerations
Trade creditors	• Existing suppliers may be necessary to continue trade, meaning that their credit balances need to be settled or assumed by the buyer. • Certain creditors may hold important information or assets that require 'ransom' payments to be made to the creditor.

continued overleaf

Creditor or liability	Considerations
Leasehold properties	• If there are common landlords of both profitable and loss-making sites, it may not be possible to secure assignments of only the profitable sites. Loss-making units may need to be included as part of the transaction.
Loss-making contracts	• Loss-making contracts may need to be retained if they serve an important ongoing customer.

The analysis of which liabilities need to be taken into account in the valuation is situation specific and typically requires a line-by-line review.

(c)   *Pensions*

A defined-benefit pension scheme may be the largest single creditor on a company's balance sheet. The treatment of the pension scheme will have a significant impact on the enterprise valuation of a business.

When considering a defined-benefit pension scheme which is transferring to the buyer as part of the transaction, it is important to treat past liabilities and the funding for future service benefits separately. Past liabilities should be considered as an additional debt and factored into the enterprise valuation. The funding for future service liabilities should be included in the forecast profits and cash flows considered in the DCF and comparable multiples analysis.

Past liabilities are held on the company's balance sheet and carried at a value calculated under the provisions of Financial Reporting Standard 17 (United Kingdom only) or International Accounting Standard 19 (international accounting standard). This is normally used as the starting point for the quantification of the debt value to be included as part of the enterprise valuation.

When executing a transaction, however, the terms of the servicing of the historic deficit and future service benefits are agreed with the pension trustees as part of the deal. The terms agreed can then be analysed on a DCF basis to assess the impact on value and an actuarial valuation should then be carried out to estimate the historic liability.

If a business is being acquired out of insolvency, then the defined-benefit pension scheme may remain with the seller. If certain conditions are met, the scheme will fall into the pension protection fund, which will then provide 90% of the expected employee benefits to the majority of scheme members.

In this insolvent scenario, the buyer will need to factor in only the future pension costs of a replacement scheme into the financial forecasts. No allowance needs to be made for the historic liability.

Defined-benefit pension schemes are highly complex products and specialist advice should be obtained when considering their valuation impact.

(d) *Financing*

An important driver for value in a distressed transaction is the availability of debt financing. In this area of the market, the most common source of debt finance is asset-based lending. Asset-based lending provides debt finance secured on specific assets. The most common assets secured by asset-based lending are stock and debtors, due to their relatively high level of liquidity, and also freehold property due to its security and marketability. In very specific circumstances, asset-based lending can be raised using other assets as security such as plant and machinery.

The level of debt financing available affects valuation due to its impact on potential equity returns. The greater the proportion of acquisition value sourced from debt rather than equity, the higher the eventual returns will be for the equity provider. This is due to the reduced amount of equity required and the lower returns paid to debt providers as interest compared with the capital growth that accrues to equity holders.

3. Conclusion

The bottom line is that although the valuation of a distressed business follows the same fundamentals as that of a healthy business, it is essential to apply the various methodologies to the right data, and to select the most appropriate methodologies for the particular circumstances.

The facts of the matter that typically need to be taken into account when valuing a distressed business are as follows:

- Distressed businesses are higher risk than healthy businesses;
- The probability of failure is real;
- Investors require higher returns to compensate for the increased risk and this drives down their entry value;
- The level of distress and associated damage to the business impacts on value; and
- The underlying financial data needs to be adjusted to reflect future net maintainable earnings, given the new reality facing the business.

With these facts in mind and using the tools suggested in this chapter, you should be well placed to value a distressed business.

Schemes of arrangement

Alan Augustin
Mark Batten
PwC

1. Introduction

A scheme of arrangement is a flexible and powerful tool used extensively in the context of corporate reorganisations or restructurings.

The statutory provisions for implementing a scheme can be found in Sections 895 to 899 of Part 26 of the Companies Act 2006 whereby a company can make a compromise or arrangement with its members or creditors, or any class of them.

Schemes are commonly used in takeovers, mergers or reconstructions and may be used to alter shareholder or creditor rights. In these instances, proposals are put to, and voted on by, members or creditors, as the case may be. For example, schemes have been used frequently as an alternative to compulsory acquisition of minority interests (following a takeover) under Part 28 of the Companies Act (squeeze-out rights) and as a means of delisting the target company.

At the more distressed end of the corporate viability spectrum, schemes have also been applied often to achieve compromises with different stakeholders – for example, in the restructuring of a company's debt or to deal with liabilities owed to third-party claimants. In a distressed context, the use of schemes has also extended to insolvent companies where schemes have been proposed either instead of, or in conjunction with, a formal insolvency procedure, such as an administration. When combined with a pre-packaged administration, it has proved possible to achieve the sale and continuation of a business, generating future value for those who retain the financial interest.

A recent phenomenon has been the use of schemes by continental European companies due to the lack of a local equivalent that would enable them successfully to restructure their debt without the unanimous consent of their creditors. There are examples where companies have been able to demonstrate 'sufficient connection' with the United Kingdom to enable a scheme to be promoted in accordance with the Companies Act.

It should be noted that a scheme is not a formal insolvency procedure and is not deemed to be an insolvency proceeding for the purpose of the EU Insolvency Regulation 2000/1346. *Prima facie*, this means that a scheme may not be automatically recognised in another EU jurisdiction and it also does not constitute a foreign judgment under EU Regulation 44/2001 (the Brussels Convention) or UNCITRAL model law (the New York Convention). However, it has proved possible in certain circumstances to instigate separate proceedings to achieve wider recognition.

Schemes have been used extensively in the financial services sector. In the recent past, well over 100 schemes have been implemented in the insurance sector, enabling insurance companies to accelerate the payment of current and future claims and achieve an early final settlement of those liabilities that, in the normal course, would have continued for many years. Schemes have similarly been used as a mechanism to settle once and for all misselling claims – for example, those relating to the misselling of investment products.

Schemes have therefore proved themselves to be a very flexible tool in the restructuring toolkit. Nothing in the Companies Act prescribes the subject matter of a scheme or the manner in which it is formulated. In practice, therefore, a scheme can be proposed for any matter upon which the company may wish to agree a compromise or arrangement with its creditors or members. As a result, each scheme proposal can be tailored to a company's specific circumstances and stakeholders, and can be adapted to deal with, for example, competing interests or the formal disenfranchisement of those with no economic interest.

The remainder of this chapter considers the use of schemes in the restructuring context of creditor compromises and arrangements rather than shareholder and member proposals.

2. Key elements of a scheme

A scheme is essentially a proposal or a deal that is offered to interested creditors for their consideration and approval. It is a legally binding procedure governed by the provisions of the Companies Act and, as part of this process, also requires the approval of the courts.

When implemented, a scheme can create new rights or obligations between the parties affected by the scheme and must involve a compromise of existing creditors' rights – that is, the proposal must have elements of 'give and take' rather than being a one-sided deal. As such, a scheme cannot compel creditors to do something (eg, to provide further funding) without giving something back (eg, the creation of an equity interest or right thereto).

The key part of the implementation of a scheme is the required sanction by the court, which details two court hearings:

- the initial hearing to approve the process for convening meetings of creditors; and
- the subsequent hearing to consider whether the results of the scheme meetings are fair and reasonable and, if so, to sanction the scheme.

In between these court hearings is a meeting of the creditors, or groups of creditors, that are affected by the scheme. The purpose of the creditors' meetings(s) is for them to consider the terms of the scheme and to vote formally on the scheme proposal.

A scheme commences formally with an application to court for an order convening meetings of the creditors, or any class of them (the convening hearing). An application to court can be made by the company (through its directors), any creditor or member of the company, a liquidator or an administrator (if one is appointed). The application must be supported by a witness statement from the scheme proponent to explain the reasoning for the scheme, and to provide an outline of the scheme proposal. Drafts of an explanatory statement setting out the principal features of the scheme and the proposed scheme document would also be submitted to court at the convening hearing.

At the convening hearing, an important issue that the court will consider is the division of creditors into classes and the number of classes being proposed.

The test to be applied when considering the number of classes to adopt is that each class should comprise those persons whose rights are not so dissimilar as to make it impossible for them to consult together with a view to their common interest. It is recognised that a class of creditor may include creditors that have different interests; however, if their rights are being treated equally by the scheme they would not necessarily comprise a separate class. The constitution of classes therefore requires careful consideration and each case needs to be considered on its own particular circumstances and merits. For example, if one creditor has access to security and another not, as long as their prevailing rights are not being amended by the scheme, they can still constitute and vote as a single class, but if the first creditor's security rights were being changed then two classes would be required.

The court issued a practice statement in 2002[1] to enable any issues relating to the composition of classes to be identified and resolved as early as possible. This commonly means that creditors will be informed of the proposed number and composition of classes in advance of the convening hearing so that any objecting creditors can make representations at the convening hearing should they disagree with the proposed class structure. By dealing with potential class issues upfront, the risk of challenges to the scheme later in the process on grounds of an incorrect composition of classes is significantly reduced as the court will have less sympathy for any arguments on classes that could and should have been raised at this earlier stage.

Once the court is satisfied that the classes have been reasonably constituted at the convening hearing, the court will order that a meeting or meetings of creditors be convened to vote on the scheme. The court will also issue directions on the notification of creditors of the creditors meeting(s). The fairness of the scheme will not be considered at the convening hearing, and will be addressed only at the hearing to sanction the scheme.

At the creditors' meeting(s), and in order for the scheme to proceed, a resolution in favour of the scheme must be supported by more than 50% by number and at least 75% by value of those creditors that vote in each class at the creditors' meeting(s). Failure to meet these majorities in all of the classes proposed at the creditors' meeting(s) means that the scheme would be unable to proceed; however, amendments to the scheme terms can still be made up until the time of the vote if this is necessary to obtain the majorities required.

Following creditor approval at a level of at least the majorities required, an application to court can then be made for the court to sanction the scheme (the sanction hearing). The application is supported by a witness statement setting out

---

1   [2002] 1 WLR 1345.

the results of the creditors' meeting(s) and a copy of the scheme (including any amendments) as voted on and approved by creditors. Creditors may make representations at the sanction hearing regarding matters such as the overall fairness of the scheme or the conduct of the voting process.

In considering whether to sanction the scheme, the court must initially be satisfied that it has, and should, exercise jurisdiction. For example, in England and Wales, the court will need to be satisfied that the scheme will apply, in at least large part, to contracts governed by English law. It must also be satisfied that:

- the provisions of the Companies Act have been complied with, such as the correct constitution of classes and whether the resolutions in favour of the scheme have been properly passed at the creditors' meeting(s); and
- sufficient time and information has been provided to creditors so they may make an informed decision on the merits of the scheme.

The court will also consider the overall fairness of the scheme – in particular applying the test as to whether an intelligent and honest creditor acting reasonably in its own self interests would be minded to vote in favour of the scheme. If the court is so satisfied on all these points, it has discretion to make an order to sanction the scheme.

Once the scheme has been approved by the court and an order made by it, this, together with the final copy of the scheme, must be filed with Companies House before the scheme becomes effective. Once the scheme is effective, the terms of the scheme will then become binding on all creditors, irrespective of whether they voted on the scheme or not.

A summary of the key elements and requirements for a scheme are summarised in Figure 1.

Figure 1: Key elements and requirements for a scheme

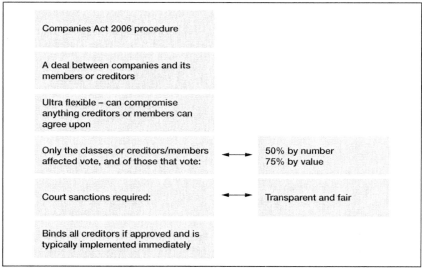

The length of time between each of the court hearings for creditors to consider and vote on the scheme proposals will depend on what is considered reasonable and necessary in the circumstances. The complexity of the scheme, the number and type of creditors affected and the timeframe within which a compromise is required (eg, in distressed circumstances) will all be factors that the court will consider in determining if sufficient time has been allowed. The length of time that a court has allowed for a scheme to be proposed and sanctioned can and has ranged from as little as four weeks to over six months, depending on the above circumstances.

3. **Creditors voluntary arrangements and comparison with schemes of arrangement**

A creditors' voluntary arrangement (CVA) is an alternative and flexible process for compromising claims but is a procedure under the Insolvency Act 1986. There are similarities to schemes under the Companies Act, but also some important differences – some of which are considered in Figure 2.

Figure 2: Distinctive features of schemes and CVAs

Scheme	CVA
• Only affects creditors for which scheme is proposed • Creditors must form separate classes where different rights exist and obtain requisite majority in each class • Can vary rights of minority (non consenting) secured and preferential creditors • Procedure under the Companies Act • No automatic moratorium • No automatic recognition under EU Insolvency Regulations (as not a procedure under the Insolvency Act) but precedent for recognition in non-EU jurisdictions (eg, United States) • Cannot set aside once approved by court	• Covers whole company • No requirement to distinguish classes of creditors and all creditors are entitled to vote • Requires 100% support from secured lenders • Process under the Insolvency Act • Moratorium for small companies but onerous on supervising IP assets • Automatic recognition under EU Insolvency Regulations • Creditors challenge a CVA within 28 days of chairman reporting result to court

For a CVA to be approved, all secured creditors and 75% by value of all others would need to support the proposal before it can be implemented. In a scheme, secured creditors often comprise a separate class, and a scheme could still proceed even if certain secured creditors did not support the proposal if the voting majorities required for that class have been achieved (ie, 75% by value and 50% by number). Therefore, dissenting minority creditors – whether secured or unsecured, preferential or otherwise – can be bound to the terms of a scheme if sufficient other creditors in their class vote in favour of the scheme. This feature has often been referred to as 'cramming down' of minority creditors, although the involvement of the court is intended to ensure fairness, rather than simply relying on creditor democracy.

A scheme will usually be proposed to, and voted on by, only those creditors that are affected by the terms of the scheme. Other creditors, whose rights are not affected by the scheme, can therefore be excluded from the scheme altogether, which is often desirable in an ongoing trading environment where it is advantageous to keep disruption to a minimum. A good example of this in practice is where a company may have costly long-tail liabilities arising from past business activities and a scheme is proposed to deal with such obligations without affecting current supplier and ongoing commercial contracts.

In a CVA, as all of the company's creditors have to be notified of the proposals and have the right to vote, there is no discretion to exclude certain creditors from the proposals. Accordingly, where a CVA proposal affects only a proportion of the creditor base, creditor groups unaffected by the proposed CVA potentially have the ability to vote either through or down the proposal if they have a sufficient proportion of the votes. As a result, commentators have argued that this has, on a number of occasions, resulted in unfairness, where a sufficient number of high-value unaffected creditors have reached the voting majority required for the CVA proposal to proceed, and their views have prevailed over the views of those actually affected by the proposal.

In the case of a scheme and as a consequence of active court involvement and required class structure, once a scheme has been sanctioned by the court there can be no further challenge from creditors. A CVA, by contrast, may still be objected to by creditors, even after a successful vote and being reported to court, with a 28-day window available after this time where any creditor can still make representations on matters such as undue prejudice or unfairness. Such a challenge may come from, for example, a contingent creditor that has no existing claim, but that may be prevented from bringing a claim in the future by the CVA terms.

As a scheme is not an insolvency process under the EU Insolvency Regulation, a possible disadvantage of a scheme over a CVA is that it is not automatically recognised in other jurisdictions, as is the case with CVAs and other insolvency procedures. It is, however, possible to apply for overseas recognition for a scheme – for example, in the United States – and such protection has been successfully obtained for many schemes (eg, where there are assets in the jurisdiction in question).

When dealing with small companies, a CVA can include a moratorium that prevents creditors from enforcing their claims against the company, which is not available for a scheme. However, a scheme for a company of any size could be proposed in conjunction with an administration under the Insolvency Act, which would provide an automatic moratorium to relieve creditor pressure. A CVA could equally be used for a large company in conjunction with an administration in order to obtain the benefit of a moratorium.

This may not, however, be desirable in certain circumstances and is a particular consideration in a solvent restructuring. When considering the merits of a scheme against a CVA, there may be reputational issues in proposing a procedure that implies insolvency or financial distress, which is more likely to be the case with a CVA proposed in accordance with the provisions of the Insolvency Act than with a scheme formulated under the provisions of the Companies Act. It is also possible that a CVA may trigger termination clauses in company contracts whereas a scheme may not, although a well-drafted termination clause may include a composition or arrangement with creditors as an event of default, which would almost certainly also be triggered by a scheme.

It is not intended to suggest that either a scheme or CVA possesses distinct advantages over the other, because both have their particular advantages and drawbacks depending on the circumstances. The intention is rather to highlight some of the principal differences and considerations that need to be taken into account when deciding which procedure may be more relevant and appropriate to a company's circumstances in the course of a restructuring.

4.   Schemes in action

Schemes have been employed in various guises across the restructuring spectrum, for a variety of purposes, and have achieved favourable outcomes for a range of different stakeholders. The following provide some examples of their different application.

In Internacionale, as part of the restructuring and subsequent sale of this high street retailer, a scheme was used to resolve reservation of title (ROT) claims of suppliers covering over 80% of the company's stock. The stock was the only significant asset of the business and a sale of the business out of insolvency where the stock could not be offered on an unencumbered basis would have made a sale of the business almost impossible to achieve. For the suppliers, there were considerable challenges in collecting and reselling the stock.

A scheme was therefore formulated and proposed in which suppliers would accept a payment of 25% of their potential claim in exchange for relinquishing any ROT claim that they may have had. Over 90% of suppliers saw this to be in their commercial interests and voted in favour of the compromise proposal. This allowed a sale to proceed and ensured a future for the business.

IMO Carwash was a global car cleaning group in default of its debt facilities and which could not service the loans advanced for its acquisition. The loan financing documentation required, in effect, 100% consent from all of the lenders (including senior lenders and subordinated mezzanine debt holders) in order to implement the restructuring proposals, which involved a transfer of the business to a Newco, the novation of a large proportion of debt and the issuing of equity in the Newco to senior lenders.

A scheme was proposed by the company alongside a pre-packaged administration, which effectively disenfranchised the subordinated mezzanine debt holders and certain minority senior lenders that were not in favour of the proposals. The proposal was founded on the premise that the subordinated mezzanine debt holders were out of the money (on the basis of a series of different going-concern valuations), and therefore had no further economic interest in the group. It was thus contended that they should not be entitled to vote on the scheme proposal and would not have any rights in Newco going forward. The out-of-the-money creditors objected to the basis on which the classes for the scheme were formulated, but the court allowed the proposed scheme to proceed with a single class (that only comprised the senior lenders), which overwhelmingly voted in favour of the scheme proposal. While a minority of dissenting senior lenders did have a vote, and voted against, they were unable to overturn the scheme majorities required for the proposal to proceed in the face of over 90% support from the other senior lenders.

Following the sanction of the scheme, the business was transferred to the Newco through a share sale, allowing IMO Carwash to survive with restructured debt arrangements. The scheme was then closely followed by the administration of Oldco, with the subordinated mezzanine creditors left within Oldco without any recourse.

Debt-for-equity swaps have also featured regularly in scheme proposals. This was the case in Teeside Gas and Transportation, an Enron group company operating in the oil and gas industry, where a substantial proportion of the company's debts, which may have otherwise caused the company to fail if repayment was demanded, was exchanged via a scheme for a *pro rata* shareholding in the company going forward, giving creditors a stake in the entity and cleaning up the balance sheet in preparation for a future sale. The scheme route was preferred to avoid the stigma of an insolvency, which may have affected the business going forward, and to bind in all creditors, should an unknown (*sic*) creditor be subsequently discovered. Similar examples of debt-for-equity schemes have been implemented for Drax and Marconi, which also benefitted from the restructuring of their debt obligations, and enabled the businesses to trade out of their difficulties with a restructured (and serviceable) debt obligation.

Preserving and enhancing enterprise value through the use of a scheme was also seen in Cape Plc's scheme proposal. Cape's historic activities involved (among other things) the manufacture and use of asbestos products and, as a consequence, many former employees and other third parties had been or might be diagnosed in the future with asbestos-related conditions resulting in significant claims for compensation against the company. The unquantifiable nature of these liabilities created financial uncertainty for the company, manifesting itself in underperformance of Cape's share price and the loss of customer confidence.

Safeguarding the company for employees and management, customers, shareholders and asbestos claimants was paramount, and options available for dealing with the uncertain claims against the group were explored. A scheme was developed as an alternative way of funding the payment of asbestos claims by ringfencing the claims in a subsidiary company, creating a fund to pay future claims and transferring the obligation to pay claims to the fund. New cash was injected into the fund by shareholders (which would not otherwise have been available) and obligations were imposed on the company to top up the fund as required, but only to the extent that the company could afford these payments out of its future profits. Safeguards were also implemented, via a special share issued by Cape and held by a trustee, providing rights that prevented the dissipation of Cape's assets without the fund's consent. In return, the scheme required future claimants to bring claims only against the fund rather than Cape, ensuring that Cape could not become insolvent as a result of any escalation in the number and value of asbestos claims.

The scheme was overwhelmingly supported by the then current and potential future claimants. By proactively dealing with the uncertainty and de-risking the company, Cape was able to regain market and customer confidence, resulting in new long-term business contracts being entered into, which in turn also contributed to a dramatic uplift in its share price. With a healthier business, the upside for claimants was maximising the potential for claims to be paid whenever they arose into the future.

Significant value has also been created in many solvent schemes formulated for insurance companies in run-off, allowing insurance companies with old books of business to exit the market much earlier than would otherwise have been the case.

Insurance liabilities are by their nature often very long term as latent claims can arise on contracts decades after the original policy was issued. Long after insurance companies stop writing business, reserves would still have had to be retained and capital committed until the last claim was notified, agreed and paid. By the use of schemes, the terms of the original insurance contracts were modified to allow for accelerated settlements to be made, potential future liabilities were valued and one-off payments made to the policyholder in full and final settlement of obligations under the contract. By imposing a 'bar date' (time limit for claims to be made) as part of the scheme proposal, any policyholder that had not submitted its claim by that date was no longer able to bring a claim under the insurance policy and all liabilities to that policyholder were extinguished. Once these obligations to policyholders had been settled, the insurance company was then able to be wound up and any surplus capital returned to shareholders.

A particular difficulty encountered when developing insurance exit schemes of this nature was in dealing with creditors that had no claims experience and/or wished to maintain cover for exposure to possible future claims that had not been reported. By ensuring a fair and robust actuarial methodology to value contingent claims of this nature within the scheme and illustrating the overall benefits to the stakeholders of the scheme proposals, it was possible to persuade the court that the overall scheme proposal was fair, and that the scheme should be sanctioned.

Significant amounts of capital release and savings in ongoing administration costs have been achieved by the promotion of schemes for insurance companies, and schemes continue to be a favoured method for closing out these long-tail books of business. A particular feature of insurance company schemes is that they typically apply to many thousands of policyholders that have been issued policies over the years; the scheme provides absolute certainty and finality that all obligations are settled or compromised, irrespective of whether policyholders participate in the scheme or not. It is not unusual to find that a few hundred creditor votes can bind many thousands of others that do not respond.

A recent example where significant benefits were obtained from an insurance exit scheme is Minster Insurance, where a scheme enabled an over 30-year claims run-off to be accelerated and ongoing administrative costs eliminated while ensuring that all policyholders with valid claims were paid in full.

Similarly constructed schemes have also been used to distribute the assets of insolvent insurance companies – for example, North Atlantic, where the scheme offered the advantages of flexibility, cost savings and increased speed of distribution over an alternative liquidation of the company. A liquidation would have attracted significant *ad valorem* charges on depositing cash assets into an insolvency services account at the Bank of England, restricted investment returns and enforced mandatory currency conversion; the scheme ultimately delivered value and increased returns to creditors.

However, it has not been just the domain of insurance companies to use schemes as a mechanism to make distributions out of insolvency, with companies as diverse as Maxwell, Ionica and Rafidain Bank also using a similar process to take advantage of the flexibility of a scheme and maximise returns to creditors.

A criticism has been levelled that schemes are applicable only to large companies, take considerable time and are costly. The scheme for Assetco demonstrated that this is not the case, and that a scheme can be equally applicable to small and medium-sized organisations.

Assetco was an AIM-listed company that supplied fire-fighting equipment and clothing and had an annual turnover of £35 million. Its financing arrangements were misaligned with the needs of the business and faced severe cash-flow pressures. Prospects of new contracts in the Middle East were good if funding could be found and a compromise agreed with its financial creditors.

A CVA was considered as an alternative, but there was a risk that it might have been challenged as there were significant contingent liabilities. A scheme was therefore proposed which compromised only the financial creditors and paved the way for new money to be injected into the company.

With dispensation being granted by the court on the length of time required for creditors to consider the proposals, given the cash-flow pressures on the company and the limited number of creditors, the scheme was able to become effective within six weeks of the idea of a scheme first being floated as a viable restructuring option. This was particularly important in ensuring that the company was still perceived as a going concern, and another reason why it was beneficial to have not implemented the restructuring via an insolvency process.

The above examples illustrate the breadth of application of schemes. Through innovation and careful planning, schemes can ensure that value is generated for a wide variety of companies (large and small), circumstances and stakeholders.

5. International application

The schemes cited here are some of those that have been proposed by UK companies. However, schemes are not solely the domain of UK-registered companies; they are generally available in Westminster (ie, Commonwealth) countries (as a result of the enactment of similar provisions by those countries). In addition, schemes are being applied increasingly within Europe where the circumstances are such as to make this a viable option. As noted earlier, this is because there is no comparable mechanism in most EU states.

The general principle is that a UK-based scheme can be implemented for any overseas company that is capable of being wound up in the United Kingdom and there have been many recent instances of overseas companies promoting a UK scheme as part of a restructuring plan.

The test for whether a non-UK company can be wound up in the United Kingdom is derived from the Insolvency Act; the court can be held to have jurisdiction to wind up a foreign entity if:

- there is sufficient connection with the United Kingdom; this has been held to be the case where, for example:
  - the relevant contracts are subject to English law;
  - there is a branch or other operations in the United Kingdom; or
  - there are assets within the jurisdiction;
- there is reasonable possibility of a benefit accruing to those applying for the winding-up order; and
- one or more parties interested in the distribution of assets of the company are subject to UK jurisdiction.

This is more commonly referred to as the 'sufficient connection' test and is arguably less demanding than the centre of main interest (COMI) test, which must be satisfied (ie, that the COMI is in the United Kingdom) to instigate certain insolvency proceedings in the United Kingdom for an overseas-registered company.

In order to propose a scheme in the United Kingdom there is no need, under the sufficient connection test, to demonstrate the existence of an establishment in the jurisdiction. As noted above, there is no equivalent mechanism in most jurisdictions in Europe, or many other jurisdictions, that provides the same flexibility as a scheme. Given that a scheme is a tried and tested procedure in the United Kingdom, with experienced and commercially minded judges presiding over scheme proposals brought before them, many overseas companies (which have been able to demonstrate sufficient connection to the United Kingdom) have sought to promote a UK-based scheme through this route.

An example of this is La Seda, a Spanish company involved in food and beverage packaging, which was seeking to implement a financial restructuring of its business. The financing documents associated with the senior lenders, whose rights it was intended be compromised, were subject to English law and, in addition, La Seda had an English subsidiary.

The court determined that on the basis of sufficient connection, it had the jurisdiction to sanction a scheme. A complex financial restructuring involving a debt-for-equity swap, a refinancing and the provision of new equity could then proceed. The scheme enabled La Seda to cram down within one class minority dissenting creditors that would have been able to derail the process in the absence of the scheme, and to complete the restructuring.

The English court has further endorsed the scope of a scheme proposal for overseas companies in Primacom, a German cable network operator, which, similarly to La Seda, had English law governed financing documents. Notably, in this case, virtually all creditors were domiciled outside England and Wales, but the court determined that it still had jurisdiction to sanction the scheme on the basis of the English law contracts.

The court has also accepted jurisdiction in relation to many solvent insurance company schemes where the companies that were the subject of the proposed scheme were overseas registered insurance companies:

- doing business in London;
- with UK-based creditors; or
- whose contracts of insurance were subject to English law.

In these cases the companies were able to argue successfully a sufficient connection to the United Kingdom in order to implement a scheme to exit their business. Schemes proposed in the United Kingdom by various ING Group companies located across the world are prime examples of how schemes for non-UK companies have now become a recognised and established process.

Schemes proposed by overseas companies are not recognised as an EU Insolvency Regulation proceeding so there is no automatic recognition of the procedure across the European Union unless combined with a recognised insolvency proceeding such as an administration. While a scheme will afford protection against challenges in the UK courts, separate proceedings may be required to obtain recognition in other jurisdictions – for example, if contracts compromised by the scheme are not subject to UK law and a claim can be brought under those contracts that may attach to assets also outside the jurisdiction of the UK court, then recognition of the scheme where assets are at risk may be required. There is, however, established precedent for the recognition of schemes in other territories – for example, in the United States under Chapter 15 of the Bankruptcy Code, which can provide protection against potential actions by creditors against the entity or its assets in that jurisdiction.

Although this chapter focuses on UK schemes, it should also be recognised that similar provisions are incorporated into the legislation of a number of other jurisdictions, being mostly Westminster countries such as Australia, New Zealand, Singapore, Bermuda and the Cayman and British Virgin Islands. Various schemes have been proposed along similar lines in accordance with the local law; an interesting recent example of this was a scheme proposal by ACS (NZ), a New Zealand insurance company impacted by liabilities arising out of the Christchurch earthquakes.

ACS faced unknown ultimate liabilities and was not certain that it could continue as a going concern, so the directors took the step of implementing a scheme to avoid the possibility of the company having to be wound up, which would have been in the interests of neither the company nor its creditors The scheme included provisions whereby if ACS's estimated liabilities ever exceeded its assets, ACS would be able to pay claims at a *pro rata* level until such time as it may be able to top up these payments, as a result of, for example, an overall improvement in claims experience. ACS was therefore able to continue to trade as a solvent entity, and to date continues to do so, but with the protection of being able to revert to *pro rata*, on-account settlements if the position ever worsens without the adverse implications of formal winding up.

The scheme for ACS was overwhelmingly supported by creditors and provides a suitable contingency arrangement should ACS's financial position deteriorate in the future.

6.   Application to long-tail liabilities

A common use of schemes has been to deal with a company's potential or future (contingent) liabilities where there can be long gestation periods for claims to emerge, often many years after the initial event giving rise to a potential claim. A feature of these so-called 'long-tail liabilities' is that there are often multiple potential claimants, but with the added uncertainty as to the identity of all possible claimants and the unknown timing and value of their potential claims (eg, they may have been exposed to asbestos but where no symptoms had thus far manifested themselves). A situation such as this gives rise to uncertainty both in terms of the overall potential solvency but also liquidity strain, particularly if the core business is already under pressure. A solution may therefore be required to provide some breathing space for the company; the Cape and ACS schemes are examples of how problems such as this can be managed.

Figure 3 sets out some sectors where contingent liability exposures may exist and current and potential claims may arise.

Figure 3: Contingent liability exposure

Landlord/lease obligations	Financial
Retail – high street/out of town Property Automotive Transportation	Misselling Guaranteed return Duplicate payments Professional services
Industrial	Products
Asbestos Personal injury Environmental Pollution	Loyalty schemes (eg, vouchers) Pharmaceutical Recall Warranties

In all of the above cases, adverse claims arising or onerous obligations have the potential to create stress for ongoing businesses in terms of ultimate liability, as well as the administrative cost and management distraction; a scheme may provide a buffer between when claims are recognised and when they have to be paid in full. Schemes of this nature are advantageous to all parties as they are based on the premise that the long-term ongoing viability of the business is in the interest of all stakeholders, and for contingent creditors in particular that will want to ensure that their claims on the company can be paid whenever they arise in the future, rather than be faced with the prospect of an unwelcome insolvency.

A scheme may therefore offer a practical, balanced and robust solution to help deal with prevailing uncertainty, especially if there is the possibility of imminent or future financial distress.

7. Conclusion

We have seen that schemes, as a result of their flexibility and the requirement that they are approved by the courts, are an essential tool in the restructuring professional's toolbox. They have been used regularly and increasingly as a means of, for example, restructuring companies, businesses or selected liabilities – all with the aim of removing uncertainty and enabling those companies to trade out of their difficulties. A scheme can be invaluable in reconciling divergent interests and, if necessary, imposing on a minority what is in the commercial best interests of the majority.

The circumstances in which schemes may be appropriate require certain preconditions – for instance, short-term financial stability (since there is no automatic moratorium) – to provide sufficient time to enable the scheme to be promoted. There also needs to be reasonable prospects of the scheme proposals being approved and time needs to be taken to sell the proposals to those affected and to ensure that the scheme is fair to the majority of those affected by it. Otherwise, it will not be sanctioned by the court.

Schemes can offer a credible and flexible means of resolving a company's financial difficulties outside of formal insolvency, which may otherwise have detrimental effects on the business. Where the circumstances of the company are such that it cannot continue to trade (eg, by reason of its liabilities), schemes may also be an effective and flexible means of dealing with creditor claims in the course of the insolvency.

In view of this flexibility, it is quite likely that the use of schemes in restructuring will continue to grow and that we shall see continuing innovation as they are applied to a multiplicity of business issues.

Forum shopping

Christine L Childers
Jenner & Block LLP

---

1.   Introduction

We live in a 'grass is greener' culture. This sentiment has not escaped the international insolvency world, and perhaps for good reason. The laws governing insolvency in individual countries are sometimes as different as the cultures of those countries. Some regimes favour the debtor, while others favour banks, creditors and employees.[1] As a result, forum shopping (selecting the most favourable place for insolvency proceedings to occur) – is thriving in the international insolvency arena. A debtor (or creditor that forces a debtor into bankruptcy) can access the set of remedies and procedures most fitting to its situation by choosing the appropriate country in which to proceed. Just how easy forum shopping is may depend on the approach to international insolvency jurisdiction employed by the country or set of countries under a treaty or model law, or the debtor's ability to control the location of its home country or 'centre of main interests' (COMI).

The approaches to international insolvency jurisdiction fall into two opposite (and extreme) camps: territorialism and universalism. The international bankruptcy laws of every nation (or group of nations), however different and dramatic they may be, incorporate some form of territorialism or universalism, pure or modified, in their approach to jurisdiction. Territorialism is, basically, the traditional idea that courts in each nation exercise exclusive jurisdiction over, and apply their insolvency laws to, debtors or assets within their borders. Forum shopping under this type of regime seems more difficult, unless a company can easily move its assets. Universalism, by contrast, dictates that one court in the debtor's home country will apply its domestic bankruptcy law to all of the debtor's assets and creditors worldwide, wherever located. Forum shopping under this type of regime seems manipulable because it comes down to the location of the debtor's home country, a concept that may be elusive.

This chapter discusses territorialism and universalism and considers which, if either, is more prone to allow forum shopping. It then discusses some of the existing legal structures in the European Union and the United States, each of which is taking the international insolvency world towards a universalist approach by incorporating the 'home country' concept of universalism into its legislation.[2] The first, passed in 2000 by the European Union, is the EU Regulation on Insolvency Proceedings.[3] The

---

1   "The US favours the company; the French protect the employee; the British, the creditors", *British Am Bus* 2007, available at www.british-american-business.com/2007/p_052.php (last visited May 2 2012).

second, promulgated in 1997 by the UN Commission on International Trade Law (UNCITRAL), is the Model Law on Cross-Border Insolvency,[4] which has been enacted in modified form in the United Kingdom as the Cross-Border Insolvency Regulations 2006[5] and in the United States in modified form as Chapter 15 of Title 11 of the US Code (11 USC, Sections 101–1532, Bankruptcy Code).[6] Lastly, this chapter reviews several cases in which forum shopping has been utilised by debtors in the international insolvency arena.

2. The two competing approaches to international insolvency jurisdiction

There are two opposite approaches to jurisdiction in international insolvencies.[7] The first, territorialism, involves the practice of nations exercising exclusive jurisdiction over parties and assets within their borders.[8] The second, universalism, involves the practice of nations resolving a debtor's insolvency under the laws of the debtor's home country.[9] Each involves a fight for control and each allows room for forum shopping by debtors, creditors and other stakeholders.

2.1 Defining 'territorialism'[10]

Territorialism is the traditional approach to jurisdiction in which courts exercise jurisdiction over assets and parties within their borders. Each country utilises its own laws to decide how the debtor's assets located within its borders will be treated in an insolvency proceeding. Hence, territorialism operates under what is referred to as the 'grab rule', because the courts of each nation seize the assets within their jurisdiction for distribution to creditors under national laws.[11]

A modified version of territorialism is referred to as 'cooperative territorialism'. It

---

2   In 2002 the American Law Institute (ALI) promulgated the Principles of Cooperation in Transnational Insolvency Cases among the Members of the North American Free Trade Association. This, too, is a universalist set of principles. Lynn M LoPucki, "Global and Out of Control?", 79 *Am Bankr L J* 79, 86 (2005) ('LoPucki, "Out of Control" ').

3   EU Regulation 1346/2000, 2000 OJ (L160). All countries in the European Union, excluding Denmark, have adopted the EU Insolvency Regulation. Accordingly, Denmark is neither bound by it nor subject to its application. Here, when reference is made to 'member states' having duties under the EU Insolvency Regulation, this is intended to exclude Denmark.

4   Model Law on Cross-Border Insolvency 52/158 (UNCITRAL 1997).

5   See the Cross-Border Insolvency Regulations 1030/2006.

6   See 11 USC, Sections 1501–1532.

7   There is one other model, contractualism, which receives scant discussion in the literature. Under contractualism, a debtor and each of its creditors would, by contract, choose the law that would apply to their relationship. John J Chung, "The New Chapter 15 of the Bankruptcy Code: A Step Toward Erosion of National Sovereignty", 27 *Nw J Int'l L & Bus* 89, 96 n 20 (2006); see also Robert K Rasmussen, "A New Approach to International Insolvencies", 19 *Mich J Int'l L* 1 (1997); Robert K Rasmussen, "Debtor's Choice: A Menu Approach to Corporate Bankruptcy", 71 *Texas L Rev* 51 (1992). Contractualism "seeks to finesse the choice between universalism and territoriality". Lynn M LoPucki, "The Case for Cooperative Territoriality in International Bankruptcy", 98 *Mich L Rev* 2216, 2244 (2000) ('LoPucki, "Cooperative Territoriality" ').

8   Chung, above note 7, at 93.

9   *Ibid* at 93–94.

10   One of the most outspoken territorialists is Lynn M LoPucki, the Security Pacific Bank professor of law at the University of California, Los Angeles Law School. LoPucki has proposed a system of cooperative territoriality in place of universalism. See, for example, LoPucki, "Cooperative Territoriality", above note 7; Lynn M LoPucki, "Cooperation in International Bankruptcy: A Post-Universalist Approach", 84 *Cornell L Rev* 696 (1999) ('LoPucki, "Post-Universalist Approach" ').

11   Andrew T Guzman, "International Bankruptcy: In Defense of Universalism", 98 *Mich L Rev* 2177, 2179–80 (2000).

encourages cooperation between different territories when a dispute arises and contemplates the use of international conventions to govern the return of assets to their proper jurisdiction if improperly relocated just prior to bankruptcy for the purposes of manipulating jurisdiction.[12]

The advantages of territoriality include:

- protection of local creditors;
- simplicity, since the local court does not have to cooperate with courts in other jurisdictions; and
- a "rough-justice allocation of assets among nations, because the location of assets at the time of the general default may fairly often reflect to some extent the debtor's commercial level of activity in each country".[13]

On the other hand, territorialism has been noted to have the following defects:

- It causes greater costs for an international business due to the need for parallel insolvency cases in each country in which assets are located;
- It enhances the difficulty of reorganisation since it decreases liquidation values and makes coordination of cases extremely complex;
- It allows for conflicts between courts and jurisdictions to develop easily;
- It creates a less efficient *ex ante* allocation of capital because creditors cannot know in advance where assets will be located at the time of bankruptcy;
- It results in uneven and unpredictable distribution, which increases the cost of capital; and
- It allows debtors and creditors to advance their private interests at the expense of the general interests of creditors.[14]

2.2 Defining 'universalism'[15]

There are at least two forms of universalism: pure universalism and modified universalism. In its purest form, universalism is based on the concept of 'one law, one court'.[16] Under the universalist approach, there is a single bankruptcy proceeding in the debtor's home country.[17] The home country court applies its bankruptcy law, has global jurisdiction over all of the debtor's assets and creditors, wherever located,

---

12   John A E Pottow, "Procedural Incrementalism: A Model for International Insolvency", 45 *Va J Int'l L* 935, 954–55 (2005).

13   Liza Perkins, "A Defense of Pure Universalism in Cross-Border Corporate Insolvencies", 32 *NYU J Int'l L & Pol* 787 (2000); Jay L Westbrook, "Choice of Avoidance Law in Global Insolvencies", 17 *Brook J Int'l L* 499, 514 (1991).

14   Hon Samuel L Bufford, "Global Venue Controls are Coming: A Reply to Professor LoPucki", 79 *Am Bankr L J* 105, 114 (2005) ('Bufford, "Global Venue Controls" ').

15   Westbrook is widely acknowledged as the "most eloquent and effective proponent of universalism". Guzman, above note 11, at 2179–80. The Hon Samuel L Bufford, US bankruptcy judge for the Central District of California, also has been an outspoken universalist, supporting an effort toward a modified universalist approach. See, for example, Bufford, "Global Venue Controls", above note 14.

16   Frederick Tung, "Is International Bankruptcy Possible?", 23 *Mich J Int'l L* 31, 40 (2001). One author has argued that the United Kingdom asserts bankruptcy universalism in Section 221 of the Insolvency Act 1986. Gerald McCormack, "Universalism in Insolvency Proceedings and the Common Law", *Oxford J L Stud*, April 4 2012, at 1, 5. He says that this section, which gives UK courts the power to wind up foreign companies despite the absence of main insolvency proceedings, grants "broad winding up jurisdiction in respect of foreign companies not limited to cases where the company has its principal place of business or centre of main interests in the UK". *Ibid.*

and makes a unified distribution to creditors. As such, universalism requires the non-home country court to defer to the home country court's decisions with respect to the property located and legal relationships formed and conducted within its own borders. The home country counts on the courts of other countries to carry out its decisions relative to the assets and creditors located in those other countries.

Under modified universalism, courts can refuse, under certain circumstances, to defer to the home country court. The most common circumstance is where the home country court's decision or process offends the public policy of the non-home country court. Most countries (and the existing legal structures) incorporate a modified universalist approach, thereby maintaining some control over whether foreign legal proceedings must be recognised in the non-home country.

The benefits of universalism have been deemed to include:

- a more efficient allocation of capital;
- a reduction in confusion over competing domestic priority rules;
- a reduction in the lender's costs of monitoring foreign assets;
- reduced administrative costs due to a reduction in the number of proceedings;
- avoidance of forum shopping and the race to file;
- facilitated reorganisations;
- increased reorganisation or liquidation value; and
- the provision of clarity and certainty to all parties.[18]

On the other hand, universalism has been noted to have the following problems:

- in a universalist system, foreign law and courts govern wholly domestic relationships, confusing domestic markets;
- the home country standard is indeterminate in many cases;
- no workable rule can be devised for determining the extent to which the home country is to have jurisdiction over corporate groups; and
- the home country standard is vulnerable to strategic manipulation.[19]

Additionally, universalism requires countries to cede national sovereignty.[20]

---

17   LoPucki indicates that the home country standard has four fatal flaws: many of the largest multinational companies do not have home countries in any meaningful sense; it can, and is, easily changed, even for multinational companies; since courts compete for bankruptcy cases, they cannot be trusted to determine fairly and in good faith whether they are the home country; and mechanisms do not exist to fix the problem of out of control international forum shopping. LoPucki, "Out of Control", above note 2, at 81.

18   Chung, above note 7, at 95 (citations omitted); see, for example, LoPucki, "Post-Universalist Approach", above note 10, at 706–08.

19   LoPucki, "Post-Universalist Approach", above note 10, at 709. See also *Ibid* at 709–23 (discussing each of the 'problems' in turn); Chung, above note 7, at 110–28 (same).

20   Chung, above note 7, at 103. "Section 1508 explicitly commands American courts to maintain, as much as possible, uniformity of interpretation with other countries of the Model Law, and the statute directs the courts to look to the decisions of other countries that have adopted it … Section 1508 opens the door wide for the introduction of foreign law, and moves the courts away from the primacy of American law." *Ibid* 103–04 (citations omitted).

2.3 Which approach promotes greater forum shopping?

Given that territorialism leaves countries to decide what happens to the debtors and assets within their borders, it would seem that territorialism provides the least chance for forum shopping. However, assets can be moved. But moving is not always practical, especially for a debtor whose operations, employees and assets have long been located in a particular country. Yet even in a territorialist regime, forum shopping can thrive.[21]

Universalism, by contrast, appears to provide an easier mechanism for forum shopping. The home country of a corporation – or, for that matter, a corporate group – is not always easily distinguishable and in today's global economy can be located almost anywhere. Is it the country of incorporation? The location of the company's headquarters? Where all of the employees, operations and customers are located? Or, when separate from operations, where the majority of its assets are located? The concept becomes more difficult when dealing with a multinational corporation. What home country controls parent and subsidiary? The elusiveness of the home country concept seems to enable forum shopping.

Of course, as sophisticated creditors become more aware of the trend for distressed companies to consider forum shopping, they may begin (if they have not already), under either approach to jurisdiction, to eliminate contractually the opportunity for forum shopping.[22] In that case, perhaps legislation is not necessary, but instead case protocols should be used to coordinate international bankruptcies, particularly multinational corporate group insolvencies.[23]

3. The existing legal structures

The existing legal structures in the European Union, the United Kingdom and the United States have a bent towards universalism. As such, the risk of forum shopping, if it is in fact any greater under universalism, remains. What will happen in this regard remains to be seen as case law is developed under the EU Insolvency Regulation, the UK Cross-Border Insolvency Regulations 2006 and Chapter 15 of the US Bankruptcy Code.

3.1 EU Insolvency Regulation (effective May 31 2002)

In 2000 the European Union passed the EU Insolvency Regulation in order to enhance cooperation among countries within the European Union in insolvency proceedings and to harmonise conflict-of-law issues.[24] The regulation was specifically

---

21   In fact, one author has indicated that territorialism may be just as bad as universalism, if not worse, because of the predictability of its choice of law rule and the likely greater ease with which assets, rather than COMIs, can be moved. John A E Pottow, "The Myth (and Realities) of Forum Shopping in Transnational Insolvency", 32 *Brook J Int'l L* 785, 816 (2006–07) ('Pottow, "Myth (and Realities)" ').

22   Joseph A McCahery, "Creditor Protection in a Cross-Border Context", 7 *Eur Bus Org L Rev* 455, 458 (2006).

23   Susan Power Johnson and John Han, "A Proposal for Party-Determined COMI in Cross-Border Insolvencies of Multinational Corporate Groups", 16 *J Bankr L & Prac* 5 Article 7 (October 2007) (proposing that insolvency professionals and courts explore, as a first option, the negotiation of appropriate protocols to govern case administration and restructuring, which can provide a wealth of creative *ad hoc* approaches to fit particular facts); see also Horst Eidenmüller, "Free Choice in International Company Insolvency Law in Europe", 6 *Eur Bus Org L Rev* 423, 431 (2005) (advocating looking for "an alternative approach that gives more room to freedom of choice in international company insolvency law in Europe").

promulgated to eliminate forum shopping: "It is necessary for the proper functioning of the internal market to avoid incentives for the parties to transfer assets or judicial proceedings from one Member State to another, seeking to obtain a more favorable legal position (forum shopping)."[25] The regulation relies on a debtor's COMI to determine which member state's courts will have jurisdiction to open main insolvency proceedings, which must be recognised in all other member states. The regulation also recognises the need for secondary proceedings in other member states in order to assist the functioning of the main proceeding. Hence, the regulation, which incorporates the home country concept of universalism, adopts a universalist view,[26] since it provides for one main jurisdiction in charge of insolvency proceedings, but also employs a territorialist view (or modified universalism), since it allows secondary, territorially based proceedings.

(a)   COMI

The regulation permits the national court of any EU member state within which the debtor's COMI is located to open insolvency proceedings, which under the regulation are main proceedings. Article 3(1) of the regulation provides:

> In the case of a company or a legal person, the place of the registered office shall be presumed to be the centre of main interests in the absence of proof to the contrary.[27]

'COMI' is not defined in the regulation, but paragraph 13 of the recital to the regulation indicates:

> The centre of main interests should correspond to the place where the debtor conducts the administration of his interests on a regular basis and is therefore ascertainable by third parties.[28]

The European Court of Justice (ECJ) has held that "in determining the centre of main interests of a debtor company, the simple presumption laid down by the Community legislature in favour of the registered office of that company can be rebutted only if factors which are both objective and ascertainable by third parties enable it to be established that an actual situation exists which is different from that which locating it at its registered office is deemed to reflect".[29] Accordingly, even

---

24   EU Insolvency Regulation, Preamble, at paras 2-3.
25   EU Insolvency Regulation, Preamble, at para 4.
26   See LoPucki, "Out of Control", above note 2, at 87 ("As a principle matter, universalism is now the law in the European Union").
27   The COMI provision of the regulation was first interpreted in *BRAC Rent-a-Car International Inc*. In that case, the court held that under the regulation, the UK courts had jurisdiction to open insolvency proceedings for BRAC, although incorporated in Delaware, because its COMI was in the United Kingdom. *In re BRAC Rent-a-Car Int'l Inc* [2003] EWCH (Ch) 12, 1 WLR 1421, para 31, 2 All ER 201 (Chancery Division). The court reasoned that BRAC's US address was not an address from which it traded, or ever traded, its operations were conducted almost entirely in the United Kingdom, it had no employees in the United States, and all of its employees (except a few in a branch office in Switzerland) were in England. *Ibid* paras 4–5.
28   See also Case C-396/09, *Interedil Srl* [2011] ECR I-0000, at para 48 ("[T]he presumption in the second sentence of Article 3(1) of the Regulation that the place of the company's registered office is the centre of its main interests and the reference in recital 13 in the preamble to the Regulation to the place where the debtor conducts the administration of his interests reflect the European Union legislature's intention to *attach greater importance* to the place in which the company has its central administration as the criterion for jurisdiction") (emphasis added).
29   *Bondi v Bank of Am (In re Eurofood IFSC Ltd)*, Case 341/04, 2006 ECR I-3813, at paras 34 and 37 (ECJ, May 2 2006).

where a debtor is a subsidiary company with a registered office in a different member state from its parent company, the presumption of Article 3(1) of the regulation can be rebutted only if factors that are both objective and ascertainable by third parties enable it to be determined that the COMI should be other than where the subsidiary is registered.[30] So, for instance, if the subsidiary is not engaged in any business in the member state, then its COMI may be in the member state of its parent.[31] By contrast, if the subsidiary is carrying on business, "the mere fact that its economic choices are or can be controlled by a parent company in another Member State is not enough to rebut the presumption laid down by the Regulation".[32]

Once a debtor's COMI has been determined by the courts of a member state, all other member states must recognise that decision.[33] Only the ECJ can overrule a final COMI order. Nonetheless, because of the fuzziness of the COMI standard,[34] companies in financial difficulty may seek to change their COMI to enable a restructuring of their debt in a more company-friendly jurisdiction.[35]

The COMI standard has been identified as having several shortcomings, including the following:

- It is extremely fact sensitive, thus allowing forum shopping;
- It is detrimental to creditors, which cannot protect themselves because of the room for manipulation;
- The COMIs of members of a corporate group are not necessarily identical and, therefore, jurisdiction over the group may or may not be in a single jurisdiction;[36] and
- It leads to discrepancies between applicable insolvency and company law rules.[37]

---

30   *Ibid* para 37.
31   *Ibid.* Further, the ECJ has held that the mere finding that two companies have intermixed property is not enough to establish that the COMI of the one concerned by the action is the same as the other: Case C-191/10, *Rastelli Davide e C Snc v Hidoux* [2011] ECJ (1st Chamber).
32   *Ibid.* Even after the ECJ's decision in *Eurofood*, the meaning of 'COMI' still lacks clear definition. The ECJ attempted to add some clarity in a 2011 decision. See *Interedil Srl*, above at paras 50–51 (explaining when the rebuttable presumption of Article 3(1) of the regulation may and may not be rebutted with reference to the location of the bodies responsible for the management and supervision or central administration of the company).
33   The last place in which the debtor's COMI was located is regarded as the relevant place for determining the court having jurisdiction to open main insolvency proceedings. *Interedil Srl*, above at para 54. Further, once a request to open insolvency proceedings has been lodged, a change in COMI thereafter does not divest the original court of jurisdiction to open proceedings even if proceedings have not yet been opened under the national law of the member state. Case C-1/04, *Susanne Staubitz-Schreiber*, 2006 ECR I-701 (Judgment of the Court).
34   McCahery, above note 22, at 458 ("With regard to the Regulation, the evidence indicates that debtors and creditors have the ability to exploit the fuzziness of the statute in order to shift a company's COMI"); Eidenmüller, above note 23, at 430 ("[T]he standard is fuzzy and manipulable, allowing forum shopping in the immediate vicinity of bankruptcy").
35   The restructurings of Schefenacker and Interedil (see below) are successful examples of the use of a change in COMI through a corporate migration. Hans Brochier (see below) provides a failed example.
36   The discussion (below) of Parmalat SpA/Eurofood IFSC Ltd is an example of the ineffectiveness of COMI as applied to multinational corporate groups. For a proposal for dealing with this shortcoming, see Gabriel Moss, QC, *Proposal for Group COMI and its Consequences*, in *Coordination of Multinational Corporate Group Insolvencies: Solving the COMI Issue* (International Insolvency Institute, Tenth Annual International Insolvency Conference June 7–8 2010).
37   Eidenmüller, above note 23, at 430–31. For a complete exploration of insolvency considerations of cross-border corporate groups and the problems of dealing with multinational corporate groups under the regulation, see Irit Mevorach, "The Road to a Suitable and Comprehensive Global Approach to Insolvencies within Multinational Corporate Groups", 15 *Norton J Bankr L* 455 (2006).

(b)   Main and secondary proceedings

According to Article 1(1) of the regulation, insolvency proceedings to which it applies must:

- be collective proceedings;
- be based on the debtor's insolvency;
- entail at least partial divestment of the debtor; and
- involve the prompt appointment of a liquidator.[38]

When a proceeding having these characteristics[39] is opened in the member state where the debtor's COMI is located, it is the 'main proceeding' under the regulation. The most important aspect of main proceeding status is that, according to Article 4(1), the law applicable to the proceedings is that "of the Member State within the territory of which such proceedings are opened". And under Article 16, this consequence must be recognised automatically in all other member states.

In accordance with Article 3(2), other member states can have jurisdiction only if "the debtor possesses an establishment within the territory of that other Member State". An 'establishment' is defined in Article 2(h) as "any place of operations where the debtor carries out a non-transitory economic activity with human means and goods". Any proceedings opened in other member states based on these provisions are 'secondary proceedings'.[40] In accordance with Articles 3(2) and 27, the effects of secondary proceedings are restricted to the assets of the debtor situated in that member state.

3.2   Model Law on Cross-Border Insolvency

The Model Law on Cross-Border Insolvency was adopted by UNCITRAL in 1997. National insolvency laws generally are not designed to deal with cross-border insolvencies, which makes it difficult to administer these insolvencies both quickly and effectively. Recognising this, UNCITRAL designed the model law to assist states in managing transnational insolvency cases in an efficient, fair and cost-effective manner.[41] The model law does not attempt to harmonise local insolvency law, but instead expressly empowers courts to extend cooperation in the areas covered by the model law.[42] Specifically, it addresses issues of:

- recognition of foreign proceedings;
- coordination of proceedings concerning the same debtor;
- rights of foreign creditors;
- rights and duties of foreign insolvency representatives; and
- cooperation between authorities in different states.

The model law is not binding on any state and must therefore be enacted

---

38   Article 2 of the regulation defines a 'liquidator' as one "whose function is to administer or liquidate the assets of which the debtor has been divested or to supervise the administration of his affairs", as listed in Annex C to the regulation.

39   Annex A of the regulation lists the insolvency proceedings of each member state to which the regulation applies.

40   Annex B of the regulation lists the allowed secondary proceedings in each member state.

41   Model Law Resolution (January 30 1998).

42   Ibid.

locally.[43] It has been enacted, in modified form to take account of established local requirements, in the United Kingdom and the United States.

A modified form of the model law, known as the Cross-Border Insolvency Regulations 2006 ('UK Model Law') became effective on April 4 2006 in the United Kingdom. The UK Model Law, the EU Insolvency Regulation and Section 426 of the Insolvency Act 1986 operate in parallel in the United Kingdom in insolvency proceedings. In accordance with Article 3 of the UK Model Law, to the extent that the UK Model Law conflicts with an obligation under the regulation, the requirements of the regulation prevail.

Likewise, Chapter 15 of the US Bankruptcy Code, which became effective on October 17 2005, essentially implements the UNCITRAL Model Law.[44] Chapter 15 specifically states that it is intended to:

- facilitate cooperation between US courts, trustees, examiners, debtors and debtors in possession, and the courts and other competent authorities of foreign countries;
- provide greater consistency in the law for trade and investment; and
- promote fair and efficient administration of cross-border insolvencies while protecting the interests of all creditors and other interested parties, including the debtor.[45]

The UK Model Law and Chapter 15 apply where:

- assistance is sought by a foreign court or a foreign representative in connection with a foreign proceeding;
- assistance is sought in a foreign country in connection with a case under the applicable insolvency law;
- a foreign proceeding and a case under the applicable insolvency law with respect to the same debtor are pending concurrently; or
- creditors or other interested persons in a foreign country have an interest in requesting the commencement of, or participating in, a case or proceeding under the UK Model Law or Chapter 15.[46]

---

43   Legislation based on the model law has been adopted in: Australia (2008), Canada (2009), the British Virgin Islands (an overseas territory of the United Kingdom and Northern Ireland) (2003), Colombia (2006), Eritrea (1998), Great Britain (2006), Greece (2010), Japan (2000), Mauritius (2009), Mexico (2000), Montenegro (2002), New Zealand (2006), Poland (2003), [South Korea (2006)] Romania (2003), Serbia (2004), Slovenia (2007), South Africa (2000), and the United States (2005). www.uncitral.org/uncitral/en/uncitral_texts/insolvency/1997Model_status.html (last visited May 2 2012).

44   11 USC, Section 1501(a).

45   11 USC, Section 1501(a)(1)–(5).

46   UK Model Law, Article 1(1); 11 USC, Section 1501(b).

47   A 'foreign proceeding' is defined as "a collective judicial or administrative proceeding in a foreign State, including an interim proceeding, pursuant to a law relating to insolvency in which proceeding the assets and affairs of the debtor are subject to control or supervision by a foreign court, for the purpose of reorganisation or liquidation". UK Model Law, Article 2(i); see also 11 USC, Section 101(23) (similarly defined). A 'foreign main proceeding' is defined as a foreign proceeding that takes place where the debtor's COMI is located. UK Model Law, Article 2(g); 11 USC, Section 1502(4). A 'foreign non-main proceeding' is defined as any other foreign proceeding, other than a main proceeding, that is pending in a country where the debtor has an establishment. UK Model Law, Article 2(h); 11 USC, Section 1502(5). An 'establishment' means any place of operations where the debtor carries out a non-transitory economic activity. UK Model Law, Article 2(e); 11 USC, Section 1502(2).

Generally, a case under the UK Model Law and Chapter 15 is ancillary to a 'foreign proceeding'.[47] A case is commenced by a foreign representative filing a petition for recognition of a foreign proceeding.[48] The petition for recognition must be accompanied by evidentiary documents, which are presumed to be authentic in the absence of evidence to the contrary.[49] A foreign representative may request recognition of the foreign proceeding as either a 'foreign main proceeding' or a 'foreign non-main proceeding'.[50]

In the absence of evidence to the contrary, the location of the debtor's registered office is presumed to be its COMI.[51] Pursuant to the introductory clause, however, that presumption may be rebutted. The legislative history to Chapter 15 makes it clear that "[t]he ultimate burden as to each element [of recognition] is on the foreign representative, although the court is entitled to shift the burden to the extent indicated in section 1516".[52] The legislative history to Chapter 15 also indicates that the statutory presumption of COMI may be of less weight in the event of a serious dispute: "The presumption that the place of the registered office is also the [COMI] is included for speed and convenience of proof where there is no serious controversy."[53]

The type of evidence required to rebut the presumption that the COMI is the debtor's place of registration or incorporation is not stated in the UK Model Law or Chapter 15.[54] Under the UK Model Law, the concept of COMI is similar to that under the regulation, so guidance can come from cases decided under the regulation. US courts have stated that various factors, singly or combined, could be relevant to the COMI determination:

- the location of the debtor's headquarters;
- the location of those who actually manage the debtor (which, conceivably, could be the headquarters of a holding company);
- the location of the debtor's primary assets;

---

48   UK Model Law, Articles 11, 15; 11 USC, Sections 1504, 1515. Under Chapter 15, the COMI analysis is made as of the date of the chapter 15 petition. See *Lavie v Ran (In re Ran)*, 607 F 3d 1017, 1025 (5th Cir 2010); *In re Betcorp Ltd*, 400 BR 266, 291–92 (Bankr D Nev 2009); but see *In re Millennium Global Emerging Credit Master Fund Ltd*, 458 BR 63, 76–77 (Bankr SDNY 2011) (finding, among other things, that use of Chapter 15 date as date for determining recognition leads to possibility of forum shopping and therefore concluding that the appropriate date to use is the date of commencement of the foreign proceeding for which recognition is sought).
49   UK Model Law, Articles 15(2), 16; 11 USC, Sections 1515(b), 1516(b).
50   UK Model Law, Article 17(2); 11 USC, Section 1517(a)(1). Although the court has the power to grant, under appropriate circumstances, extensive relief regardless of whether the foreign proceeding is recognised as 'main' or 'non-main', recognition of the proceeding as a foreign main proceeding triggers some additional relief. See UK Model Law, Article 20; 11 USC, Section 1520.
51   UK Model Law, Article 16(3); 11 USC, Section 1516(c). The determination of COMI under the regulation and the Model Law, although similar in concept, serve distinct purposes. Under the regulation, the purpose is to determine the jurisdiction in which main proceedings should be commenced, whereas under the Model Law the purpose relates to recognition. See "The UNCITRAL Model Law on Cross-Border Insolvency: The Judicial Perspective", at 22 (UNCITRAL July 20 2011), available at www.uncitral.org/pdf/english/texts/insolven/V1188129-Judicial_Perspective_ebook-E.pdf (last visited June 24 2012) ('UNICITRAL: A Judicial Perspective').
52   HR Rep No 109–31, at 112–113 (2005), reprinted in 2005 USCCAN 88, 175.
53   *Ibid.*
54   The Preamble to the UK Model Law and the legislative history to Chapter 15 both indicate that courts may look to the Guide to Enactment of the UNCITRAL Model Law on Cross-Border Insolvency, UN Gen Ass UNCITRAL 30th Sess, UN Doc ACN9/442 (1997) for guidance on how to interpret the provisions of the UK Model Law and Chapter 15. See UK Model Law, Preamble at para 2(2)(c); HR Rep No 109–31(I), at 106 n 101, reprinted in 2005 USCCAN 88, 169 n 101.

- the location of the majority of the debtor's creditors or of a majority of the creditors that would be affected by the case; and
- the jurisdiction whose law would apply to most disputes.[55]

However, these factors are not to be mechanically applied, but instead "should be viewed in light of Chapter 15's emphasis on protecting the reasonable interests of parties in interest pursuant to fair procedures and the maximisation of the debtor's value".[56] Read in conjunction with the EU Insolvency Regulation,[57] under the UK Model Law and Chapter 15, an analysis of COMI for purposes of determining whether a foreign proceeding is main or non-main also should consider the place where the debtor conducts the administration of its interests on a regular basis as is ascertainable by creditors.

Upon the application for recognition, at the request of the foreign insolvency representative to protect the assets of the debtor or in the interests of the creditors, the court may grant relief of a provisional nature, such as:

- staying execution against the debtor's assets;
- entrusting the administration or realisation of the debtor's assets located within its jurisdiction to the foreign representative;
- suspending the right to transfer, encumber or dispose of assets;
- providing for the examination of witnesses and taking of evidence concerning the debtor; and
- granting certain additional relief otherwise available under the insolvency laws.[58]

---

55 *In re SPhinX Ltd*, 351 BR 10, 117 (Bankr SDNY 2006). One US court has found that the debtor's COMI is comparable to the concept of 'principal place of business' under US law. *In re Tri-Continental Exch Ltd* 349 BR 627, 634 (Bankr ED Cal 2006); see also *Betcorp* 400 BR at 290 (including principal place of business in the objective factors to be discerned when determining a debtor's COMI). In *In re Bear Stearns High-Grade Structured Credit Strategies Enhanced Leverage Master Fund Ltd* Judge Lifland, relying on the ECJ's decision in *Eurofood*, set forth the following analysis of the COMI presumption: "As noted by the European Court of Justice, the COMI presumption may be overcome "particular[ly] in the case of a 'letterbox' company not carrying out any business in the territory of the Member State in which its registered office is situated." See *In re Eurofood IFSC Ltd*, above at para 35; see also *In re SPhinX, Ltd* 371 BR 10 (SDNY 2007). In addition, the Guide to Enactment of the UNCITRAL Model Law on Cross-Border Insolvency explains that the presumption does "not prevent, in accordance with applicable procedural law, calling for or assessing other evidence if the conclusion suggested by the presumption is called into question by the court or an interested party". 374 BR 122, 129 (Bankr SDNY 2007) (citing the Guide to Enactment of the UNCITRAL Model Law on Cross-Border Insolvency para 122). The fact is, differences in approach to deciding COMI have arisen in the case law. However, the courts have adhered to the principle that the debtor's COMI must be ascertainable by third parties. See, for example, *In re British Am Ins Co Ltd* 425 BR 884, 909 (Bankr SD Fla 2010); *Betcorp* 400 BR at 291 ("COMI is affected not only by what a debtor does, but by what a debtor is perceived as doing"). Some US courts even have indicated that the activities of the debtor conducted for the purpose of winding up its business, even those of a liquidator, are relevant and important to the COMI determination. *In re Fairfield Sentry Ltd*, 2011 WL 4357421, at *4 (SDNY September. 16 2011); *British Am Ins Co* 425 BR at 914.
56 *SPhinX*, 351 BR at 117.
57 In keeping with its international context, Chapter 15 directs courts to obtain guidance from the application of similar statutes by foreign jurisdictions: "In interpreting this chapter, the court shall consider its international origin, and the need to promote an application of this chapter that is consistent with the application of similar statutes adopted by foreign jurisdictions." 11 USC, Section 1508; see also 11 USC, Section 1501(a) (noting Chapter 15's incorporation of the model law); UK Model Law, Article 8 ("In the interpretation of this Law, regard is to be had to its international origin and to the need to promote uniformity in its application and the observance of good faith").
58 UK Model Law, Article 19(1); 11 USC, Section 1519.

These protections are extended once a proceeding has been recognised, either as main or non-main.[59] Additionally, upon recognition either as main or non-main, the recognising court may entrust the distribution of all or part of the debtor's assets located in the recognising country to the foreign representative or another person authorised by the foreign court.[60]

Under the UK Model Law, upon recognition as a foreign main proceeding:

- commencement or continuation of individual actions or individual proceedings concerning the debtor's assets, rights, obligations or liabilities is stayed;
- execution against the debtor's assets is stayed; and
- the right to transfer, encumber or otherwise dispose of any assets of the debtor is suspended.[61]

The scope and effect of the stay and suspension are the same as if the debtor had been made the subject of a winding-up order under the Insolvency Act 1986.[62] Under Chapter 15, upon recognition as a foreign main proceeding:

- the automatic stay under Section 362 of the Bankruptcy Code (as well as the creditors' right to adequate protection and relief from the automatic stay under Sections 361 and 362(d) of the Bankruptcy Code) applies with respect to the debtor and its property within the territorial jurisdiction of the United States;
- Sections 363 (relating to the use, sale or lease of property), 549 (relating to post-petition transactions) and 552 (relating to the post-petition effect of security interests) of the Bankruptcy Code apply to restrict the ability to transfer such property in the absence of court approval; and
- unless the court orders otherwise, the foreign representative may operate the debtor's business and exercise the rights and powers of a trustee under Sections 363 and 552 of the Bankruptcy Code.[63]

The UK Model Law and Chapter 15 are universalist in approach, but contain provisions that allow the national court to protect the interests of its creditors and other interested parties.[64]

---

59   See UK Model Law, Article 21(1); 11 USC, Section 1521(a).
60   UK Model Law, Article 21(2); 11 USC, Section 1521(b).
61   UK Model Law, Article 20(1).
62   *Ibid*, Article 20(2)(a).
63   11 USC, Section 1520(a)(1)–(3). Recognition of a foreign proceeding as 'main' has limited specified consequences under Chapter 15 particularly since the court is given the ability to grant substantially the same types of relief in assistance of foreign non-main proceedings as main proceedings, and to condition the foreign representative's ability to operate the business and dispose of the debtor's assets under Section 1520(a)(3): moreover, recognition itself is subject to review and modification under Bankruptcy Code, Section 1517(d).
64   For instance, the national court can satisfy itself that the interests of creditors and other interested persons or entities are protected. See UK Model Law, Article 22(1); 11 USC, Section 1522(a); see also Chung, above note 7, at 101 ("There appear to be sufficient safety valves [in Chapter 15] to protect American interests").

4.   Case examples: forum shopping in action

Since the enactment of the above legal structures, many companies have attempted to control their insolvency fate by controlling the location of their COMI. As the following case examples illustrate, such control is not always an easy – or successful – task.

4.1   Parmalat SpA/Eurofood IFSC Ltd[65]

At the beginning of 2003, Parmalat was a successful multinational food company operating through subsidiary companies in more than 30 countries worldwide. In late 2003 the empire collapsed in deep financial crisis, with charges of massive financial fraud and the arrest in Italy of its principal managers. On December 23 2003 Parmalat SpA – the parent company of the Parmalat group of companies, with its seat in Parma, Italy – filed its request for extraordinary administration with the minister of productive activities in Italy.[66] The request was immediately granted and an administrator was appointed. On December 27 2003 the Parma court confirmed that Parmalat was insolvent and placed it into extraordinary administration proceedings. Thereafter, 66 Parmalat entities filed extraordinary administration cases in Parma, including Eurofood IFSC Limited on February 9 2004.

Eurofood, a subsidiary of Parmalat created to arrange finance for companies in the Parmalat group in Venezuela and Brazil, was incorporated and registered in Ireland. Eurofood's day-to-day operations were conducted by Bank of America in Ireland pursuant to an administration agreement governed by Irish law. On January 27 2004 creditors of Eurofood filed an involuntary winding-up case under Irish law in the High Court in Dublin, Ireland. The Dublin court appointed a temporary liquidator. Because the case was involuntary, the Dublin court neither issued an order to open a winding-up of Eurofood nor made a determination of whether the case was a 'main proceeding' within the meaning of the regulation or where Eurofood's COMI was located.

Thirteen days later, the Italian administrator sought an order from the Italian minister of productive activities for extraordinary administration of Eurofood. The application was approved and the Italian administrator was appointed as administrator of Eurofood. The next day, the Italian administrator filed a case for Eurofood in the Parma court and, upon only a few days' notice (and questionable notice to the Dublin liquidator), the Parma court opened a main case, finding that the activity of Eurofood management and the COMI of the enterprise was located in Parma. The Parma court further found that the proceeding in Ireland had not proceeded to such a point that it was precluded under the EU Insolvency Regulation

---

65   The facts and details presented in this section have been taken from the published decisions of the various courts in the *Eurofood* cases, as well as from the following sources: Gabriel Moss QC, "Group Insolvency – Choice of Forum and Law: The European Experience Under the Influence of English Pragmatism", 32 *Brook J Int'l L* 1005, 1014–17 (2007); McCahery, above note 22; Mevorach, above note 37; Hon Samuel L Bufford, "International Insolvency Case Venue in the European Union: The Parmalat and Daisytek Controversies", 12 *Colum J Eur L* 429, 438–453 (2006); Bufford, "Global Venue Controls", above note 14, at 126–129.

66   Ultimately, insolvency proceedings for the Parmalat group of companies were filed in Italy, Brazil, Ireland, the United States, the Czech Republic and Hungary.

from opening a main proceeding. Hence, the Parma court issued a judgment that seems to have opened insolvency proceedings, declared Eurofood insolvent and determined its COMI to be in Italy.

Thereafter, the Dublin court decided that the Parma court acted without jurisdiction and that recognition of that court's decision to open a main case for Eurofood violated Irish public policy due to the court's failure to observe due process principles. The Dublin court issued its decision to open a proceeding on March 23 2004, which it said related back to its prior order of January 27, and held that Eurofood's COMI was in Ireland and the Irish proceeding, having been opened on January 27 2004, was the main proceeding since it pre-dated the Parma court's opening decision.

The decisions of both courts were appealed. The Italian appeals court heard oral argument and dismissed the appeals of the Irish liquidator and Bank of America on July 16 2004. The Italian appeals court found that the opening of Italian extraordinary administration proceedings is a two-step process, which occurred for Eurofood on February 9 and February 20 2004. For the purposes of mandatory recognition under the regulation, the Italian appeals court found that no proceeding for Eurofood had been opened in Ireland by either of those dates because the Dublin court's January 27 decision was too limited to constitute an 'opening' of a proceeding under Irish law, since all the court did was appoint a provisional liquidator.[67]

The Italian administrator appealed to the Irish Supreme Court. On July 27 2004 the Irish Supreme Court affirmed the Dublin court, insofar as its decision was based on Irish law, and referred the matter to the ECJ,[68] insofar as its decision was based on the EU Insolvency Regulation. To assist the ECJ in deciding the referred issues, the Irish Supreme Court made rulings on relevant facts and issues of Irish law with respect to, among other things, the opening of insolvency proceedings and COMI. The Irish Supreme Court made it clear, in its opinion and referring questions, that it thought the Dublin court was correct.

The judgment of the ECJ was eagerly awaited as one that should interpret the COMI provisions in the regulation and clarify the application of the definition, such as to instances where COMI can be found outside a company's jurisdiction of incorporation, as well as to determine what is necessary for a judgment opening insolvency proceedings under Article 16(1) of the EU Insolvency Regulation. On May 2 2006 the ECJ issued its judgment.[69] The ECJ's answers essentially reflect that it agreed with the Dublin court that the proceedings were correctly opened in the Dublin court and should have been recognised by the Parma court.

In rendering its opinion, the ECJ first addressed COMI and concluded that in the

---

67   The Italian appeals court also placed significance on the fact that the Italian legislature had enacted legislation the day before Parmalat's filing to deal with the financial crisis of large groups of global companies. The Italian appeals court certainly was advocating a universalist approach to an international insolvency case.

68   The Court of Justice of the European Communities, usually called the European Court of Justice or ECJ, is the highest court in the European Union. It has the ultimate say on matters of EU law in order to ensure equal application across the various EU member states. The court is composed of 27 judges and eight advocates general, who are appointed by common accord by the governments of the member states for a renewable term of six years. The advocates general assist the court and are responsible for presenting, with complete impartiality and independence, an 'opinion' in the cases assigned to them. See http://curia.europa.eu/jcms/jcms/Jo2_7024/#avantpropos (last visited May 2 2012).

situation where the subsidiary and parent company are registered in two different member states, the presumption of COMI "can be rebutted only if factors which are both objective and ascertainable by third parties enable it to be established that an actual situation exists which is different from that which location at that registered office is deemed to reflect".[70] The ECJ pointed out that the COMI could be the same as the parent where a company is not engaging in any business where its registered office is located (a 'letterbox' company); but that, by contrast, where a company engages in business where its registered office is located, the mere fact that a parent company located in another member state controls or can control its economic choices is not enough to rebut the regulation's presumption.[71] With respect to the opening of main proceedings, the ECJ first concluded that the opening of main proceedings by a court of a member state must be recognised by other member states without a review of the jurisdiction of the court of the opening state.[72] However, the ECJ concluded that pursuant to Article 26 of the regulation, a member state may refuse to recognise the opening of insolvency proceedings by a member state "where the decision to open the proceedings was taken in flagrant breach of the fundamental right to be heard, which a person concerned by such proceedings enjoys".[73] Next, the ECJ concluded that the opening of insolvency proceedings, the conditions and formalities of which are a matter for national law, is deemed to have occurred where a decision is formally described as an opening decision by the legislation of the member state or where, following an application seeking the opening of proceedings (as referred to in Annex A to the regulation), the decision involves divestment of the debtor and the appointment of a liquidator (referred to in Annex C to the regulation).[74]

---

69   See Case C-341/04, *In re Eurofood IFSC Ltd*, 2006 ECR I-3813 (Judgment of the Court). Prior to the ECJ issuing its decision, detailed written arguments are submitted and a brief oral argument is held, after which the advocate general, who is part of the ECJ, gives an opinion. This opinion is considered by the judges of the ECJ. In most cases, the opinion is accepted and the ECJ gives a brief judgment, and the opinion can be looked to for further reasoning. In a minority of cases, the opinion is rejected by the ECJ and becomes a minority opinion: Moss, above note 65, at 1015–16. In *Eurofood*, the advocate general issued his opinion on September 27 2005. See Case C-341/04, *Eurofood IFSC Ltd*, (Op of Advocate General; September 27 2005). The advocate general, reasoning that the appointment of a provisional liquidator is the first form of court order that possibly can be made in a compulsory winding-up procedure under Irish law, *Ibid* para 60, concluded that the appointment of the Irish liquidator had in fact constituted the opening of main proceedings for purposes of Article 16 of the regulation. *Ibid* para 88 and 152. Further, the advocate general concluded that since the Dublin court first opened insolvency proceedings, thereby declaring Ireland as Eurofood's COMI, the Parma court should have recognised such opening without scrutinising the Dublin court's opinion, and did not have jurisdiction to open main proceedings. *Ibid* paras 102, 105, 152. However, where a member state's courts opine that another member state's decision to open insolvency proceedings was not based on fair procedures and a fair hearing, such as is contrary to public policy, the member state does not have to give legal effect to and recognise such opening of proceedings: *Ibid* paras 142, 145 and 152. Finally, the advocate general concluded that the presumption that a subsidiary debtor's COMI is in the member state of its registered office where it conducts the administration of its interests on a regular basis in a manner ascertainable by third parties is "not rebutted merely because the parent company is in a position, by virtue of its shareholding and power to appoint directors, to control, and does in fact control, the policy of the subsidiary and the fact of control is not ascertainable by third parties": *Ibid* paras 123 and 152. The ECJ essentially followed the advocate general's opinion.

70   Case C-341/04, *In re Eurofood IFSC Ltd*, 2006 ECR I-3813, at para 34 (Judgment of the Court).

71   *Ibid* paras 35-36.

72   *Ibid* para 44. The ECJ based its conclusion on the principal of mutual trust set out in the 22nd recital of the EU Insolvency Regulation. *Ibid* paras 39–42.

73   *Ibid* para 67.

The *Eurofood* cases evidence a failed attempt by the Italian administrator to bring the insolvency proceedings of each member of a corporate group in one place (Italy) by massaging COMI or winning the race to the courthouse to have main proceedings opened. The ECJ's decision does not bode well for corporate groups. In fact, in line with its decision, the COMI of each legal entity in a corporate group must be separately determined in order to determine the national venue for each member's insolvency.[75] Such a process means that insolvency proceedings of corporate groups will continue to be dispersed in numerous countries and subject to divergent legal regimes and procedures. Additionally, a group solution to the corporate group's financial woes will be much more difficult to negotiate.

The hoped-for guidance, for a world where multinational corporations are the norm, was not given by the ECJ in *Eurofood*. For now, the insolvency world will have to await another ECJ decision on COMI generally, or specifically with respect to another multinational corporation.

4.2 Hans Brochier Holdings Limited[76]

Hans Brochier Holdings Limited is a member of a large manufacturing and construction group in Germany. Its existence arose out of a migration from a German company to a UK company, by operation of a universal succession under German law whereby the assets and liabilities of the German parent company were moved to a UK company.

Hans Brochier specialised in plant engineering and the construction and maintenance of pipelines. It had approximately 720 employees, 120 of whom were part of its plant engineering business based throughout Germany. After failing to pay wages owed to its workers, the workers engaged in protest at Hans Brochier's Nuremberg office, which ended in its legal advisers and shareholder representatives being barricaded in the office for several hours. Several days later, the employees began removing assets from the Nuremberg office.

Thereafter, on August 4 2006 at 12:34pm, joint administrators were appointed under the UK Insolvency Act 1986. Forty-five minutes later, a preliminary administrator was appointed under German law. After reconsidering the facts, initially provided by the company's directors and later by speaking with the employees, the UK administrators sought a declaration from the High Court that Hans Brochier's COMI was in Germany and not in the United Kingdom. The UK

---

74   *Ibid* paras 54 and 58. The divestment involves the debtor losing powers of management over its assets: *Ibid*. Further, the fact that a liquidator may be appointed only provisionally has no effect: *Ibid* para 55. Under Irish law, the first form of court order that can possibly be made in a compulsory winding-up procedure is the appointment of a provisional liquidator: Case C-341/04, *Eurofood IFSC Ltd*, at para 60 (Opinion of Advocate General; September 27 2005).

75   *Ibid* para 30 ("[E]ach debtor constituting a distinct legal entity is subject to its own court jurisdiction"); see also *In re BRAC Rent-a-Car Int'l Inc* [2003] EWCH (Ch) 12, 1 WLR 1421, at para 27, 2 All ER 201 (Chancery Division) ("[T]he Regulation contains no provisions dealing with affiliated companies or groups of companies, so that each debtor must be considered separately.").

76   The facts and details presented in this section have been taken from *Hans Brochier Ltd v Exner* [2006] EWHC 2594 (Chancery) Case 5618/06 (Eng); Robert Hickmott, "View From Here: Tailored Migration", Legalweek.com (February 22 2007), available at www.legalweek.com/legal-week/analysis/1159102/view-tailored-migration (last visited May 2 2012).

77   *Hans Brochier Ltd v Exner* [2006] EWHC 2594 (Ch) Case 5618/06, para 28 (Eng).

court held that, based on a totality of the evidence, Hans Brochier's COMI was at all material times in Germany.[77] The UK court found persuasive that:

- the majority of the employees worked in Germany;
- a large part of Hans Brochier's business was run from Germany; and
- most of Hans Brochier's banking occurred through German accounts.[78]

So, the UK court concluded that main insolvency proceedings were not possible in the United Kingdom.

The directors of Hans Brochier did not give up and appointed a second set of administrators on the basis that there was an 'establishment' in the United Kingdom. This would allow for the opening of secondary proceedings to deal with the assets in the United Kingdom. The Nuremberg administrator applied to the UK court for a finding that the appointment of the second set of administrators was invalid. The Nuremberg administrator argued that although the company's registered office was in London, its link was tenuous and not strong enough to be an 'establishment' because there was little genuine economic activity. The UK court agreed and entered a judgment finding that the appointment of the second administrators was invalid.[79] A German court also agreed that the migration did not shift COMI from Germany to the United Kingdom.[80]

Hans Brochier involved a failed attempt to establish its COMI in the United Kingdom after engaging in a universal succession under German law. It is also a lesson in the power of employees. Companies should take heed that if they are going to engage a shift in their COMI, they need to follow the steps and ensure that they move the most important parts of their operations. Unfortunately, the case law has not yet established what those important parts are. Nonetheless, as discussed next, *Schefenacker* figured it out and breathed some life into forum shopping by COMI shifting.

4.3   Schefenacker[81]

Schefenacker AG is a German company that moved its headquarters to the United Kingdom to restructure the debt of the holding company by a debt-for-equity swap

---

78   *Ibid* para 25. Upon the UK administrators' original appointment, and their reasoning for determining that the COMI was in the United Kingdom, were the following facts provided to them by the directors of Hans Brochier: the employment contracts were with Hans Brochier; creditors knew that they were owed debts by a UK company; Hans Brochier's bank account was in the United Kingdom; the financial statements were prepared in the United Kingdom; and a creditor had issued a statutory demand in London and was threatening a petition. *Ibid* para 9. The new facts learned by the UK administrators, and the reasoning for their seeking a declaration that Hans Brochier's COMI was in Germany, included the following: Hans Brochier effected most of its transactions from its German bank accounts and not from its UK bank account; there was a strong feeling among a significant proportion of the employees that the Nuremberg administrator (who was appointed on the application of the employees, and not the UK administrator) was the appropriate office holder; and the financial statements of Hans Brochier were not always prepared in the United Kingdom: *Ibid* para 24.

79   Hickmott, above note 76.

80   Pottow, "Myth (and Realities)", above note 21, at 797–98 n 53 (citing *Hans Brochier Holdings Ltd*, WEiR2007, 177; NZI2007, 187 (UK proceedings before High Court in London); EWiR2007, 177; ZIP2007, 81; NZI2007, 185 (German proceedings before insolvency court at Nuremberg)).

81   The facts and details presented in this section have been taken from pleadings and papers filed in *In re Schefenacker plc*, No 07-11482 (Bankr SDNY 2007).

through a company voluntary arrangement (CVA). It had to take this action because, under German law, it would have been forced into bankruptcy since its third-quarter 2006 results breached the terms of its bond covenant and it would not have been allowed to cram down a reluctant minority of bondholders. Ultimately, this is the story of successful forum shopping.

Schefenacker AG was a German holding company for an international automotive mirrors and lighting business. The mirrors business supplied about 28% of the world's production of wing and rearview mirrors for automobiles. Its principal operating mirrors businesses were located in the United Kingdom, the United States, Korea, Hungary, Australia and Germany, along with six other countries. The much smaller lighting businesses operated in Germany, the United States and Slovenia.

Beginning in August 2006, the management of Schefenacker AG became concerned with the operational performance of the company and its subsidiaries and the sustainability of its capital structure. It retained financial advisers to assist with formulating a restructuring plan. Over the ensuing months, Schefenacker AG, Dr Alfred Schefenacker (the sole beneficial owner of the equity interests in Schefenacker AG), its senior secured lenders and an *ad hoc* committee of bondholders, along with their advisers, discussed potential restructuring scenarios. A binding term sheet was reached in February 2007 by all parties, including major customers, except the bondholders.

The financial restructuring contemplated that, by operation of a universal succession under German law, the assets and liabilities of Schefenacker AG would be transferred to Schefenacker plc (Schefenacker), which was incorporated on October 11 2006 in the United Kingdom and had its registered office in Portchester, Hampshire. To effect this, Schefenacker AG had to become a German limited partnership, with Schefenacker as one of its general partners, and the other general and limited partners had either to withdraw from the partnership or to transfer their interests in the partnership to Schefenacker. Under German law, this resulted in the German limited partnership ceasing to exist and its assets and liabilities being transferred, by operation of German law, to Schefenacker as the remaining general partner. This 'migration'[82] was approved by the senior secured lenders, Dr Schefenacker, the major customers and a majority of 57.78% in value of the bondholders, accomplished by way of an amendment of the bond covenants by consent solicitation to the bondholders. Hence, on February 9 2007 Schefenacker assumed all of the assets and liabilities (including the bonds and the obligations under the indenture) of Schefenacker AG.

On March 9 2007 Schefenacker issued its proposal for a CVA under the Insolvency Act, which was modified and re-issued on April 5 2007 due to renegotiations with the informal committee of bondholders. The CVA was approved

---

[82] A migration involves a legal entity in one jurisdiction being transformed into a legal entity established in another jurisdiction. The United Kingdom's flexible insolvency law and restructuring mechanisms have led to a strong trend for companies to migrate to the United Kingdom, particularly from Germany. See Adam Gallagher, "Migration Nation: Keeping the Wheels Turning", 26 *Am Bankr Inst J* 30, 30 (September 2007) ("England, with its user-friendly insolvency regime, is seen as sort of European mecca for restructuring and insolvency possibilities"): *Ibid* at 56 (stating that some in Germany believe that the United Kingdom is trying to establish itself as the New York of Europe for restructurings).

at a meeting held on May 2 2007 by the requisite creditor and member majorities under the Insolvency Act. Once approved and upon the filing of the chairman reports on May 4 2007 in the UK High Court, Chancery Division, the 28-day period commenced for creditors to challenge the CVA on the grounds of unfair prejudice or material irregularity at, or in relation to, the meetings.[83] No creditor – and, importantly, no bondholder – commenced any challenge before the UK court. Accordingly, pursuant to Articles 3 and 16 of the EU Insolvency Regulation, the courts of the EU member states are obliged to recognise the CVA because Schefenacker's COMI is located in the United Kingdom and the CVA is listed as a 'collective insolvency proceeding' in Annex A to the regulation. As such, creditors with effective notice were precluded from filing and maintaining a challenge to the CVA in any EU member state. Thus, all claims against Schefenacker in respect of any liability covered by the CVA were dealt with pursuant to the terms of the CVA.

A condition precedent to the implementation of the CVA was the recognition of the CVA in the United States pursuant to Chapter 15. Therefore, on May 15 2007 the appointed supervisors of the CVA initiated a voluntary petition under Chapter 15 in the Bankruptcy Court for the Southern District of New York and moved for recognition of the CVA as a foreign main proceeding and to enforce the CVA in the United States through a permanent injunction.

A group of bondholders objected, claiming, among other things, that Schefenacker's COMI was not in the United Kingdom, but instead was in Germany because the reconstituted UK company continued to have the majority of its creditors, assets, operations and employees in Germany. The bondholders claimed that Schefenacker "devised a stratagem to seek to 'migrate' the company to England for the primary purpose of circumventing or subordinating the rights of bondholders".[84] The US bankruptcy court focused on the fact that the bondholder group's objections relating to the solicitation of bondholders to approve the migration or the CVA should have been directed to the UK court. The US bankruptcy court granted the application for recognition of the CVA in the United States, giving it full force and effect and making it binding upon all parties within the US bankruptcy court's jurisdiction. Additionally, the US bankruptcy court granted the permanent injunction, permanently enjoining and restraining all persons within its jurisdiction from taking any action inconsistent with the CVA and from continuing or commencing any action against the joint supervisors under the Schefenacker CVA.

Because the US bankruptcy court did not decide the issue of whether the CVA was a foreign main proceeding or foreign non-main proceeding under Section 1517 of Chapter 15, it did not address the COMI issue raised by the bondholders.[85] The issue was, however, fully briefed by the parties in the Chapter 15 case.

---

83   In the Chapter 15 proceedings, commenced in the United States for recognition of the UK CVA proceeding, the petitioners took the position that the bondholders should have raised their issues related to alleged irregularities in the voting process or procedure and their challenge to Schefenacker's COMI during this 28-day period: see *In re Schefenacker plc*, No 07-11482, Decl of Mark Sterling, Docket No 75, at para 36 (Bankr SDNY 2007).

84   See *In re Schefenacker plc*, Case No 07-11482, Memorandum of Law in Support of Bondholder Group Objection to Chapter 15 Petition, Docket No 41, at 2–3 (Bankr SDNY 2007).

The petitioners pointed out that Schefenacker, a pure holding company registered in the United Kingdom with its only office located in Portchester in the United Kingdom, functioned to hold equity interests in its subsidiaries and restructure its financial indebtedness. Its principal asset was its equity interests in Schefenacker Management UK Limited, also registered in the United Kingdom. All operating assets of Schefenacker and its subsidiaries were held through operating subsidiaries located in 12 different countries including the United Kingdom, the United States, Spain, Germany, Slovenia, Hungary, Australia, Korea, India and China, and none was held by Schefenacker, so this could not be used, petitioners argued (relying on *Eurofood*), to determine its COMI. Schefenacker had only two employees, who were resident in the United Kingdom and employed under employment contracts subject to UK law. All of these facts, the petitioners argued, were insufficient to establish that an actual situation existed which is different from that which locating Schefenacker's COMI at the UK registered office is deemed to reflect. Schefenacker had to be viewed separately from its subsidiaries when determining its COMI and, thus, its activities were in the United Kingdom and its COMI was the United Kingdom.

The bondholders argued that Schefenacker was not truly a UK company, so its COMI could not be located in the United Kingdom. They maintained that a misleading consent solicitation allowed certain creditors to "forum-shop their way over to England to improve their leverage in a workout".[86] Because Schefenacker had far more creditors, employees, facilities and assets in Germany, the bondholders argued that its operations clearly were centered in Germany.

The fight under Chapter 15 of the real difference between recognition as a foreign main or foreign non-main proceeding is left for another case. What is known, however, is that objectors to recognition under Chapter 15 need to consider whether their objections should properly be before the foreign court or the US court where recognition is being sought.

4.4   Bear Stearns[87]

Bear Stearns is the story of a Cayman Islands-registered company that tried to twist the definition of 'COMI' to get a US court to recognise its insolvency proceedings in the Cayman Islands as foreign main or non-main proceedings. Essentially, Bear Stearns took the position that since its request for recognition was unopposed, it

---

85   At the hearing on the application for recognition, the US bankruptcy court indicated that it did not seem to matter for the purposes of the relief that it could grant whether it made the finding of fact as to whether the CVA was a main or non-main proceeding. Counsel for Schefenacker indicated that it would confirm that such a finding was not important to the CVA and, if it was, it would notify chambers so that a trial on the issues could be had. See *In re Schefenacker plc* Case No 07-11482, Transcript of Motion, Docket No 90, at 27–30 (Bankr SDNY 2007). A trial never occurred. A notice of appeal of the order granting recognition was filed, but later withdrawn. See *In re Schefenacker plc* Case No 07-11482, Notice of Appeal, Docket No 88, Notice of Withdrawal of Appeal, Docket No 98 (Bankr SDNY 2007).

86   See *In re Schefenacker plc*, Case No 07-11482, Memorandum of Law in Support of Bondholder Group Objection to Chapter 15 Petition, Docket No 41, at 12 (Bankr SDNY 2007).

87   The facts and details presented in this section have been taken from pleadings and papers filed in *In re Bear Stearns High-Grade Structured Credit Strategies Master Fund Ltd (In Provisional Liquidation)*, No 07-12383 and No 012384 (Bankr SDNY 2007) and *In re Bear Stearns-High-Grade Structured Credit Strategies Master Fund Ltd (In Provisional Liquidation)*, No 07-08730 and No 07-08746 (SDNY 2007), as well as from the reported decisions of the US courts.

should get recognition. The US courts did not accept the invitation to be mere rubber stamps under Chapter 15.

Bear Stearns High-Grade Structured Credit Strategies Master Fund Ltd and Bear Stearns High-Grade Structured Credit Strategies Enhanced Leverage Master Fund Ltd (together, 'Bear Stearns' or 'funds') were open-ended investment companies incorporated in the Cayman Islands as limited liability companies. The funds were registered as 'exempted' companies under Cayman Islands law, which allows qualifying companies to trade in the Cayman Islands provided that they seek to further business outside of the Cayman Islands and not to compete with local businesses. The funds maintained their registered offices in the Cayman Islands.

A Massachusetts corporation acted as the administrator, registrar and transfer agent of the funds, and provided the day-to-day administrative services to the funds, including:

- undertaking accounting and clerical functions;
- processing the issuance, transfer and redemption of shares;
- maintaining all appropriate shareholder registers and ledgers;
- distributing annual reports and account statements to shareholders;
- responding to inquiries from shareholders and prospective investors, as well as from the general public;
- maintaining the funds' principal administrative records;
- disbursing payment of expenses of the funds; and
- notifying the funds' investment manager of redemption requests.

The books and records of the funds were maintained and stored in Delaware by the administrator. A New York corporation acted as the funds' investment manager, which managed assets in New York. Other assets of the funds consisted of receivables from broker dealers and all (or virtually all) were also located in New York. An affiliate of the administrator in Dublin, Ireland, held the investor registers.

Due to the volatility in the markets, the funds suffered significant devaluations in their asset portfolios in 2007, which led to margin calls from many of their trading counterparties. The funds were ultimately unable to meet the margin calls. This resulted in the issuance of default notices by trading counterparties and their exercise of rights under their respective agreements to seize and/or sell those assets of the funds that had been the subject of repurchase agreements or over which they held security interests.

On July 31 2007 the funds' boards of directors passed resolutions authorising each of the funds to file petitions seeking orders that the funds be wound up under the provisions of the Companies Law of the Cayman Islands and to apply for the appointment of joint provisional liquidators of the funds, subject to the supervision of the Grand Court of the Cayman Islands. On July 31 2007 the Cayman court entered orders appointing the petitioners as the joint provisional liquidators of the funds. On September 14 the Cayman court entered orders converting the proceedings from provisional to official liquidations and directing a winding-up of the funds under the Companies Law. In accordance with this order, the joint provisional liquidators became joint official liquidators.

Also on July 31 the joint provisional liquidators sought recognition of the Cayman Island proceedings as foreign main or non-main proceedings under Chapter 15 of the Bankruptcy Code in order to protect the funds' US assets from attachments by creditors. The joint provisional liquidators argued, basically, that because no objections were filed and the funds' registered offices were in the Cayman Islands, the US bankruptcy court should recognise the Cayman proceedings as foreign main proceedings. The US bankruptcy court did not agree, and denied recognition of the Cayman proceedings as either foreign main or non-main proceedings.[88] The US bankruptcy court reasoned that the Cayman proceedings were not foreign main proceedings because the funds' COMIs were in the United States, relying on the following facts:

- The funds' investment manager was located in New York;
- The administrator that ran the back-office operations of the funds was in the United States;
- The funds' books and records were maintained in the United States;
- Prior to the commencement of the Cayman proceedings, all (or virtually all) of the Funds' liquid assets were located in New York;
- The investor registries were maintained and located in Ireland;
- Accounts receivable were located throughout Europe and the United States; and
- Counterparties to master repurchase and swap agreements were based both inside and outside the United States (but none was claimed to be in the Cayman Islands).[89]

The US bankruptcy court noted that the only business that the funds did in the Cayman Islands was to take steps necessary to maintain the funds in good standing as registered Cayman Islands companies.

With respect to the determination that the Cayman proceedings also were not foreign non-main proceedings, the US bankruptcy court concluded that the funds did not have an 'establishment' in the Cayman Islands within the meaning of Chapter 15 – that is, the funds did not conduct non-transitory economic activity in the Cayman Islands and no bank accounts were kept there until after the Cayman proceedings were commenced, so the funds did not have a "seat for local business

---

88   *In re Bear Stearns High-Grade Structured Credit Strategies Master Fund Ltd* 374 BR 122, 129–30 (Bankr SDNY 2007), *aff'd*, 389 BR 325 (SDNY 2008) (determining that the funds' "real seat and therefore their COMI is the United States, the place where the Funds conduct the administration of their interests on a regular basis and is therefore ascertainable by third parties ... and, more specifically, is located in this district where principal interests, assets and management are located").

89   *Ibid* at 124–25, 130.

90   *Ibid* at 131–32. Perhaps the keeping of a bank account in the Cayman Islands would have been enough for the US bankruptcy court, which pointed out that the account migrated there after the Cayman proceedings were initiated. *Ibid* at 131; but see *In re Yukos Oil Co*, Case No 04-47742-H3-11, Memorandum Opinion, at 3, 22, 31 and 33 (Bankr SD Tex Feb 24 2005) (dismissing Chapter 11 bankruptcy case for cause, using a "totality of the circumstances" approach, even though debtor had a bank account in the United States, which the court found to be property of the estate and concluded gave debtor standing to be a debtor under Section 109(a) of the Bankruptcy Code, where court found one circumstance for dismissal to be that debtor transferred funds to accounts in the United States one week prior to filing and for purpose of creating jurisdiction).

activity".[90] The US bankruptcy court equated 'establishment' with local business activity, which the funds could not have in the Cayman Islands because under Cayman law the funds could not operate locally.[91]

The joint official liquidators appealed the decision to the US district court.[92] The US district court affirmed the US bankruptcy court's decision. The US bankruptcy court held that the COMI presumption had been rebutted by evidence to the contrary, and the US district court opined, in response to the joint official liquidators' argument that the presumption was not overcome because no one objected, that a court could do so on its own accord without opposition.[93]

The district court held that the bankruptcy court employed the proper standard for the COMI determination.[94] The district court said that it properly relied on and applied the concept of the EU Insolvency Regulation that the COMI is "the place where the debtor conducts the administration of his interests on a regular basis and is therefore ascertainable by third parties", which is properly equated to the US concept of 'principal place of business'.[95] With respect to the decision in *Eurofood*, the district court stated that it "more or less amounts to another non-barking dog ... the opinion itself states few relevant facts and the development of the facts critical to its COMI decision have been gleaned from commentary".[96] With respect to the US bankruptcy court's decision not to grant main recognition, the district court upheld the finding of facts as sufficient to rebut that the funds' COMI was in the Cayman Islands.[97] With respect to the bankruptcy court's decision not to grant non-main recognition, the district court concluded that auditing activities, preparation of incorporation papers and review of insider transactions are not operations or economic activity.[98]

The *Bear Stearns* opinions seem to indicate that US courts will not merely rubberstamp recognition proceedings.[99] Accordingly, foreign representatives should take heed that they will be required to meet their burden of proof under Chapter 15, even without objectors to the recognition. Additionally, these opinions evidence that

---

91   *Bear Stearns,* 374 BR at 131. If US courts accept the definition of 'establishment' to mean 'a local place of business', then exempted companies under Cayman law could be barred from Chapter 15 proceedings. Ronald DeKoven, Mark Fennessy & Brian Hauck, "US Chapter 15 Application Refused", *Int'l Corp Rescue,* Issue 5, Vol 4, at 277 (November 2007). The US bankruptcy court did not, however, forget to point out that the foreign representative had access to the Bankruptcy Code through Section 303(b)(4), which allows a foreign representative to bring an involuntary petition under Chapter 7 or Chapter 11: *Bear Stearns,* 374 BR at 132–33; DeKoven, above, at 277.

92   Unfortunately, perhaps, for the joint official liquidators, the US bankruptcy court judge was among the authors of the UNCITRAL Model Law and Chapter 15. Also unfortunately, the appeal brought *amici* to the proceedings, including Professor Jay L Westbrook and Daniel M Glosband, who also were among the authors of the model law and Chapter 15, and both of whom write extensively in the area of international insolvency. A lot of knowledge of the process was brought to bear in these proceedings, so the *Bear Stearns* opinions should be studied by future petitioners, objectors, practitioners and judges.

93   *In re Bear Stearns High-Grade Structured Credit Strategies Master Fund Ltd (In Provisional Liquidation),* 389 BR 325 at 335 (SDNY 2008); see also *In re Tri-Continental Exch Ltd,* 349 BR 627, 635 (Bankr ED Cal 2006) ("[I]f the foreign proceeding is in the country of the registered office, and if there is evidence that the center of main interests might be elsewhere, then the foreign representative must prove that the center of main interests is in the same country as the registered office"); *In re Basis Yield Alpha Fund (Master),* 381 BR 37 at 46 (Bankr SDNY 2008) (denying unopposed summary judgment on issue of COMI, regardless of presumption, based on failure of foreign representative to submit sufficient evidence to the court).

94   *Bear Stearns,* 389 BR at 336.

95   *Ibid* at 336.

96   *Ibid* at 337.

97   *Ibid* at 338.

98   *Ibid* at 339.

a company's registered office is not all that matters in COMI determinations, and that there is life in the rebuttable presumption. Lastly, the *Bear Stearns* decisions show that US courts are not afraid to put a stop to forum shopping.

4.5   Interedil Srl[100]

Interedil Srl was an Italian company that successfully changed its COMI for the sole purpose of preparing a restructuring. It had been formed and registered its office in Italy. In 2001 Interedil transferred its registered office to the United Kingdom and was removed from the Italian companies register. At that time, it also was engaged in transactions that concluded in Interedil being acquired by a UK company, and contracts being negotiated and entered into for the transfer of a business concern. Additionally, certain of its Italian-owned properties were transferred to another entity. In 2002 the company ceased all activity and was removed from the UK register. A year later Intesa Gestione Crediti SpA filed insolvency proceedings against Interedil in Italy. Interedil challenged the jurisdiction of the Italian court on the grounds that only the UK courts would have jurisdiction following the company's transfer of its registered office to the United Kingdom. The ECJ was asked by the Italian court to provide guidance on how the COMI under Articles 2 and 3 of the EU Insolvency Regulation was to be interpreted.[101]

The ECJ, following its earlier decision in *Re Eurofood IFSC Ltd*, first, stressed that the definition of 'COMI' must be interpreted in a uniform way and by reference to EU law.[102] Next, relying on the guidance provided by the preamble to the regulation and the second sentence in Article 3(1) of the regulation, the ECJ held that "greater importance" must be attached to the place of the company's central administration.[103] This place must be identified by reference to criteria that are both objective and ascertainable by third parties, such that where the debtor company conducts the administration of its interests on a regular basis is made public or made sufficiently accessible to creditors.[104]

---

99   The US Bankruptcy Court parted with the dicta in the *SPhinX* decision opining that if the parties in interest had not objected, recognition would have been granted under the sole grounds that no party objected and no other proceeding had been initiated anywhere else: *Bear Stearns* 374 BR at 130 (citing *In re SPhinX Ltd*, 351 BR at 117). It will be interesting to see whether other US courts follow the lead of *Bear Stearns* in this regard. DeKoven, above note 91, at 277 ("When all parties agree that a certain process would best facilitate a resolution, and there is no evidence that they chose that process for improper reasons, other courts may be loath to reject the recognition opportunity [like that done by the court in *Bear Stearns*].").

100   See Case C-396/09 *Interedil Srl* [2011] ECR I-0000 (Judgment of the Court).

101   *Ibid* paras 10–13. There was some internal conflict between the *Corte Suprema di Cassazione* (Italy's court of last resort) and the *Tribunale di Bari*, wherein, while the Supreme Court was deciding the issue of jurisdiction to open insolvency proceedings, the tribunal, without awaiting the decision of the court and taking the view that the jurisdictional objection was unfounded, ordered that Interedil be wound up: *Ibid* para 14. Following that order, Interedil appealed: *Ibid* para 15. The court, ruling on the preliminary issue of jurisdiction, held that the Italian courts had jurisdiction. *Ibid* para 16. It reasoned that the second sentence on Article 3(1) of the EU Insolvency Regulation that the centre of main interests corresponded to the place of the registered office could be rebutted as a result of such things as immovable property in Italy owned by Interedil, the existence of a lease agreement on two hotel complexes, a contract with a banking institution, and not notifying the Bari register of companies of the transfer of the registered office: *Ibid* para 16. Doubting this ruling in light of *Eurofoods*, the Bari Tribunal stayed the proceedings and referred questions to the ECJ. *Ibid* para 17.

102   *Ibid* paras 43 and 44.

103   *Ibid* paras 48 and 59.

In a somewhat clarifying act, the ECJ set parameters around the rebuttable presumption of Article 3(1). "Where the bodies responsible for the management and supervision of a company are in the same place as its registered office and the management decisions of the company are taken, in a manner that is ascertainable by third parties, in that place," then the presumption in Article 3(1) cannot be rebutted.[105] That is, "it is not possible that the centre of the debtor company's main interests is located elsewhere."[106] Alternatively, where a company's central administration is not in the same place as its registered office, the presence of company assets in a different EU member state could suffice to rebut the presumption in Article 3(1).[107] The ECJ reiterated that a comprehensive assessment of all the factors needed to be conducted in order to "establish, in a manner that is ascertainable by third parties, that the company's actual centre of management" is located elsewhere.[108] For example, the location in another member state of immovable property and the existence in that state of a contract with a financial institution could be regarded as objective factors – and factors that are ascertainable by third parties since they are in the public domain.[109] According to the ECJ, however, such facts alone would not be sufficient to rebut the presumption of Article 3(1) unless a comprehensive assessment of all factors led to the conclusion that the company's actual centre of management and supervision and of the management of its interests is located in that other member state.[110]

As to the transfer of a debtor's COMI, the ECJ, relying on the general wording of Article 3(1) and Staubitz-Schreiber,[111] inferred that the last place in which the debtors' COMI was located at the date on which the request to open insolvency proceedings was lodged is what is relevant for the purpose of determining the court having jurisdiction to open main insolvency proceedings.[112] Given this, the ECJ concluded that greater importance should be given to the location of the last COMI such that when a registered office is transferred or the debtor company has been removed from the register of companies and has ceased all activity before a request to open insolvency proceedings, there is a presumption that the debtor's COMI is located at the place of the new registered office.[113]

With respect to secondary proceedings, the ECJ held that the term 'establishment' must also be determined on the basis of objective factors ascertainable by third parties.[114] The ECJ opined that an 'establishment' requires the "presence of a structure consisting of a minimum level of organisation and a degree of stability necessary for the purpose of pursuing an economic activity."[115] It held that

---

104   *Ibid* para 49.
105   *Ibid* paras 50 and 59
106   *Ibid* para 50.
107   *Ibid* paras 51 and 59.
108   *Ibid* paras 52-3.
109   *Ibid* para 53.
110   *Ibid*.
111   Case C-1/04 *Staubitz-Schreiber* [2006] ECR I-701 at para 29 (holding, where a transfer occurred after a request to open insolvency proceedings, that the courts of the member state within the territory of which the COMI was situated at the time when the request was lodged retained jurisdiction to rule on the proceedings).
112   *Ibid* paras 54-55.
113   *Ibid* paras 56–59.
114   *Ibid* para 63.

"the presence alone of goods in isolation or bank accounts does not, in principle, meet that definition."[116]

The *Interedil* case provides some helpful insight following *Eurofoods*. The ECJ reiterated the importance of carrying out a comprehensive assessment of all relevant factors in determining the right jurisdiction in which to open insolvency proceedings, and to focus not solely on the place of registration of the debtor company. While it did not define or interpret 'COMI', which is what practitioners have been hoping for, the ECJ did put some parameters around the rebuttable presumption. Unfortunately, those parameters continue to require a comprehensive analysis of factors. Importantly, however, in *Interedil*, the ECJ expressly sanctioned a COMI shift from Italy to the United Kingdom for the purpose of preparing for a restructuring. Accordingly, a debtor, by shifting its registered office and ceasing activities in its current member state, now has the *imprimatur* of the ECJ to forum shop.

5. Conclusion

Given the direction of laws such as the EU Insolvency Regulation, the UK Model Law and Chapter 15, COMI or the 'home country' concept seems to be the driving force behind a determination of where a debtor's insolvency proceeding should occur. Unfortunately, these concepts are not defined in the laws themselves. Although the jurisprudence is beginning to develop, thus far there is not enough case law to determine with any certainty how the courts will define 'COMI'. Furthermore, given the cases already decided in the short time since these laws were enacted, multinational corporations have a significant challenge: the *Eurofood* precedent of determining the COMI of each and every entity in a corporate group does not lend itself to a coordinated restructuring of a multinational corporation. Only time will reveal how individual countries' laws will help to establish a company's COMI in times of distress, such as the failed attempt by Hans Brochier and the successful migrations by Schefenacker and Interedil.

Lastly, the road to recognition under Chapter 15, while potentially curtailed by *Bear Stearns*, likely remains wide open while US and foreign courts continue to grapple with the definition of 'COMI' and 'establishment' with respect to recognition of foreign proceedings. Recently, that road was apparently widened to allow for forum shopping (albeit as long as the other Chapter 15 factors can be satisfied) when two US courts determined that the activities of a liquidator or foreign representative could be relevant and important to the COMI determination.[117]

When it comes to restructuring, one thing is certain: parties have always sought the remedies and procedures most fitting to their situation. Even the promulgation of laws aimed at curbing forum shopping will not put an end to the practice.[118] No

---

115   *Ibid* para 64.
116   *Ibid*.
117   *In re Fairfield Sentry Ltd*, 2011 WL 4357421, at *4 (SDNY September 16 2011); *British Am Ins Co* 425 BR at 914.
118   UNCITRAL has suggested an alternative way of dealing with forum shopping: refusing to grant recognition on grounds of public policy, thereby treating it as an abuse of the processes of a court. *UNCITRAL: A Judicial Perspective*, above note 51, at 30.

matter what approach is followed – territorialism or universalism, or some modified or mixed version thereof – where an insolvency proceeding should take place will continue to be a part of the insolvency decision.

France

Matthieu Barthélemy
Philippe Dubois
Jacques Henrot
De Pardieu Brocas Maffei

French insolvency law was significantly reformed by the so-called 'Safeguard Law' (Law 2005-845) of July 26 2005 and its implementing decree of December 28 2005 which came into force on January 1 2006. The Safeguard Law was further amended by an ordinance dated December 18 2008 and its implementing decree of February 12 2009. Most provisions of the amendment took effect on February 15 2009.

The main innovation of the reform is the safeguard procedure, which was inspired to an extent by the US Chapter 11 procedure. Its primary aim is to encourage reorganisation at a stage when insolvency might be prevented: any debtor still solvent but facing difficulties that could lead to insolvency may initiate safeguard proceedings to restructure under court protection, thus benefiting from an automatic stay.

The new statute has also reformed existing procedures and provisions. For example, the regime governing pre-bankruptcy proceedings (*mandat ad hoc* and conciliation) has been clarified and modified. While conciliation proceedings were previously available only to debtors that were not yet technically insolvent, they are now also available to entities that have been insolvent for fewer than 45 days. In addition, under the new statute the workout agreement entered into between the debtor and its major creditors within the framework of conciliation proceedings can be formally approved through a court judgment (homologation), which has certain effects on creditors' rights (including a high-ranking priority granted to new money providers).

Rehabilitation proceedings have also been reformed and most mechanisms of the safeguard procedure are now also a feature of rehabilitation proceedings, including the creditors' committees introduced by the new statute.

Lastly, the new statute has introduced an exemption from liability in favour of credit providers, albeit subject to certain exceptions. The ability of secured and unsecured creditors to enforce their rights against the debtor is still subject to certain limitations within the framework of safeguard, rehabilitation and liquidation proceedings.

A recent law of October 22 2010, effective as of March 1 2011, and its implementation decree of March 3 2011 created a new safeguard procedure called the 'expedited safeguard procedure' intended to be a quick, simplified process allowing the speedy reorganisation of a company with essentially financial debt.

1. Overview of rescue and insolvency procedures

French rescue and insolvency proceedings apply to all 'private' (as opposed to government) legal entities and individuals carrying on trade activities.

1.1 Pre-bankruptcy proceedings

(a) Ad hoc *proceedings*

Ad hoc proceedings are voluntary, flexible, non-coercive and confidential proceedings in which the president of the commercial court appoints an agent to assist a solvent debtor in informal negotiations with its major creditors.

The creditors participate in *ad hoc* proceedings on a voluntary basis. The agreement entered into between the debtor and its creditors within the framework of *ad hoc* proceedings is purely contractual and is not binding on creditors that are not party to the agreement. Debt rescheduling and debt forgiveness cannot be imposed on creditors by the debtor, the agent or the court.

Ad hoc proceedings are not available to insolvent debtors. Under French law, a debtor is deemed insolvent when it is unable to meet its current debts out of its current assets (those in the form of cash or those that can be quickly turned into cash).

(b) *Conciliation proceedings*

Like *ad hoc* proceedings, conciliation proceedings are confidential, voluntary, flexible and non-coercive, aimed at reaching a workout agreement between the debtor and its major creditors, under the supervision of a court-appointed agent.

Conciliation is available to any solvent debtor that faces legal, economic or financial difficulties, whether current or foreseeable. Unlike *ad hoc* proceedings, conciliation is also available to any debtor that has been insolvent for fewer than 45 days.

The debtor must file a petition for conciliation proceedings with the president of the commercial court. The president then issues an order appointing the agent and opening conciliation proceedings, which cannot last more than five months.

Conciliation proceedings do not automatically stay creditors' actions. In addition, the court or the president of the court cannot order a general stay within the framework of conciliation proceedings. However, at the request of the debtor or agent, the president of the court can order creditors that have initiated steps or actions (by way of legal action or even by way of a simple formal notice) against the debtor aimed at collecting their claims while conciliation proceedings are ongoing to accept a moratorium for up to two years.

Shareholders of the debtor and new credit providers may be invited to participate in the negotiations. Social and tax authorities may be asked to consent to a debt rescheduling plan or a cancellation of part of their claims.

The workout agreement sets out the loans extended by existing creditors, new credit providers or shareholders, and/or any waiver, rescheduling or cancellation of existing claims agreed to by the creditors. It may be subject (if the parties agree), to formal court approval at the debtor's request (homologation). If the court approves the workout agreement, those parties that have provided new money or goods/services to allow the business to continue to operate will be granted priority of payment – the so-called 'new money priority' – in respect of the corresponding claims, which will thus rank senior to any other claims in the event of subsequent bankruptcy proceedings (except for employees' super-privileged claims and the so-called '*coûts de la procedure*' – essentially, the fees of the trustee and creditors' representative, plus those of any expert appointed by them). In addition to this new money priority, the court approval has certain other legal effects, the most notable of which is to protect the transactions, payments and agreements made prior to the court approval from future voidance in the framework of bankruptcy proceedings, since the insolvency date (which is the starting point of the 'suspect/hardening period') may not be set back at a date that is prior to that court approval (see below).

Formal court approval is not automatic. It is granted in a formal, publicly available judgment rendered after an adversarial hearing with the debtor's legal representatives and employees' representatives, the agent, the public prosecutor and those creditors that are party to the workout agreement. However, the workout agreement itself is not made available to the public and remains confidential.

If no new money priority is required and/or the parties agree that the conciliation proceedings should remain totally confidential, the parties may alternatively decide to request a simple stamp (*constatation*) from the president of the court instead of a formal court approval.

Once the conciliation proceedings have closed, no new conciliation may be opened in respect of the debtor until after the expiry of a three-month period starting from the closing date of the initial conciliation.

1.2   Safeguard proceedings

(a)   *Standard safeguard procedure*

Safeguard proceedings are voluntary proceedings that aim to encourage reorganisation at a preventive stage by enabling solvent debtors to restructure under court supervision.

Any debtor still solvent but facing difficulties that it cannot overcome may initiate this debtor-in-possession type of proceedings to restructure under court protection and preserve the business as a going concern.

Although available to solvent debtors only, safeguard proceedings are usually classified as bankruptcy proceedings, as the main rules applicable to rehabilitation proceedings (eg, automatic stay, creditors' filing of proofs of claim, creditors' committees) also apply to safeguard proceedings.

Safeguard proceedings are opened by the commercial court on the petition of the debtor only. As an exception, a debtor can be placed into safeguard proceedings at the request of the administrator, creditors' representative, public prosecutor or *ex officio* by the court, as a result of the extension of existing safeguard proceedings opened in respect of another debtor in the case of consolidation of the estates with that of the debtor or of a fictitious legal entity (ie, an entity that is found to be no more than a corporate veil; see 1.4 below).

In the judgment opening the safeguard proceedings, the court will appoint:

- a supervising judge, who oversees the proceedings and approves or rejects the creditors' proofs of claim;
- an administrator/trustee, who supervises and assists the management in preparing a safeguard plan; and
- a court agent, who represents the creditors' interests and assesses the creditors' proofs of claim; this agent can be assisted by up to five supervising creditors appointed by the court.

Safeguard proceedings begin with an observation period of up to six months, during which the court-appointed administrator assesses the debtor's financial position and reports to the court. This period can be extended once by six months and, in exceptional circumstances, can be further extended at the public prosecutor's request for an additional six-month period. The court can convert safeguard proceedings into rehabilitation or liquidation proceedings at any time if it appears that the debtor is insolvent.

The opening of safeguard proceedings triggers an automatic stay of all pending actions and enforcement proceedings aimed at obtaining payment of a sum of money or terminating a contract due to a payment default. It also prevents creditors from initiating such proceedings. Therefore, all creditors whose claims arose prior to the safeguard judgment are barred from enforcing their rights against the debtor.

Any interest (whether contractual or statutory) ceases to accrue from the date of the safeguard judgment, except interest accruing on loans with an initial maturity of one year or more or in respect of deferred payment terms contracts with an initial maturity of one year or more. However, the safeguard judgment does not trigger a stay of actions against corporate entities that are guarantors of, or joint debtors with, the debtor.

Once the safeguard judgment has been issued, the debtor is prevented from paying any pre-filing debts, except by way of set-off against 'connected' claims of the debtor. The Supreme Court has held that debts are deemed connected when resulting from a single contract or from separate contracts that constitute a single global contractual arrangement.

Since the law of March 12 2012, enacted within the context of the *Petroplus* case and the financial difficulties faced by the holding company, it is now possible, where the extension of proceedings is order in case of consolidation of estates (see above), protective measures may be ordered by the president of the court to freeze the assets of the legal entity to which safeguard proceedings (as well as rehabilitation and liquidation proceedings, see below) are extended, and avoid asset misappropriation. These protective measures may be ordered at the request of the administrator, creditors' representative, public prosecutor or *ex officio*.

All creditors (except employees) must file proof of their claims within two months (four months for foreign creditors) of publication of the safeguard judgment in the French legal *Gazette*.

For companies of a certain size (with over 150 employees and €20 million turnover) and for smaller companies subject to court approval, the new statute has created two classes of creditors (credit institutions and major suppliers), each of which is organised through a committee that must be set up by the administrator. The two committees are entitled to discuss and vote on the safeguard plan proposed by the debtor and the administrator.

Bondholders are not members of a committee but will form part of a third separate group. The bondholders' group votes on the draft safeguard plan after that plan has been approved by the two committees. All bondholders will (once the plan has been approved by the committees), vote in one single meeting – regardless of currency, security and seniority.

All suppliers that are not members of the suppliers' committee will be consulted on an individual basis, as well as the public creditors (eg, tax authorities or social security administration).

Social and tax authorities are invited to negotiate and may agree to a debt rescheduling and/or debt cancellation.

The safeguard plan may provide for debt restructuring, recapitalisation of the debtor, debt-for-equity swaps, and/or asset sales or partial sale of the business. The sale of the entire business is not an option in safeguard proceedings. Where creditors are organised in committees, the safeguard plan will be deemed approved by all members of each committee if in each committee the required percentage votes in favour of the plan. The required majority is a two-thirds majority in value of the creditors in each class attending or represented at the meeting.

If the draft plan is approved by both committees, it is then submitted to the bondholders' group (if any) for approval. In those circumstances, all bondholders – whatever the currency or the law applicable to their indenture – will vote together in one single group at a two-thirds majority in value (of those attending or represented at the meeting). The two-thirds majority in the bank class and the trade class (or in the bondholders' group) can approve a debt-for-equity swap that will then be imposed on the dissenting minority within the classes (or within the bondholders' group). However, the approval of the shareholders of the debtor will also be required for such debt-equity-swap in the same manner as for any regular capital increase transaction.

The plan prepared by the debtor will be deemed rejected if it is not approved by one of the committees or by the bondholders' group, and the negotiation process will then begin again on a one-to-one basis with each member of the committees and of the bondholders' group.

Once approved by the court, the plan is enforceable against all members of the creditors' committee, including the dissenting minority.

The plan is negotiated on a one-to-one basis with each creditor that is not a member of a committee.

The court can impose new maturity dates and debt rescheduling plans (for a period of up to 10 years) on dissenting creditors, but cannot impose any debt cancellation. This also applies where the committees and the bondholders' group fail to reach agreement or reject the plan proposed by the debtor, or where the court does not approve such a plan.

During the observation period, the debtor can sell assets with the prior consent of the supervising judge appointed by the court in the safeguard judgment. The supervising judge must verify that the assets to be sold are not integral to the anticipated safeguard plan.

A sale of part of the debtor's business may also be ordered at the close of the observation period when the court approves the safeguard plan. According to legal commentators, a sale may not be ordered without the debtor's consent. However, as the Safeguard Law does not specify that the debtor's consent is required, this point remains to be confirmed by the courts. In the authors' opinion, however, the debtor's management has the upper hand when proposing a safeguard plan involving the partial disposal of a business line.

(b) Expedited safeguard procedure

The *sauvegarde financière accélérée* (SFA) has been created essentially to accelerate and facilitate the treatment of financial difficulties faced by leveraged buyout holding companies.

Pursuant to the new law of October 22 2010, the eligibility criteria allowing the opening of a SFA are the following:

- Conciliation proceedings must be "pending": whatever the company's situation, the status of the negotiation with creditors, any direct access to the SFA without pending conciliation is strictly prohibited;
- As with the regular safeguard procedure, the company must not be insolvent;
- The company's accounts must be certified by statutory auditors or prepared by chartered accountants;
- The company must have at least 150 employees or an annual turnover of €20 million minimum; and
- The company must have prepared a draft plan likely to receive sufficient support from its creditors that would lead to its adoption.

The 150-plus employees/€20-million turnover requirement *de facto* excludes holding companies from the scope of the SFA. An amendment was proposed, but finally rejected by the French Constitutional Council on May 12 2011. The law of March 22 2012 therefore created a new article in the Commercial Code that provides that a debtor having a total balance sheet in excess of a certain threshold (set by a decree yet to be enacted and which should be around €15/€25 million) is deemed to meet the 150-plus employees/€20-million turnover requirement. This new balance-sheet requirement constitutes an alternative for holding companies to benefit from the opening of an SFA.

The opening of the SFA has effects only vis-à-vis financial creditors – that is, the creditors that are members of the credit institutions committee and, as the case may be, the members of the bondholders' group.

As a consequence, all the other creditors – including the members of the trade committee (as well as the public creditors) – are not affected by the opening of the SFA. Their claims should be repaid when falling due with no obligation to file proof of claim (see below).

The draft plan prepared by the debtor is submitted to the financial creditors. The voting process is the same as in safeguard, except that the trade committee is not invited to participate. The plan must be approved by the court within one month of the opening of the SFA. This one-month period can be renewed only once. In the event that the credit institutions committee and, as the case may be, the bondholders' group rejects the plan, the court would close the SFA. If, as a result of such closure, the debtor becomes insolvent, it will have no option other than filing for either rehabilitation proceedings or liquidation proceedings.

1.3   Insolvency proceedings

(a)   Rehabilitation proceedings
The objectives of rehabilitation proceedings, in order of priority, are:
- to protect the debtor's activities and prospects of recovery;
- to save jobs; and
- to pay creditors.

Rehabilitation proceedings are available to any insolvent debtor, provided that it has not ceased operating and that rescue seems possible. The debtor must file for rehabilitation within 45 days of the date on which it becomes insolvent, unless conciliation proceedings have been opened within this 45-day period.

The court can open rehabilitation proceedings on its own initiative if it becomes aware that the debtor is insolvent. In particular, if conciliation proceedings have been opened and the parties have failed to reach a workout agreement, and if it appears from the court-appointed agent's report that the debtor is insolvent, the court must decide on the opening of rehabilitation proceedings in respect of the debtor.

Rehabilitation proceedings can also be opened by the court at the request of the public prosecutor or at the request of any unpaid creditor, whether secured or unsecured (regardless of the amount of its claim).

If it is clear to the court that rehabilitation proceedings will not succeed and that a rescue may not be achieved, the court can order the pending rehabilitation proceedings to be converted into liquidation proceedings.

In the judgment opening rehabilitation proceedings, the court appoints:
- a supervising judge, who oversees the proceedings;
- an administrator/trustee, who assists the debtor's management or takes control of the debtor's management; and
- an agent, who represents the creditors' interests and assesses proofs of claim filed by the creditors. Between one and five supervising creditors can be appointed by the court to assist the agent.

Rehabilitation proceedings begin with an observation period of up to six months. This period can be extended in the same way as in safeguard proceedings.

The judgment opening rehabilitation proceedings has the same effects as a judgment opening safeguard proceedings – that is, it triggers an automatic stay of proceedings and prevents the debtor from making any payments in respect of any pre-filing debts, except via set-off against connected claims.

As in safeguard proceedings, the debtor and/or administrator can sell assets during the observation period with the prior consent of the supervising judge appointed by the court in the rehabilitation judgment. The supervising judge must verify that the relevant assets are not integral to the debtor's expected rehabilitation.

All creditors other than employees must file proofs of claim.

Subject to the same conditions as in safeguard proceedings, the creditors are organised through committees (credit institutions' committee and major suppliers' committee) and the bondholders through one single group. The rehabilitation plan proposal is negotiated with the creditors' committees and the bondholders' group on the one hand and with those creditors that are not members of a class on the other, in the same way as in safeguard proceedings.

The rehabilitation plan can involve debt restructuring, recapitalisation, debt-for-equity swaps, changes in shareholdings, sale of certain assets or partial sale of the business.

The court can impose new maturity dates and debt rescheduling plans (for a period of up to 10 years) on dissenting creditors, or where the committees and/or the bondholders' group fail to reach agreement or reject the proposed plan, or where the court does not approve the negotiated plan. However, the court cannot impose debt forgiveness.

Based on the reports filed by the administrator on the debtor's financial situation and prospects, the court can order the sale of all or part of the debtor's business (transfer plan) – without the debtor's consent – if it finds that the debtor will be unable to achieve rehabilitation on its own. The transfer plan is carried out according to the rules applicable to liquidation proceedings.

The sale of business is carried out pursuant to a process initiated by the court (where the court considers that the sale of the business may be a viable option), in which third parties are invited to submit acquisition offers to the administrator. The court will order the sale to the bidder whose offer is deemed to be the most likely to ensure rehabilitation, save jobs and facilitate the payment of creditors.

The debtor, the *de jure* and *de facto* managers of the debtor and the supervising creditors appointed by the court cannot submit a purchase offer to the administrator.

(b) Liquidation proceedings

The aim of liquidation proceedings is to sell the debtor's business, either in whole or in part, and/or its assets, in order to satisfy creditors' claims in their order of priority.

The debtor can apply for liquidation proceedings. Liquidation proceedings can also be opened by the court at the request of the public prosecutor or any unpaid creditor, whether secured or unsecured (regardless of the amount of its claim).

The court can further order liquidation proceedings on its own initiative. The court will order liquidation where the rescue of the insolvent debtor appears to be impossible. Liquidation can be ordered at any stage of safeguard or rehabilitation proceedings, or without any prior safeguard or rehabilitation proceedings.

The judgment ordering liquidation triggers an automatic stay of proceedings against the debtor and prevents the debtor from paying pre-filing claims, as in safeguard and rehabilitation proceedings. Creditors must file proofs of claim (see above).

Notwithstanding the stay that results from the opening of the liquidation proceedings, secured creditors are allowed to enforce their security rights against the debtor under certain conditions.

In the judgment opening rehabilitation proceedings, the court appoints:

- a supervising judge, who oversees proceedings; and
- a liquidator, who collects all of the company's assets and pays the creditors to the extent that funds are available. The liquidator also assesses proofs of claim and represents the creditors' interests. Between one and five supervising creditors can be appointed by the court to assist the liquidator.

Where the court considers that the sale of the debtor's business as a whole is an option, it starts a bidding process (as in rehabilitation proceedings) in which third parties are invited to submit offers to the liquidator. The court will order the sale of the business to the bidder whose offer is deemed to be the most likely to ensure rehabilitation, save jobs and facilitate payment of the creditors. The debtor, the *de jure* and *de facto* managers of the debtor and the supervising creditors appointed by the court cannot submit a purchase offer to the administrator. Any assets that are not included in a sale of the debtor's business are sold by the liquidator under the supervision of the supervising judge. The assets are generally sold through public auction, although the supervising judge can allow the liquidator to sell any assets pursuant to private contracts.

Liquidation proceedings last until no further proceeds can be realised from selling the company's business and/or assets. Once two years have elapsed since issuance of the judgment ordering liquidation, any creditor can request the court to terminate all proceedings. The new statute has created a simplified form of liquidation proceedings available to small businesses. Those simplified proceedings can last for up to one year. Liquidation proceedings conclude when the business (either in whole or in part) and assets have been sold to pay the creditors.

1.4 Consolidation of proceedings

The court may order the consolidation of proceedings (safeguard, rehabilitation or liquidation proceedings) so that debts of two (or more) different companies (irrespective of whether those companies belong to the same group) can be paid from a larger consolidated pool of assets, when either of the following conditions is met:

- One of the companies is found to be a 'fictitious corporate entity' – that is, a pure corporate veil created deliberately to try to isolate one company's assets from another, without an independent management running a real business enterprise. Theoretically, a fiction can be found where one of the essential elements of the contract to form a company – that is, the actual intent to share profits and losses – is missing. Most of the time, however, it is found as a result of fraud.
- The 'commingling' of the assets and liabilities, bank accounts or cash flows of two non-fictitious entities is such that, in terms of operations, management and accounting, it is impossible to separate one company's activities from the other's. The existence of such a commingling of assets

usually results from a finding by the court that two tests, theoretically alternative but usually used cumulatively by the courts, are satisfied: a commingling of accounts and/or abnormal finance streams.

Provided that one of the above conditions is met, a company (even a solvent one) may be consolidated into another company's safeguard, rehabilitation or liquidation proceedings. In such a case the extension or consolidation of proceedings will be ordered by the court that opened the initial proceedings, and consolidated proceedings in respect of all the concerned companies are conducted under the supervision of that court as if one single debtor were actually in bankruptcy.

2. Preference and avoidance issues

In rehabilitation and liquidation proceedings, certain transactions, payments, transfers and rights over assets (including mortgages) can be challenged by the administrator, the agent, the liquidator or the public prosecutor if they were entered into or established during the so-called 'suspect period'.

The suspect period, if it applies, is a period prior to the bankruptcy judgment that runs from the date on which the company is found to be effectively insolvent (the insolvency date) to the date on which the bankruptcy judgment is issued.

The bankruptcy court may set the insolvency date retrospectively at a date up to 18 months prior to the date of the bankruptcy judgment. However, if the debtor and all or some of its creditors entered into a workout agreement prior to the opening of rehabilitation or liquidation proceedings, and if the court formally approved such agreement in a homologation judgment, the bankruptcy court cannot set the insolvency date at a date prior to that of the homologation judgment (unless it can be demonstrated that the court issued the judgment as a result of fraud). These provisions do not apply in safeguard proceedings as the court sets no insolvency date (safeguard proceedings are not available to insolvent debtors).

2.1 'Automatic' avoidance

French law sets out a list of transactions, payments and rights that, if executed or perfected during the suspect period, will be automatically avoided by the court at the request of the administrator, agent, liquidator or public prosecutor. This list includes:

- transfers of movable or immovable assets without consideration (as an exception to the principle that the suspect period cannot exceed 18 months, such transfers can be avoided if they were entered into in the six months prior to the insolvency date);
- agreements in which the debtor's obligations materially exceed those of the other party;
- payments in any form made on account of debts that have not fallen due;
- payments on account of debts that have fallen due, if they were not made by 'normal' means (ie, methods of payment commonly used in business transactions, including cash, bank transfers and Dailly Law assignments of receivables (see below));
- any security interests, including mortgages and pledges, perfected over the

debtor's assets to secure pre-existing debts; and
- any protective or provisional measures.

2.2 'Optional' avoidance

Transactions, payments, rights or actions that are not listed in the automatic avoidance provisions may also be challenged by the administrator, agent, liquidator or public prosecutor if they were made/perfected/initiated during the suspect period. The avoidance is not automatic and lies within the court's discretion. These optional avoidance provisions apply to the following:
- any payments made by the debtor on account of matured debts;
- any transaction for consideration, including assignment, transfer, sale, security or other rights over the debtor's assets; and
- any seizure (eg, on claims or bank accounts).

The administrator, liquidator or public prosecutor must demonstrate that when the relevant transaction/payment/right/action was made/perfected/initiated, the other party (eg, the lender) actually knew, or was in a position to know, of the company's insolvency. If this test is met, the court can (but is not obliged to) render an avoidance decision.

3. Enforcement of security interests in bankruptcy

3.1 Main security interests

(a) Real estate

The main security interests over real estate properties in France are mortgages and lender's privilege (the latter being granted where the lender's claim results from a loan solely used by the borrower for the purpose of paying the acquisition price of the property).

For the purposes of perfection, French law requires that legal documentation pursuant to which a lender's privilege or mortgages shall be granted:
- be drafted in French;
- contain certain information and provisions in a specified format; and
- take the form of an instrument recorded by a French notary (who shall thus be responsible with respect to the lender as regards the validity and enforceability of those security interests).

The notary must register both lender's privileges and mortgages with the mortgage registry located in the same district as the relevant property. It may take up to two months to complete registration of the security interest.

(b) Fixtures

Under French law, no specific global security interests over fixtures can be perfected (the floating charge does not exist under French law). However, French law provides for a large range of security interests concerning specific fixtures (eg, cars, boats, aircraft, machines, inventory), to each of which specific legal provisions apply as regards grant, registration (as the case may be), perfection and/or enforceability.

Moreover, French law recognises the concept of *fonds de commerce*, usually translated as 'goodwill', which mainly comprises a universality of intangible and tangible assets on the basis of which a commercial business is carried on. Pledge over a *fonds de commerce* is available under French law. The agreement pertaining to the security interest must be registered with the tax authorities and the registrar(s) of the commercial court with which the business (and its related branches) has been registered.

In addition, where IP rights (eg, trademarks and trade names) are included in the going concern, an additional filing must be made with the French National Institute of Industrial Property within 15 days of filing the pledge with the registrar of the commercial court. The registration of a pledge over a *fonds de commerce* remains valid for 10 years and expires if not renewed prior to the end of such term.

(c) **Intangibles**

The main security interests over intangibles in France are security interests over shares and security interests over receivables.

Security interests over shares: These comprise pledges of shares or, where the company is a *société anonyme* (SA) or a *société par actions simplifiée* (SAS), pledges over the security accounts on which the shares issued by that company are registered.

Where the pledged shares are issued by a corporation other than an SA or an SAS, French law requires that the pledge be notified to the issuer of the shares and registered with the registrar of the commercial court (the registration remains valid for five years and expires if not renewed prior to the end of this term). Where the pledged shares are issued by a *société civile*, French law requires that the pledge also be registered with the tax authority.

Where a pledge of securities account can be granted, no formalities are required other than mere execution of a pledge declaration by the pledgor.

In both cases the shareholders of the entity whose shares have been pledged remain the registered and legal owners of those shares until the pledge is enforced. From a practical perspective, and where necessary (ie, for *sociétés civiles*, *sociétés à responsabilité limitée* and, if so provided by the articles of association, other types of company), a decision of the company's relevant corporate body approving in advance the first beneficiary of the pledge, as well as its successors and assignees in that respect, as a shareholder of the company in case of enforcement of the pledge shall be required.

Security interests over receivables: These mainly comprise pledges over receivables and Dailly Law assignments of receivables.

A pledge over receivables becomes valid and binding between the pledgor and the pledgee, and enforceable against third parties, upon execution of a pledge agreement. However, for the pledge to be enforceable against the debtor of the pledged receivables, the debtor of the pledged receivables must either be notified of the pledge agreement or execute the pledge agreement as a party thereto. In addition, notification of the pledge to the debtor of the pledged receivables entitles the secured creditor to require that the pledged receivables be paid directly into its hands (in satisfaction of the secured claim), unless otherwise provided for in the notification. The same provisions apply where the debtor executes the pledge agreement.

Under a Dailly assignment, the borrower assigns to the lender receivables that it holds against one or several third parties (eg, tenants that have entered into a lease agreement with the borrower). Such assignment can be used as a security interest. A Dailly assignment is perfected upon execution by the borrower (which assigns the receivables) of a private deed; notification to the debtors of the assigned liabilities is not required. However, notification of the Dailly assignment to the debtors of the assigned liabilities results in those debtors being obliged to pay the assigned receivables directly to the beneficiary/lender instead of the borrower (ie, the original creditor of those debtors in respect of the assigned liabilities).

Dailly assignments are available only where:

- the beneficiary of the assignment is a credit institution licensed in France or carrying out activities in France through the European passport;
- the Dailly assignment is made by the borrower to secure financing extended by that credit institution to the borrower; and
- the assigned receivables relate to business or professional activities.

3.2 Enforcement rights of the secured creditors

(a) Safeguard or rehabilitation proceedings

Secured creditors cannot enforce their security interests, as the judgment opening the proceedings results in an automatic stay.

However, in light of recent French Supreme Court decisions in connection with contracts with deferred performance (including its decision dated November 22 2005), the enforcement of a Dailly assignment in respect of future receivables (ie, receivables resulting from the performance after the opening of bankruptcy proceedings of ongoing contracts such as lease agreements) is still possible once bankruptcy proceedings have been opened in respect of the borrower. Nonetheless, the enforceability of Dailly assignments in bankruptcy is still debated among certain scholars and practitioners.

In safeguard and liquidation proceedings, all secured claims that arose prior to the judgment are automatically subordinated to certain senior claims that will rank ahead, including:

- so-called 'super-privileged' employees' claims;
- the costs of the proceedings (ie, the fees, costs and expenses incurred by the debtor, administrator and liquidator for the purpose of the proceedings);
- new money resulting from a prior conciliation workout agreement; and
- any claims that arose subsequent to the bankruptcy judgment, provided that they arose for the purpose of the proceedings or as a result of transactions entered into for the purpose of the debtor's business activity.

Employees' 'super-privilege' essentially protects the last 60 days of wages in arrears before the judgment opening bankruptcy proceedings. If the bankruptcy estate cannot pay these claims from its available cash, they are pre-financed by the *Association pour la Gestion du régime de garantie des créances de Salariés* (AGS), a wage insurance organisation that is financed by a levy on all employers and run and supervised by the Employers' Association. Once the AGS has paid, it is subrogated in the employer's rights and, save for one exception, in the employees' ranking.

(b)   Liquidation proceedings

A creditor with a security interest over collateral can enforce its rights as a secured creditor against the debtor provided that the liquidator has not undertaken the sale of the relevant collateral within three months of the liquidation judgment.

The security interest can be enforced by applying to the court for judicial appropriation of the collateral – that is, an order transferring ownership of such collateral to the secured creditor in satisfaction of its claim – provided that appropriation is an available remedy in respect of the relevant type of security interest (essentially, where possession of the collateral was transferred to the beneficiary and/or where specifically provided for by law).

Judicial appropriation is available only until the collateral has been liquidated by the liquidator. For the purpose of appropriation, the value of the collateral will be assessed by a court-appointed expert.

The secured claim shall be deemed satisfied up to the value of the appropriated collateral. If the value is higher than the secured claim, the secured creditor must pay the difference to the liquidator.

The main advantage of judicial appropriation is that it enables the secured creditor to obtain full title to the collateral in satisfaction of its secured claim without taking into consideration the rank of that secured creditor and notwithstanding the rights of higher-ranking creditors (eg, employees, liquidator, tax authorities) with senior claims.

Judicial appropriation has been an available remedy with respect to mortgaged properties only since the entry into force of the new statute adopted on March 23 2006 that reformed the French security regime. However, as French bankruptcy law provides for judicial appropriation only in respect of pledges, and as remedies under the French security regime do not automatically apply in bankruptcy proceedings, there is uncertainty as to whether judicial appropriation of a mortgaged property is available in liquidation proceedings.

In liquidation proceedings, subject to judicial appropriation (if applicable), all secured claims that arose prior to the bankruptcy judgment are automatically subordinated to certain senior claims that will rank ahead, including:

- 'super-privileged' employees' claims;
- costs of the proceedings (ie, fees, costs and expenses incurred by the debtor, the administrator and the liquidator for the purpose of the proceedings); and
- new money resulting from a prior conciliation workout agreement.

(c) *Specific rights of secured creditors*

Whatever the proceedings (safeguard, rehabilitation or liquidation), secured creditors have certain rights over the collateral and sale proceeds from such collateral, depending on whether the creditor is vested with a so-called 'retention right' resulting from the transfer of possession (whether virtual or actual) of the collateral (eg, transfer of possession resulting from a pledge over inventory or a pledge over securities account).

Security interests without a retention right: In safeguard or rehabilitation proceedings, if the collateral is sold by the administrator with the consent of the supervising judge, the sale proceeds will first be deposited with the *Caisse des Dépôts et Consignations*, a French state-owned bank. At the end of the observation period, the secured creditors will be paid from this account in accordance with their respective rank/privileges.

In rehabilitation or liquidation proceedings, if the court orders the sale of all or part of the business (including the collateral), and in the event that the security interest has been granted in order to secure a loan extended to the debtor for the purpose of financing the acquisition of the collateral, the purchaser of the business will be bound by the terms of the loan agreement and the related security agreements and shall pay to the secured creditor any overdue and unpaid amounts due as from the date of transfer of the assets (subject to any agreement that may be entered into between the purchaser and the secured creditor).

In other cases the court will allocate, at its discretion, part of the proceeds of sale of the business towards the satisfaction of secured claims.

Security interests conferring a retention right: In safeguard or rehabilitation proceedings, the supervising judge may, at the request of the administrator, require a secured creditor to surrender the collateral that is being retained to the extent that it is necessary to continue the debtor's business. In such case the secured creditor in possession of the collateral can enforce its retention right, as the judge's order is subject to full payment of the secured claim.

The same provisions apply in liquidation proceedings, essentially where the court has ordered the temporary continuation of the debtor's operations (which is possible in liquidation, subject to certain conditions) and if the collateral is necessary to the continuation of operations.

In cases of a sale of all or part of the business pursuant to a disposal plan, the French Supreme Court has held that a secured creditor vested with a right of retention over the collateral included in the sold business can enforce its retention right by retaining the relevant collateral and refusing to transfer the collateral to the purchaser until its claim is paid in full.

4. Liability issues

4.1 Lender liability

French law recognises the right of a borrower, and that of the borrower's creditors, to sue a lender alleging the lender's liabilities. However, the French Commercial Code as reformed by the Safeguard Law provides for certain exemptions from liability in the framework of bankruptcy proceedings.

Outside bankruptcy, a borrower may sue a lender alleging lender's liability pursuant to the Civil Code, which establishes a general theory of contractual liability. The borrower may claim damages on the grounds of lender's liability if it can be demonstrated that:

- the lender breached one of its obligations towards the borrower; and
- such breach directly caused the damage suffered by the borrower.

The Civil Code also establishes a general theory of liability in tort, whereby a third party (eg, a creditor of the borrower) has the right to sue the lender if it can prove that misconduct or negligence on the part of the lender was the direct cause of specific damage suffered by that third party. However, these types of liability action are rarely brought against lenders outside the bankruptcy of the borrower.

Before the entry into force of the Safeguard Law, lender's liability actions were more common in cases where bankruptcy proceedings were opened in respect of the borrower.

The court-appointed agent or the liquidator can sue a lender in the name and on behalf of the borrower's creditors, alleging lender's tort liability and requesting damages (which in most cases are equivalent to those claims that could not be satisfied from the proceeds of the bankruptcy proceedings).

The Safeguard Law has created an exemption from liability for all types of creditors (not only credit institutions), except in the event of:

- fraud;
- improper interference with the company's management; or
- security interests and/or guarantees obtained by the lender that are disproportionate to the amount of the loan (ie, security interests perfected on one or several assets the global value of which, as assessed on the date of perfection, materially exceeds the amount of the secured debt).

These provisions (Article L650-1 of the French Commercial Code) provide that if a creditor is held liable on one of the above grounds, then not only will that creditor be ordered to pay damages, but the security interests and/or guarantees granted to that lender in order to secure the claim may also be deemed null and void or reduced by the court.

4.2   Management liability

The management of an insolvent company can be held liable to pay all or part of its debts.

This liability can extend to both *de jure* and *de facto* managers.

A *de jure* manager is a formal appointee. For example:

- in an SA *avec conseil d'administration*, the chairman of the board, the CEO and/or the deputy CEOs, and the directors; individuals acting as permanent representatives of corporate entities appointed as such as members of the board of directors are *de jure* managers, as well as the company that they represent; and

- in a SAS, the president of the company and/or the CEO and deputy CEOs.

Although the concept is defined not by statute but by case law, a *de facto* manager is generally deemed to be any individual or legal entity that in practice performs in its own right positive and repeated management or leadership activities within or on behalf of the company. A parent company can also be held liable for an insolvent subsidiary's debts if it has been appointed as a manager, or can be deemed a manager of that subsidiary.

Two different actions – based on either mismanagement or a specific breach of duty – can be brought before the bankruptcy court with a view to having *de jure* and/or *de facto* managers held liable for all or part of the company's debts. These actions are available only to the liquidator, the court agent or the Public Ministry. In addition, the creditors appointed by the court as advisers can either summon the liquidator to bring an action or commence proceedings on their own initiative if the court agent does not do so.

(a)   **Actions based on mismanagement**

Liability can arise where, as a result of management errors, a company's assets do not cover its debts.

Management errors may result either from positive action or from a failure to act or negligence (eg, operating at a loss without taking adequate measures to restructure the business, while in the meantime increasing the company's total liabilities), or from any violation of applicable legal rules, in particular mandatory rules.

This action applies only in liquidation proceedings or where a safeguard or rehabilitation plan has been terminated.

(b)   **Actions based on a specific breach of duty**

During liquidation proceedings, managers can be held liable if they have contributed to the company's insolvency by:

- using company assets or credit for their own benefit or for the benefit of another corporate entity in which they have a direct or indirect interest;
- using the company to conduct and conceal business transactions for their own benefit;
- carrying out business activities at a loss to further their own interests, knowing that this would lead to insolvency;
- fraudulently applying or concealing all or part of the company's assets; or
- fraudulently increasing the company's debts.

In certain circumstances, directors found liable of the above breaches can be required to sell their equity interest in the company. In addition, they can be prohibited from managing any business for up to 15 years and from holding any public office for up to five years.

5.   International issues

French courts can open safeguard, rehabilitation or liquidation proceedings in respect of a debtor that is incorporated in another jurisdiction, provided that the debtor runs a business through one or several branches located in France and those branches are in financial difficulties or have become insolvent.

However, decisions rendered by French bankruptcy courts may conflict with other court judgments rendered in the jurisdiction of the debtor, in particular where that jurisdiction has not entered into a treaty with France providing for the mutual recognition and enforcement of court decisions (eg, EU Regulation 1346/2000). In the absence of any such treaty, foreign judgments are recognised and can be enforced only if they have been the subject of an exequatur procedure in France, which is intended to verify that the foreign court had proper jurisdiction and complied with international public policy, and that no fraud was committed.

Pursuant to EU Regulation 1346/2000, French courts can open main bankruptcy proceedings in respect of a debtor established in another EU member state if the debtor's centre of main interests (COMI) is in France. A company's COMI is presumed to be the place of its registered office, unless proved otherwise.

Once the main bankruptcy proceedings of a debtor that has its COMI in France have been commenced in France under EU Regulation 1346/2000, secondary proceedings can subsequently be commenced to liquidate the assets of a branch of the debtor located in another EU member state.

Similarly, where main bankruptcy proceedings have initially been opened in another EU jurisdiction where the debtor has its COMI, the French courts can subsequently commence secondary proceedings to liquidate assets that are part of the debtor's branches located in France.

Germany

Heinrich Meyer
Beiten Burkhardt

1. Introduction

In 2011 a total of 30,099 businesses (5.9% less than the previous year) requested the opening of insolvency proceedings. The insolvency courts have estimated the value of creditors' claims at around €31.5 billion. This continues the downward trend in corporate insolvencies since 2004, interrupted only during the crisis years of 2008/2009. Consumer insolvencies have begun to follow the same trend. In 2011 there were 103,289, 5.1% less than in 2010. Consumer insolvencies dropped for the first time following the introduction of the Insolvency Statute in 2008, by 7.1%.

German insolvency law is based on the Insolvency Statute, which entered into force on January 1 1999 and superseded the Bankruptcy Act 1877, the Law on Composition Proceedings 1935 and the Collective Enforcement Act 1990. The purpose of insolvency proceedings is the collective satisfaction of creditors through realisation of the debtor's assets, in particular with the aim of preserving the indebted enterprise (Section 1 of the Insolvency Statute).

2. Overview of insolvency proceedings

German insolvency law principally distinguishes between ordinary insolvency proceedings, consumer insolvency proceedings, insolvency plans, personal management and insolvency proceedings involving a deceased.

2.1 Ordinary insolvency proceedings

Ordinary insolvency proceedings may be opened only on the request of either the debtor or a creditor (Section 13(1) of the Insolvency Statute). If the debtor files the request, it must be accompanied by a list of creditors and their claims. With regard to debtors which have not discontinued their operations, Section 13(1)(4) of the Insolvency Statute under certain circumstances imposes binding requirements on the contents of the list to be filed by the debtor. Thus, the debtor shall – but is generally not obliged – to highlight certain claims, in particular the highest claims, the highest secured claims and financial administration, social insurance and occupational pension claims. Debtors whose assets are subject to insolvency proceedings may be natural or legal persons (eg, GmbH, AG), or undertakings without legal personality (eg, OHG, KG, GbR) (Section 11 of the Insolvency Statute). The effectiveness of insolvency proceedings is subject to the existence of a reason for their commencement, such as:

- illiquidity (Section 17 of the Insolvency Statute);

- imminent illiquidity (Section 18 of the Insolvency Statute); or
- over-indebtedness (Section 19 of the Insolvency Statute).

While a creditor requesting the opening of insolvency proceedings must establish the probable validity of such a reason, a debtor requesting the opening of insolvency proceedings must generally (an exception is made in Section 15(2) of the Insolvency Statute) point out only that this is reasonable

In the event of a corporate debtor's illiquidity, the debtor is obliged to file a request for the opening of insolvency proceedings, while a creditor is entitled to do so. If the debtor is a natural person, he has the right, but not the obligation, to request the institution of insolvency proceedings. 'Illiquidity' is defined in Section 17(2) of the Insolvency Statute, which states that a debtor is illiquid if it is no longer able to meet its due payment obligations. Where a debtor discontinues payments, illiquidity is presumed.

The debtor has the right (but not the obligation) to request the opening of insolvency proceedings in the event of imminent illiquidity. The aim is to work towards the timely opening of insolvency proceedings in the early stages of an economic crisis, when rescue is still a possibility. A debtor faces imminent illiquidity if it is likely to be unable to meet its existing liabilities as they fall due (Section 18 of the Insolvency Statute). A forecast decision must be made for a specified period, usually two years (comprising at least the current and the subsequent financial year). If it is likely that the debtor will be able to meet its existing liabilities as they fall due during the forecast period, the debtor does not face imminent illiquidity.

Only legal persons may request the opening of insolvency proceedings on the grounds of over-indebtedness. In the event of over-indebtedness, the debtor is obliged to request the opening of insolvency proceedings, while a creditor is entitled to do so. According to Section 19(2)(1) of the Insolvency Statute, over-indebtedness exists where a debtor's assets no longer cover its payment obligations, unless it is highly likely, considering the circumstances, that the enterprise will continue to exist. Therefore, insolvency proceedings cannot be opened on the grounds of over-indebtedness if continuation of the enterprise is very likely. This is the case where the company's financial plans show that a financial equilibrium will be maintained or regained during the forecast period (ie, a positive going-concern prognosis). If the financial plans for the forecast period reveal an underfunding (ie, a negative going-concern prognosis), the over-indebtedness is to be determined by means of a statement of assets and liabilities.

Until a decision on the request for the opening of insolvency proceedings has been issued, the insolvency court is obliged to take measures to secure the debtor's assets (Section 21 of the Insolvency Statute). The court may, for example, appoint a preliminary insolvency administrator or impose a restraint on alienation and prohibit execution against the debtor's assets. With the (partial) introduction of the Act on the Further Facilitation of Corporate Restructuring on March 1 2012, Section 21(2) of the Insolvency Statute now also offers the possibility to appoint a preliminary creditors' committee which can play an active part in selecting the administrator. The preliminary creditors' committee can submit to the insolvency court a list of requirements on the administrator to be appointed and can even specify the identity of the (preliminary) administrator, unless there are objective reasons why their candidate is unsuitable (Section 56a of the Insolvency Statute). A preliminary creditors' committee is mandatory only for large and mid-sized debtor companies (Section 22a(1) of the Insolvency Statute), while all others may appoint one (Section 22a(2) of the Insolvency Statute).

Where the necessary conditions are met, the insolvency court will order the opening of insolvency proceedings (Sections 27 and following of the Insolvency Statute). If a preliminary insolvency administrator has been appointed, he will generally become the final insolvency administrator.

Upon the opening of insolvency proceedings, the insolvency administrator is vested with the right to manage and transfer the debtor's assets (Section 80 of the Insolvency Statute). Individual creditors cannot enforce their claims against the debtor (Section 89(1) of the Insolvency Statute). The insolvency administrator may further, subject to Sections 129 and following of the Insolvency Statute, contest certain transactions of the debtor in order to reverse asset transfers conducted prior to the opening of insolvency proceedings.

The debtor's assets may be realised by way of liquidation or rescue. In case of liquidation, the debtor's entire assets are realised by the insolvency administrator and the proceeds deriving therefrom are used to satisfy creditors' claims. Where an undertaking is rescued, the creditors will receive all profits generated for a certain period specified in advance (eg, through equity in the undertaking; see section 2.3).

However, before creditors' claims are satisfied, the costs of the insolvency proceedings are deducted from the proceeds (Section 53 of the Insolvency Statute). These include court costs, the remuneration of the preliminary and final insolvency administrator, and any claims deriving from the activities of the insolvency administrator (Section 55 of the Insolvency Statute). Creditors' claims are then satisfied from the remaining proceeds.

After the proceeds have been distributed, the insolvency court will order the termination of the insolvency proceedings (Section 200(1) of the Insolvency Statute). If the debtor is a natural person and if the insolvency court has not announced the discharge of any residual debts, the creditors may subsequently assert their remaining claims by way of execution (Section 291 of the Insolvency Statute).

2.2   Consumer insolvency proceedings

Consumer insolvency proceedings allow natural persons to have a fresh start, free of debt. They are available to natural persons who independently carry out no or only minor economic activities. In this context, 'minor independent economic activities' can be presumed only if the debtor has fewer than 20 creditors upon the opening of insolvency proceedings.

2.3   Insolvency plan

An insolvency plan provides for the distribution of the debtor's assets for the benefit of creditors in derogation from the ordinary insolvency procedure (Sections 217 and following of the Insolvency Statute). For example, the creditors' meeting may agree, with the consent of the insolvency court, to continue the indebted enterprise if a majority of the creditors will not end up in a worse position than that which they would be in were the debtor to be liquidated. An insolvency plan cannot be concluded unless insolvency proceedings have been opened. If it is not possible to open insolvency proceedings due to a lack of assets, it is not possible to conclude an insolvency plan.

An insolvency plan may be submitted to the insolvency court either by the insolvency administrator or by the debtor (Section 218 of the Insolvency Statute).

The Act on the Further Facilitation of Corporate Restructuring has considerably expanded and thus strengthened the insolvency plan procedure. In contrast to the previous situation, there now exists the possibility, through the insolvency plan, to interfere with the shareholder or membership rights of the stakeholders in the debtor. The plan may in particular provide for the transformation of claims of creditors into shareholder or membership rights in the debtor (debt-to-equity swap) (Section 225a(2) of the Insolvency Statute).

2.4 Personal management

If the insolvency court orders personal management upon the opening of insolvency proceedings, the debtor may manage and dispose of the assets involved in the insolvency proceedings under the supervision of a custodian.

Sections 270 and following of the Insolvency Statute, as amended by the (partial) introduction of the Act on the Further Facilitation of Corporate Restructuring, are intended to promote personal management as a restructuring tool. However, so far this has hardly been used. In future, (preliminary) personal management will be ordered whenever requested, unless this is expected to leave the creditors at a disadvantage. If the debtor's illiquidity or over-indebtedness is imminent, the new 'protective shield procedure' (Section 270b of the Insolvency Statute) offers the debtor the chance to draw up an insolvency plan under the supervision of a preliminary custodian within a maximum of three months. This requires that the debtor submit to the insolvency court, together with the request for the opening of insolvency proceedings, a certificate issued by a qualified person (eg, a tax adviser, chartered accountant or lawyer with experience in insolvency matters) stating that illiquidity or over-indebtedness is imminent and the desired restructuring has a chance of success.

2.5 Insolvency proceedings involving a deceased

Under German law, heirs inherit both the assets and liabilities of the deceased (Section 1967(1) of the Civil Code). In principle, the heir is fully liable for these liabilities (ie, to the full extent of his assets). However, pursuant to Section 1975 of the Civil Code, the heir can restrict this unlimited liability to the estate by opening insolvency proceedings involving the deceased (see Section 11(2) of the Insolvency Statute). Insolvency proceedings apply exclusively to the assets of the estate, excluding the assets of the heir. Insolvency proceedings involving a deceased are principally subject to the regulations governing ordinary insolvency proceedings, unless derogation therefrom, specified in Section 315 of the Insolvency Statute, applies.

3. Domestic insolvency proceedings relating to foreign countries

German insolvency proceedings relating to foreign countries are subject to the EU Insolvency Regulation and German international insolvency law as set out in Sections 335 and following of the Insolvency Statute. Insofar as German international insolvency law derogates from the EU Insolvency Regulation, the EU regulation prevails – at least with regard to matters within Europe. For matters involving non-EU member states, German international insolvency law applies, since the EU Insolvency Regulation applies exclusively to relationships with EU member states (with the exception of Denmark).

3.1 Debtor's assets

Both the EU Insolvency Regulation and German international insolvency law are based on the principle of universality. If insolvency proceedings are opened in Germany, all of the debtor's assets are involved, including foreign assets (Section 35 of the Insolvency Statute). However, this provision can be implemented only if the foreign state acknowledges the German insolvency proceedings.

Whether an object falls within the debtor's assets is subject to the law of the state in which the proceedings are opened (Article 4 of the EU Insolvency Regulation; Section 335 of the Insolvency Statute). Insolvency proceedings opened in Germany include all assets owned by the debtor on the date on which proceedings are opened and any assets acquired during the proceedings (Sections 35 and 36 of the Insolvency Statute). However, objects not subject to execution do not form part of the bankruptcy estate (Section 36(1) of the Insolvency Statute). Neither do objects that form part of the debtor's usual household and are used in that household, if their disposition would obviously not yield proceeds largely disproportionate to their value (Section 36(3) of the Insolvency Statute). Whether an individual object is subject to coercive execution depends on the law of the state in which the object is situated on the date that the proceedings are opened, since liability to execution is a question of the respective execution law and not of insolvency law.

If, after the opening of insolvency proceedings, the debtor transfers foreign property, this transfer becomes legally invalid pursuant to Sections 80 and 81 of the Insolvency Statute, unless the foreign state does not acknowledge the German insolvency proceedings. In case of non-acknowledgement of such transfers, validity or invalidity is exclusively subject to the law of the foreign state.

Administration of the debtor's assets is conducted by the insolvency administrator. The insolvency administrator's rights are subject to the law of the state in which insolvency proceedings have been opened (Articles 4(2)(c) and 18(1) of the EU Insolvency Regulation; Section 335 of the Insolvency Statute). Thus, a German insolvency administrator has the same powers with respect to foreign assets as he has under German insolvency law. The insolvency administrator therefore must assume possession of (Section 148 of the Insolvency Statute) and liquidate (Section 159 of the Insolvency Statute) those assets of the bankruptcy estate which are situated in a foreign state. In particular, he may remove the respective objects from the state in which they are situated at the time that the proceedings are opened (Article 18(1) of the EU Insolvency Regulation; Section 335 of the Insolvency Statute).

Whether the insolvency administrator may realise any assets forming part of the bankruptcy estate is subject to the law of the place of jurisdiction of the insolvency court. With respect to the type of realisation (eg, disposal or auction), the insolvency administrator must observe the law of the state in which the assets are situated (Article 18(3) of the EU Insolvency Regulation).

If the insolvency administrator cannot access assets situated in a foreign country due to conflicting laws of the foreign state, the debtor may freely dispose of such property, unless insolvency proceedings have been opened against it in the foreign state. However, in light of the debtor's obligation to cooperate resulting from Section 97 of the Insolvency Statute, it is obliged to authorise the insolvency administrator to dispose of its assets situated in a foreign state or permit their confiscation. Such conduct is permitted only by some states (eg, Denmark, Finland, Netherlands, Sweden, Switzerland); others reject it because they consider it an abuse or circumvention of the principle of territoriality valid under their law.

3.2 Effect of insolvency proceedings on pending civil procedures and executions

Section 240 of the Code of Civil Procedure provides that pending domestic civil procedures are interrupted by the opening of insolvency proceedings if the assets concerned form part of the bankruptcy estate. Its application to German insolvency proceedings relating to foreign states and proceedings pending in a foreign state is to be decided, pursuant to Article 15 of the EU Insolvency Regulation, according to the relevant foreign procedural law.

Upon the opening of insolvency proceedings, domestic executions involving the bankruptcy estate or the debtor's other property are not permitted for the duration of the proceedings (Section 89(1) of the Insolvency Statute). In order to safeguard the principle of equal treatment of all creditors, the execution prohibition applies worldwide. In this context, attention should be paid to the fact that the foreign state will ultimately decide on the acknowledgement of the German proceedings, and thus also on the acknowledgement of an execution prohibition (because this has only immediate domestic impact). In addition to the execution prohibition, *ex lege* invalidity pursuant to Section 88 of the Insolvency Statute shall be effective worldwide. Section 88 provides that any security established in the month preceding the request to open insolvency proceedings or after such request by virtue of execution attaching assets of the debtor that form part of the bankruptcy estate becomes invalid when insolvency proceedings are opened. This is acknowledged in relation to EU member states by Article 4(2)(2)(f) of the EU Insolvency Regulation. With respect to non-member states, as with the execution prohibition, *ex lege* invalidity is subject to acknowledgement by the foreign state.

Where the foreign state allows an execution in spite of the German insolvency proceedings, the creditor is, as a consequence of Section 812 of the Civil Code, obliged to return what it has obtained at the expense of the bankruptcy estate to the insolvency administrator (Article 20(1) of the EU Insolvency Regulation; Section 342(1) of the Insolvency Statute). The claim for return is not limited to domestic creditors, but also applies to foreign creditors due to the principle of equal treatment. In general, it is impossible to enforce a claim for return against foreign creditors if the foreign state does not acknowledge such claim.

A creditor may principally retain what it has obtained in insolvency proceedings that have been opened in another state. This will be offset against its proportional share in the domestic proceedings. The creditor will be accommodated in the distributions only alongside other creditors of the same rank (Article 20(2) of the EU Insolvency Regulation and Section 342(2)(2) of the Insolvency Statute).

3.3 Claims in insolvency proceedings

Article 32(1) of the EU Insolvency Regulation and Section 341(1) of the Insolvency Statute govern the registration of claims. Any creditor (domestic or foreign) may lodge a claim in the domestic main proceedings and in any secondary proceedings in another state.

Whether such claim exists depends on the law that is applicable to the claim. Regarding whether the claim arises from insolvency proceedings, German insolvency law alone is decisive – in particular, Sections 38 to 40 of the Insolvency Statute. Since German insolvency law does not provide for higher-ranking claims (although see Section 264 of the Insolvency Statute), any existing higher foreign rank can be disregarded.

The type of registration and proceedings for the determination of insolvency claims are subject to the law of the state in which the insolvency proceedings are opened (Article 4(2)(2)(h) of the EU Insolvency Regulation; Section 335 of the Insolvency Statute). Thus, for proceedings opened in Germany, Sections 174 and following of the Insolvency Statute shall apply. Foreign creditors must register their claims with the insolvency administrator in order for these to be entered in the schedule of claims. Principally, registration must be conducted in the German language and include:

- the content specified in Article 41 of the EU Insolvency Regulation (ie, a copy of existing evidence;
- the type of claim;
- the date on which claim arose;
- the amount of claim; indication of any priority right;
- whether collateral security or retention of title was taken; and
- which assets are subject to the security).

Article 42(2)(1) of the EU Insolvency Regulation provides for an exception to the requirement to register in the German language: a creditor with its usual residence, domicile or seat in the European Union may also register its claim in the official language of its home state. In such case, however, pursuant to Article 42(2)(2) of the EU Insolvency Statute, the registration must contain at least the heading 'Registration of claim' in the German language.

3.4 Insolvency plan

According to Section 254 of the Insolvency Statute, a confirmed insolvency plan becomes binding upon all parties involved, regardless of whether they have filed claims or opposed the plan. The effects of the insolvency plan are not restricted to

Germany, but also apply in other states. As a consequence, foreign creditors cannot execute against the debtor's property situated in a foreign state to satisfy any part of their claims that has been waived due to the insolvency plan. However, observance of this depends on whether the German insolvency proceedings and the German insolvency plan are acknowledged by the foreign state.

3.5 Discharge of residual debt

The discharge of residual debt is binding for all creditors (Section 301(1) of the Insolvency Statute; but for exceptions see Section 302 – obligations incumbent on the debtor under tort as a result of wanton acts; fines and liabilities from interest-free loans granted to the debtor to cover the costs of the insolvency proceedings). The aim of a discharge of residual debt is to enable the debtor to rebuild its economic existence. However, this aim can be achieved only if the effect of the discharge of residual debt applies equally to all creditors. The discharge of residual debt is therefore assumed to have general effect in foreign states. Again, such effect also depends on whether the foreign state acknowledges the discharge of residual debt. Within the European Union, the decision on the discharge of residual debt is recognised under Article 25(1)(1) of the EU Insolvency Regulation. If a non-US state is involved, recognition depends on the laws of that specific state.

4. Effect of insolvency proceedings on security interests

Creditors often wonder about the effect that the opening of insolvency proceedings will have on any security provided to them by the debtor. Two possibilities may be distinguished in this context: the right to separation and the right to separate satisfaction. The former involves the separation of an object that does not belong to the debtor from the bankruptcy estate. The latter entitles the creditor to higher-ranking satisfaction from certain assets forming part of the bankruptcy estate (Section 170(1)(2) of the Insolvency Statute). Whether the respective creditor has a right to separation or merely a right to separate satisfaction depends on the security interest that it holds, as outlined below.

4.1 Equitable liens

Equitable liens permit a chattel mortgagor to use the security granted to satisfy its claim against the chattel mortgagee in the event of default.

Where insolvency proceedings are opened, the mortgagor has a right to separate satisfaction only with regard to its claim (Section 51(1) of the Insolvency Statute). This is because the equitable lien, although allocated *in rem* to the mortgagor, is still a non-possessory lien from an economic point of view. The equitable lien thus exists only in order to secure a claim, and any excess resulting from realisation must be added to the bankruptcy estate.

Insofar as the insolvency administrator holds possession of the item subject to a right to separate satisfaction, it is principally entitled to realise it pursuant to Section 166(1) of the Insolvency Statute. However, if the creditor has already asserted its claim over the asset prior to the opening of insolvency proceedings, it is not obliged to return the item to the insolvency administrator, but may continue the realisation.

4.2 Retention of title

In order to analyse the consequences of the opening of insolvency proceedings for a holder of retained title, it is first necessary to distinguish between the different types of retention of title.

(a) *Regular retention of title*

Regular retention of title occurs when an item is transferred from the seller to the buyer under the condition precedent of full payment of the purchase price.

If the buyer becomes insolvent and the purchase price has not yet been paid in full, the seller has the right to separation of its retained title (Section 47 of the Insolvency Statute). However, this shall apply only if the insolvency administrator does not demand fulfilment of the purchase agreement (Sections 103 and 107(2) of the Insolvency Statute), or if the seller has effectively withdrawn from the purchase agreement (Sections 449(2) and 323(1) of the Civil Code). Only in such cases is the buyer no longer entitled to possession in terms of Section 986 of the Civil Code. If the insolvency administrator decides on fulfilment, the debtor acquires title to the item upon complete payment of the purchase price and the seller's right to separation no longer applies. The seller is then also not placed in a worse position, since it receives the full purchase price as a claim incumbent on the bankruptcy estate (Section 55(1)(2) of the Insolvency Statute).

(b) *Transferred and subsequent retention of title*

Retention of title is transferred if the buyer intends to resell and thereby disposes of its anticipated right. As a consequence, the second buyer becomes the owner only upon full payment of the purchase price by the first buyer to the original seller.

Such retention of title is treated as ordinary retention of title in insolvency proceedings involving the first and second buyer.

A subsequent retention of title has different consequences. The first buyer is entitled merely to dispose to a second buyer under retention of title, so that the second buyer obtains its own anticipated right. Upon full payment of the purchase price by the second buyer, title is transferred from the original seller. If the first buyer becomes insolvent, it has no right to separation.

(c) *Enhanced retention of title*

Enhanced retention of title means that title is not transferred upon full payment of the purchase price to the seller unless certain additional requirements have been met (in particular, settlement of further claims).

For as long as the original purchase price has not been paid in full, this is treated as a case of ordinary retention of title in the event of the buyer's insolvency. The seller has the right to separate its property if it has withdrawn pursuant to Sections 449(2) and 323(1) of the Civil Code.

However, if the full purchase price has been paid to the seller, but the additional requirements have not yet been met, the seller is entitled merely to separate satisfaction. Enhanced retention of title is treated economically as an equitable lien that entitles the holder only to separate satisfaction (Section 51(1) of the Insolvency Statute).

(d)   *Extended retention of title*
Retention of title is extended if the security covers future assets that will replace the item acquired under retention of title.

Extended retention of title may include either a processing clause or a clause on the assignment of future claims and a power of resale. The former confirms that the seller is deemed a manufacturer in terms of Section 950 of the Civil Code and thus obtains title to the item, which has been newly manufactured by the buyer. Legally and economically, the owner of the new item (ie, the original seller) is to be treated as the owner of an equitable lien, which is also applicable in case of the buyer's insolvency. With regard to its secured claim, it may thus claim only separate satisfaction.

The latter authorises the buyer of the retained title to resell the item pursuant to Section 185(1) of the Civil Code. However, such resale is subject to the condition that the buyer assigns to the seller, in advance, the purchase price resulting from the resale as security. If the first buyer becomes insolvent, the buyer of the retained title may claim separate satisfaction from the claim assigned to it, just as in the case of assignment for security.

4.3   Liens

(a)   *Liens on immovables*
According to Section 49 of the Insolvency Statute, creditors whose claims are secured by immovable assets are entitled to separate satisfaction. A right to separate satisfaction is therefore granted in particular to owners of charges on real property (mortgages, land charges).

(b)   *Legal liens on movables*
Legal liens may be created over assets (Sections 1204 and following of the Civil Code), and over transferable rights (Sections 1273 and following of the Civil Code). If a lien has been effectively created, it entitles the pledgee, in the event of the insolvency of the holder of the lien, to separate satisfaction from the lien pursuant to Section 50(1) of the Insolvency Statute.

(c)   *Statutory liens and security rights of an execution creditor*
Statutory liens include the landlord's lien (Section 562 of the Civil Code), the contractor's lien (Section 647 of the Civil Code) and the lien of a commission agent on consigned goods (Sections 397 and following of the Commercial Code). Pursuant to Section 50(1) of the Insolvency Statute, holders of legal liens are also entitled to separate satisfaction. Regarding the landlord's or lessor's lien, the restrictions set out in Section 50(2)(1) must be observed. According to this provision, landlords and lessors cannot claim their liens in insolvency proceedings for rent or lease payments covering a period outside the 12 months preceding the opening of insolvency proceedings. Nor does the right to separate satisfaction apply to any claims from damages to be paid due to the termination of such lease by the insolvency administrator pursuant to Section 109(1)(3) of the Insolvency Statute.

According to Section 50(1) of the Insolvency Statute, an effective statutory lien which a creditor acquired pursuant to Section 804(1) of the Code of Civil Procedure through attachment of an asset forming part of the bankruptcy estate entitles the creditor to separate satisfaction. The attachment must have taken place before the opening of proceedings, since pursuant to Section 89(1) of the Insolvency Statute, individual execution is prohibited from that date on. Thus, no statutory lien can effectively arise.

5. Forum shopping

As essential differences exist between the insolvency laws of the EU member states, a 'competition of legal systems' arose after the introduction of the EU Insolvency Regulation, which governs the acknowledgement of insolvency proceedings in other member states. In the event of both consumer and corporate insolvencies, debtors often try to avoid the strict German insolvency law and choose a more favourable legal system.

5.1 Consumer insolvencies

Pursuant to Section 4(1) of the EU Insolvency Regulation, the applicable insolvency law is that of the place where the insolvency proceedings have been opened. The place where insolvency proceedings are to be opened is subject to the principle of the 'centre of main interests' (COMI) (Article 3(1) of the EU Insolvency Regulation).

No presumption as to COMI exists for natural persons under Article 3(1)(2) of the EU Insolvency Regulation for undertakings and legal persons. However, it may be presumed that the place of operational activities is decisive for freelancers. For other persons, the place of residence is decisive.

A combination of Articles 4(1) and 3(1) of the EU Insolvency Regulation enables the debtor to influence the applicable law and to choose the most favourable insolvency law applicable to him. By moving to another member state, the debtor can benefit from essential advantages – in particular with regard to the discharge of residual debt – that would be unavailable were insolvency proceedings to be opened in Germany. In the context of discharge of residual debt and its various ways of implementation, there is a notable divergence between the French and German regimes. Numerous websites advertise the advantages of private insolvencies in France, with the discharge of residual debt reportedly taking between 12 and 14 months, as compared to six years in Germany (Section 287(2) of the Insolvency Statute). Difficulties resulting from the avoidance of German insolvency law arise only if the debtor moves before the insolvency proceedings have been opened. If the debtor moves to another member state after insolvency proceedings have been opened, the relocation of jurisdiction based on Section 4 of the Insolvency Statute in connection with Section 261(3)(2) of the Code of Civil Procedure is excluded. If the move is executed before insolvency proceedings have been opened in Germany, the debtor faces certain risks. He needs to ensure that key elements of his life are relocated to the other country; a mere postal address in that country is insufficient. The debtor will have to lease an apartment abroad – a difficult task, given his straitened financial circumstances.

5.2 Corporate insolvencies

Articles 4(1) and 3(1) of the EU Insolvency Regulation further apply to corporate insolvencies. However, undertakings and legal persons are subject to the presumption of Article 3(1)(2) of the EU Insolvency Regulation, which provides that COMI is located at the registered seat of business, unless evidence to the contrary exists. Taking this presumption into consideration, undertakings have the opportunity to influence the applicable insolvency law by relocating their business seat. Again, however, it can be assumed that actual relocation of operational activities during a financial crisis will often be impossible, due to a lack of liquidity.

Before the Reform Act to Modernise the Law governing Limited Liability Companies became effective on November 1 2008, German corporations could not easily relocate their business seats abroad, because Section 4a of the Act on Limited Liability Companies and Section 5 of the Stock Corporation Act both stipulated that a company's business seat must be located within Germany. However, corporate law opens up various opportunities for a company to access the insolvency laws of foreign states. One such way is through a merger according to Sections 2 and following of the Transformation Act, which exclusively regulate the conditions for a merger of companies with their business seats in Germany. However, in a December 13 2005 ruling, the European Court of Justice (ECJ) held that the unequal treatment of national and cross-border mergers resulting from the Transformation Act constituted an infringement of the freedom of establishment. Although that particular case dealt with the merger of a Luxembourg *société anonyme* with a German stock corporation, the same will apply for a merger of a German undertaking with a foreign company. Since Sections 122a and following of the Transformation Act entered into force on April 19 2007, there is the additional option of a cross-border merger of corporations. This does not result in a loss of relevance for the ECJ, which still applies to legal entities that are not subject to Sections 122a and following of the Transformation Act (ie, partnerships of EU member states).

As a result, there were still possibilities for German companies to relocate their business seat. Indeed, this has frequently happened in the past (eg, insolvency proceedings of Hans Brochier Holdings Ltd). UK insolvency law seems to be particularly attractive to German undertakings. Its rescue procedure, which is considered especially flexible, is often cited as the reason for a move to the UK jurisdiction.

Since the Reform Act to Modernise the Law on Limited Liability Companies came into force, German companies no longer need to resort to these 'tricks' to disprove the presumption of Article 3(1)(2) of the EU Insolvency Regulation. Section 4a of the Act on Limited Liability Companies and Section 5 of the Stock Corporation Act no longer require that a company's registered office and headquarters be identical. Both Section 4a of the Act on Limited Liability Companies and Section 5 of the Stock Corporation Act require a registered office within Germany, but the headquarters may be located abroad, so that the presumption of Article 3(1)(2) of the EU Insolvency Regulation can be overcome.

Russia

Marina Ivanova
Anton Panchenkov
Elena Trusova
Goltsblat BLP

1.   Background

The Law on Insolvency (127-FZ) came into force on October 26 2002. The statute:

- defines the term 'insolvency';
- sets out the grounds and criteria for insolvency;
- regulates bankruptcy procedures;
- defines the status, rights and obligations of insolvency officers;
- provides rules for settlement with creditors; and
- sets out other key mechanisms for insolvency in Russia.

This is the third Russian federal law on insolvency, replacing the laws of 1998 and 1992. Since its adoption, the law has been subject to amendments introduced by more than 30 legal acts. The most significant amendments were made in 2008 and 2009, affecting more than two-thirds of the document.

The recent amendments were aimed at strengthening the protection of creditors' rights and preventing bankruptcy from constituting an unfair mechanism through which to acquire companies or company assets. Russia's insolvency legislation is becoming more complex; despite the fact that the Law on Insolvency is not ideal, it is certainly more balanced than the preceding regulations.

This chapter provides a general introduction to the Russian insolvency regime, but does not cover the specifics of rules related to particular debtor categories (eg, a special Law on Insolvency of Credit Institutions (40-FZ) relates to the insolvency of banks and other credit institutions).

The Law on Insolvency provides only general guidelines related to the bankruptcy of individuals in Russia. A separate draft federal law specifically related to the bankruptcy of individuals is under consideration by the State *Duma* (the lower house of Parliament).

2.   Overview

Under Article 2 of the Law on Insolvency, 'insolvency' (bankruptcy) is defined by arbitration courts[1] as a debtor's inability to satisfy creditors' claims and/or fulfil mandatory payment obligations.

In general, a company is considered to be incapable of satisfying creditors' claims if:

---

1   An arbitration court is a Russian state commercial court.

- its outstanding monetary obligations and/or mandatory payments exceed Rb100,000, as confirmed by a court ruling; or
- it fails to discharge its monetary obligations and/or fulfil mandatory payments within three months of their due date.

Arbitration courts enjoy exclusive jurisdiction to administer bankruptcy proceedings.

The right to file an application with an arbitration court for declaration of bankruptcy is granted to:

- the debtor;
- insolvency creditors; and
- authorised bodies.[2]

In some cases, a debtor is obliged to file an application with the arbitration court if:

- meeting the claims of one or more creditors would make it impossible for it to discharge monetary obligations or make mandatory payments and/or other payments in full to other creditors; or
- levying of execution would significantly hinder or render impossible pursuit of its economic activity.

A director who fails to perform this obligation may face an administrative penalty, which may result in his long-term disqualification (ie, a ban on performing management activities in any form for up to two years).

According to the Law on Insolvency, bankruptcy proceedings consist of five stages:

- supervision;
- financial rehabilitation;
- external administration;
- receivership; and
- amicable agreement.

Each stage has its own objectives and regulations (discussed further in section 4).

3. Insolvency officer

The key figure in insolvency proceedings is the insolvency officer, who is appointed by the arbitration court. Initially, the insolvency officer is nominated by the petitioner for bankruptcy; during bankruptcy proceedings, the insolvency officer is nominated by the creditors' meeting. The insolvency officer's tasks and powers differ from one stage to the next (discussed further below).

Since the introduction of Russian insolvency law in the early 1990s, the role of the insolvency officer has been subject to controversy and suspicion. In the past,

---

2   An authorised body is a state body that is empowered to represent state interests in insolvency procedures. The relevant legislation refers to the Federal Tax Service in this respect.

insolvency officers had more power than they do now, which many skilfully combined with certain loopholes in the previous insolvency legislation to act as independent market players, offering 'clients' attractive assets and full control over a given insolvency as a type of turnkey product. Few insolvency officers safeguarded the rights of creditors.

However, the latest set of amendments to the Law on Insolvency, adopted in 2009, sought to reverse this trend – at least in the longer term. The new version of the law explicitly states that insolvency officers must serve the creditors' interests and will be accountable to them.

3.1 Legal status

An insolvency officer must be a Russian citizen engaged in professional private practice, subject to the legislative requirements imposed by the Law on Insolvency. According to the provisions introduced into the law over the past three years, the main activity of an insolvency officer should not be deemed to be entrepreneurial; however, he can still undertake other types of professional activity, including entrepreneurial activity, provided that this does not affect his obligations under the Law on Insolvency. An insolvency officer must be a member of one (and only one) self-regulating organisation of insolvency officers.

Besides the standard criteria[3] set by a self-regulating organisation for its members (eg, a higher education qualification, professional administrative experience or completion of an insolvency officer assistant traineeship course), an organisation can impose additional requirements related to expertise, independence and reputation.[4] Moreover, in insolvency proceedings, a petitioner may demand that an insolvency officer meet additional criteria (eg, must hold a degree in the field of the debtor's activity or possess a track record of a certain number of previously conducted insolvency proceedings).

An insolvency officer should receive corresponding remuneration for his services, encompassing a fixed fee (expressly provided for by the Law on Insolvency) and an additional payment, which incorporates a fixed amount that is set legislatively, plus a fee calculated on the basis of the debtor's asset value. Creditors may decide to pay additional remuneration to the insolvency officer out of their own funds or the funds owed to them by the debtor.

The insolvency officer's legal liability is subject to mandatory standard and case-specific civil insurance, covering potential damages to be paid to the participants in the insolvency case.

Each insolvency procedure within the scope of the proceedings has its own type of insolvency officer:

- supervision – interim administrator;
- external administration – external administrator;
- financial rehabilitation – administrative manager; and
- receivership – bankruptcy receiver.

---

3   See Sections 2 and 3 of the Law on Insolvency.
4   *Ibid*, Article 20, Section 4.

3.2 Nomination, appointment, discharge and dismissal

The first insolvency officer is appointed by the state arbitration court on the basis of an insolvency application submitted by either the debtor, a creditor or an authorised body. The applicant may suggest a specific insolvency officer to be appointed during the first stage (supervision) or may delegate such nomination to a specific self-regulating organisation. In practice, this means that the first party to submit an insolvency application has a strong chance of placing at least the supervision procedure under the control of its own candidate.

It is highly recommended to try to win the 'procedural race' and promote a trusted candidate from the outset of the insolvency proceedings. The key rights and duties of an insolvency officer are discussed below in order to provide a basic understanding of how influential this figure can be.

An insolvency officer should be discharged[5] from his position if he leaves the self-regulating organisation of which he was a member. An insolvency officer should be dismissed[6] in the event of expulsion from his self-regulating organisation or improper performance of duties during the insolvency proceedings. However, such decisions are subject to a state arbitration court ruling.

3.3 Main rights and duties

In addition to certain rights and duties related to a specific procedure, during insolvency proceedings, insolvency officers shall:

- maintain the claims register (the insolvency offer also has the right to object to any creditors' claim in court);
- analyse the debtor's financial position;
- conduct an inventory of the debtor's assets;
- organise and lead creditors' meetings; and
- prepare reports on his activities during each procedure.

The key rights enjoyed by an insolvency officer include:

- challenging transactions entered into by the debtor in breach of the Law on Insolvency (discussed further in section 6);
- appealing for limitation of management powers or even dismissal of the debtor's general manager, while also exercising all powers of the general manager (during receivership); and
- receiving any necessary information related to the debtor.

4. Stages of bankruptcy proceedings

4.1 Supervision

In most cases, the first stage of bankruptcy is supervision.[7] The arbitration court initiates this stage after considering the bankruptcy application and finding it to be valid.

---

5   *Ibid*, Article 20.5.
6   *Ibid*, Article 20.4, Section 1.
7   *Ibid*, Chapter IV.

Initiation of supervision involves the following principal consequences for the debtor:

- Monetary claims and claims regarding mandatory obligations that arose during the period before the bankruptcy application was filed may be filed against the debtor only with the arbitration court administering the bankruptcy proceedings, not in the usual manner;
- Enforcement of writs of execution is suspended;
- Discharge by virtue of set-off is prohibited if this prioritises one creditor over others; and
- Payment of dividends and distribution of profit are prohibited.

The debtor's general director and management body remain in control of the debtor and continue to exercise their powers, but can undertake the following functions only with the insolvency officer's written consent:

- conclude agreements connected with the acquisition or disposal of the debtor's property amounting to more than 5% of the balance-sheet value of its assets; and
- conclude credit and/or loan agreements, agreements on the assignment of rights and/or the transfer of debts, issue guarantees and establish trusts.

During supervision, the insolvency officer must secure the debtor's property, identify the debtor's creditors, register creditors' claims, and arrange and conduct the first creditors' meeting.

One of the most important functions of the insolvency officer at this stage involves analysis of the debtor's financial standing. The insolvency officer analyses the debtor's balance sheets, profit-and-loss statements and other financial documentation. The insolvency officer then assesses whether it is possible to restore the debtor's solvency and whether the value of the debtor's property is sufficient to cover the expenses that will arise during the bankruptcy proceedings. The insolvency officer will prepare a report on the basis of this financial analysis and submit it to the first creditors' meeting for approval.

The insolvency officer will also recommend to the first creditors' meeting which bankruptcy stage it is reasonable to initiate next. The first creditors' meeting has the right to choose any of the four stages mentioned above. Once the first creditors' meeting has chosen the next stage of the bankruptcy, the insolvency officer files an application with the arbitration court to close supervision and initiate the next stage.

4.2 Financial rehabilitation

According to the Law on Insolvency, the court has the right to initiate financial rehabilitation.[8]

Financial rehabilitation is initiated only with respect to debtors whose solvency may be restored, which is why it is reasonable to do so while debtors continue to operate and generate money or other assets.

---

8   *Ibid*, Chapter V.

The parties entitled to propose initiation of financial rehabilitation to the creditors' meeting are:

- a shareholder or holder of a state enterprise's assets; or
- any third party.

The repayment schedule should include the dates on which all debts on the debtor's claims register are scheduled to be paid. The repayment schedule should be submitted to the creditors' meeting.

The shareholder or holder of a state enterprise's assets may secure the repayment schedule by pledge, guarantee or other type of security, excluding penalty, retention or deposit. However, if a third party proposes financial rehabilitation, it is obliged to secure the repayment schedule.

In general, initiation of financial rehabilitation involves the same principal consequences for the debtor as supervision.

The debtor's general director and management team remain in place and in control of the debtor, with the following limitations:

- Agreements connected with the acquisition or disposal of the debtor's property amounting to more than 5% of the balance-sheet value of the debtor's assets may be concluded only with the consent of the creditors' meeting;
- Credits, loans and guarantees may be issued and trusts may be established only with the written consent of the creditors' meeting;
- The debtor may obtain or dispose of property (other than that produced during the course of ordinary business) only with the insolvency officer's consent;
- Agreements on the assignment of rights and/or transfer of debts may be made only with the insolvency officer's consent; and
- Credits and loans may be obtained only with the insolvency officer's consent.

If the debtor repays all its debts in full conformity with the repayment schedule and no longer has any other debts, the arbitration court will terminate the bankruptcy proceedings and declare that the debtor's solvency has been restored.

If the debtor fails to meet the repayment schedule, the court may terminate the financial rehabilitation early and initiate the next stage of bankruptcy, as chosen by the creditors' meeting.

If the repayment schedule was secured and the debtor fails to repay its debts accordingly, the insolvency officer must file a claim for repayment against the party that granted the security. After this party has paid the debtor's debts, it may bring an action against the debtor in the usual manner.

4.3 External administration

The Law on Insolvency empowers the court to initiate external administration, which is also a rehabilitation procedure.[9]

External administration is initiated when the debtor's solvency can be restored.

---

9   *Ibid*, Chapter VI.

The insolvency officer must formulate an external administration plan and submit it to the creditors' meeting for approval. The plan must contain a detailed rehabilitation programme (eg, describe the actions to be performed and specify the terms and costs involved). For example, in order to restore the debtor's solvency, the insolvency officer may undertake the following measures:

- change the debtor's line of business;
- close down unprofitable business;
- collect debts receivable;
- sell the business in full or in part;
- reallocate the debtor's debt; and
- issue additional ordinary shares.

Once external administration has been initiated, the debtor is considered to be in a moratorium – that is, fulfilment of its monetary obligations and mandatory payments is suspended (apart from expenses arising during external management).

External administration involves the following principal consequences for the debtor:

- The powers of the debtor's general director and management board are revoked and the insolvency officer is put in charge of the debtor;
- A moratorium on payments comes into force; and
- Monetary claims and claims regarding mandatory obligations arising during the period before the bankruptcy application was filed may be filed against the debtor only with the arbitration court administering the bankruptcy proceedings, not in the usual manner.

The term of external administration may not exceed 24 months. In addition, the total term of financial rehabilitation and external administration may not exceed 24 months.

If external administration is effective and the debtor obtains enough funds to satisfy all claims included on its claims register, the insolvency officer will pay the debts and then terminate the bankruptcy proceedings. The debtor's solvency is considered to be restored.

If the debtor fails to pay the debts, the creditors' meeting may decide to initiate one of the two remaining stages of bankruptcy.

Financial rehabilitation and external administration are seldom used in Russia (in less than 1% of bankruptcy cases in 2010 and 2011).

The most common scenario consists of supervision followed by receivership.

4.4   Receivership

Receivership[10] is the final stage in the majority of bankruptcy proceedings in Russia. This stage is launched in relation to companies when it is obvious that their solvency cannot be restored, their business has virtually ended and creditors' claims cannot be satisfied. In this event, the arbitration court declares the debtor bankrupt and

---

10   *Ibid*, Chapter VII.

initiates receivership for a six-month period. On expiry of this term, receivership may be extended for a further six months an unlimited number of times.

The insolvency officer should publish information on the debtor's bankruptcy in the media. The debtor's creditors have two months within which to file their claims against the debtor with the arbitration court. On expiry of this term, the debtor's claims register closes; all claims filed subsequently will be paid only after all registered claims are satisfied, if any funds remain.

Receivership involves the following principal consequences for the debtor:

- The powers of the debtor's general director and management board are revoked and the insolvency officer is put in charge;
- Monetary claims and claims regarding mandatory obligations arising before the bankruptcy application was filed may be filed against the debtor only with the arbitration court administering the bankruptcy proceedings, not in the usual manner;
- All of the debtor's obligations are considered due;
- Data on the debtor's financial standing is no longer confidential; and
- Writs of execution may not be executed and should be handed over to the insolvency officer.

During receivership, the insolvency officer is required to take control of and manage the debtor's affairs. The insolvency officer must:

- verify the debtor's property and other assets and appraise their value;
- search for other property belonging to the debtor;
- collect debts receivable; and
- assess whether to make claims on the debtor's behalf for invalidation of transactions and hold controlling parties liable.

Once all of the debtor's assets have been disclosed and appraised, the creditors' meeting approves the procedure for holding a public auction to sell the debtor's property. This process should be arranged by the insolvency officer.

Proceeds received from sale of the debtor's assets should be used first to cover expenses connected with the bankruptcy proceedings (eg, court expenses, the insolvency officer's remuneration, salary of the insolvency officer's assistants, current payments). After these expenses have been covered, the insolvency officer arranges for repayment of the debtor's debts.

The Law on Insolvency establishes the following classes of payment priority:

- first class – claims by individuals relating to injury or disease, as well as non-pecuniary damages (moral harm);
- second class – former employees' salary claims; and
- third class – all other claims included on the debtor's claims register.

If the proceeds of realisation of the debtors' assets are insufficient to satisfy all claims of the same priority class, these claims will be settled *pro rata*.

After all proceeds of realisation have been distributed among the creditors, the creditors' meeting adopts a decision to close the bankruptcy proceedings and liquidate the debtor. The debtor is considered to be liquidated from the time that it is deleted from the State Companies Register.

4.5 Amicable agreement

The creditors and the debtor are entitled to conclude an 'amicable agreement' at any time.[11] The amicable agreement should contain the debt repayment procedure and terms.

In order to be effective, the amicable agreement should be approved by the arbitration court. The arbitration court will approve the amicable agreement if the debtor has paid the first and second-class priority claims. After approval of the amicable agreement, the bankruptcy proceedings against the debtor are terminated. If the debtor fails to fulfil the amicable agreement, the creditors are entitled to file claims against the debtor in relation to outstanding debts in the usual manner.

The arbitration court may terminate the amicable agreement prematurely with respect to all creditors only at the request of creditors accounting for at least one-quarter of the claims.

If the amicable agreement is terminated early, the bankruptcy proceedings are renewed from the stage at which the agreement was concluded.

5. Status of pledged creditors

From the date on which the bankruptcy proceedings commence, foreclosure on pledged property is prohibited, including extrajudicially. Creditors whose claims are secured by pledge have a specific, more privileged status in the bankruptcy proceedings than ordinary creditors.

The pledged creditor itself (not the creditors' meeting) approves the procedure for conducting an auction of the pledged property. Pledged creditors' claims are satisfied from the proceeds collected from the sale of the pledged property; specifically, 70% of the proceeds go to the pledged creditor to satisfy its claims (if the pledge secures performance of the debtor's obligations under the loan agreement, such creditor receives 80% of the proceeds). The remaining part(s) of the pledged claims should be included in the third-class priority of the debtor's claims register. The remaining portion of the proceeds collected from the sale of the pledged property is placed in the debtor's bank account and used as follows:

- Twenty percent (or 15% in the case of debt under a loan agreement) is used to pay the claims of the creditors in the first and second priority classes; and
- The remaining 10% (or 5% in the case of debt under the loan agreement) is used to pay the bankruptcy costs (eg, court fees, remuneration of trustees and third parties involved in providing services to the trustee).

6. Invalidation of transactions and liability of controlling persons

6.1 Invalidation of transactions

In general, two types of transaction (unless otherwise specified in the company

---

11   *Ibid*, Chapter VIII.

bylaws) can require preliminary approval by the board of directors and/or the shareholders' (participants) meeting:

- large-scale transactions (involving property or obligations worth more than 25% of the total asset value); and
- interested party transactions.

When the bankruptcy proceedings commence, a transaction will be deemed to be large scale if it relates to more than 5% of the total asset value (this type of transaction requires preliminary approval from the interim administrator or the creditors' meeting). The given transactions may be challenged by the company itself or its shareholders within one year of having obtained relevant information of such a transaction.

The following special types of debtor transaction challenged as voidable have recently been incorporated into the Law on Insolvency:[12]

- Suspicious transactions –
  - Undervalue – a transaction is deemed suspicious if it is effected at an undervalue during a one-year period before acceptance of the insolvency application by a court, or at any time thereafter, and provides for unequal consideration in the debtor's favour by its counterparty (eg, the transaction is not in line with comparable market conditions and prices, or the consideration provided by the debtor substantially exceeds the value received under this transaction).
  - Harm to creditors' proprietary interests – a transaction is deemed suspicious if it is effected within a three-year period ('period of suspicion') before acceptance of the insolvency application by a court, or at any time thereafter, with the intention of inflicting harm on the creditors' proprietary interests (eg, reducing the value of the debtor's property and/or increasing the amount of the debtor's obligations, resulting in the creditors' inability to settle their claims (in whole or in part) against the debtor) if a counterparty possessed actual knowledge of such intent at the time that the transaction was concluded.
- Preferential transactions –
  - Type 1 – these are transactions effected within a one-month period before acceptance of an insolvency application by a court, or at any time thereafter, which potentially result in preferential treatment for one creditor.
  - Type 2 – these are transactions effected within a six-month period before acceptance of an insolvency application by a court, which secure a creditor's existing obligations or change the priority of creditors and where the counterparty was aware of the insufficiency of the debtor's property or its insolvency (actual knowledge is presumed for an affiliated party).

---

12   *Ibid*, Chapter III.

Relevant transactions may be challenged only by the insolvency officer (external administrator or bankruptcy receiver) on his or her own initiative or by decision of the creditors' meeting. The one-year statute of limitations commences when the insolvency officer actually discovers or should have discovered indicators of a voidable transaction.

The rules for challenging transactions are expressly applied not only to deals, but to all actions and operations leading to fulfilment of obligations and duties arising in accordance with civil, labour, family, tax or customs legislation and all actions conducted in execution of a court decision, legal acts or acts of other state authorities.

Where any of the above-mentioned debtor transactions are challenged, a special type of restitution is executed in the event that a specific transaction is deemed void by the court on the grounds described above. All property (or cash compensation) returned to the debtor is included in the insolvency assets and, if returned, then:

- the creditors under suspicious transactions or Type 2 preferential transactions are granted the right to receive payments under their claims. Their claims should be settled after the claims of all the creditors included on the debtor's claims register; or
- the creditors under transactions at an undervalue or Type 1 preferential transactions are granted the right to be included on the debtor's claims register as creditors of third-class priority.

6.2 Liability of controlling persons

A certain group of persons can be held liable alongside the debtor before its creditors. All of these persons may be qualified as exerting a decisive influence on the way that the debtor carries out its activities before or after the insolvency case is initiated.

(a) Debtor's management

In the event of a breach of the Law on Insolvency, the following parties shall reimburse any damage caused by the breach:

- directors and other members of the debtor's management bodies;
- members of the debtor's liquidation commission;
- the debtor's members (shareholders); and
- the holders of property of a state enterprise's assets.

A director's failure to apply for insolvency as required by law imposes secondary liability for damage caused to the company and its creditors one month after expiry of the obligatory filing period.

A debtor's director bears secondary liability for damage caused to the company if accounting documents go missing and accounting document data as of the date of supervision enforcement is misrepresented.

(b) Controlling parties and corporate liability for a subsidiary's insolvency

A debtor's controlling party (considered to be a person issuing binding instructions to the debtor or otherwise able to determine the debtor's activities) bears secondary liability for the debtor's obligations (a debtor's controlling party should prove that it has acted reasonably and in good faith).

The debtor's controlling parties may include:

- liquidation commission members;
- representatives that have concluded transactions (on the basis of a power of attorney, special authority or legislative provisions); and
- a party holding more than 50% of the voting capital.

The damages may be reduced by a state arbitration court if it is proved that the harm caused by the instructions issued by the debtor's controlling party is substantially less than the total claims to be settled at its expense.

Insolvency proceedings may not be finalised unless the court passes a decision determining the liability of a debtor's controlling party.

Apart from the circumstances mentioned above, Russian legislation and enforcement practice provide a limited number of cases in which a person may be held liable for the insolvency of a specific entity. Such cases include premeditated insolvency (punishable under criminal and administrative law) and the insolvency of a subsidiary caused by direct instructions from its parent company (which is included in key corporate federal laws).

The legal construct of a 'shadow director', which is found in the main Anglo-Saxon jurisdictions, is absent from Russian legislation.

6.3 Administrative and criminal liability

The Administrative Code and the Criminal Code establish liability for illegal actions performed in the course of bankruptcy proceedings and/or causing insolvency.

For example, gross violations of the bankruptcy legislation – that is, fictitious bankruptcy (ie, the intentionally misleading public announcement of bankruptcy) and deliberate bankruptcy – committed by a general director, participant or shareholder of the debtor, depending on the consequences, may be punished by fine, disqualification or imprisonment for up to six years.

7. Financial rehabilitation measures

Besides financial rehabilitation, there are other 'friendly' methods for remedying a debtor's financial position, as set out in the Law on Insolvency, as well as several that are common in most western jurisdictions, but overlooked in Russia.

The Law on Insolvency includes a general provision[13] that allows the shareholders of a debtor, the holder of a state enterprise's assets or any creditor to provide the debtor with financial assistance in covering its liabilities, thus improving its financial position. This is an optional statutory provision allowing the parties to decide on the forms of and/or methods for its practical incorporation. However, legal practice states that this option has been exercised only a couple of times in the 20 years since the first Russian insolvency law was introduced.

Since the global financial crisis, foreign institutional investors have been seeking

---

13   *Ibid*, Chapter II.

standstill arrangements in relation to Russian borrowers/debtors. However, this kind of classic debt settlement is not allowed (although not explicitly prohibited) by Russian law. The main reasons for this are as follows:

- Any arrangement leading to waiver of the right to enforce one's legal rights is void; and
- Any arrangement leading to deprivation of the right to bring a claim in arbitration proceedings is void.

During 2009 and 2010 many debtors faced this problem when trying to restructure their debts in a traditional western manner. The main reason that they were unsuccessful is that Russian banks are not classic financial institutions, as in most European countries or the United States. The most powerful Russian banks either are state owned or form part of a group owned by a prominent Russian tycoon. In such circumstances, there is no need to ensure the survival of a borrower; there is merely the greedy desire to absorb it and its assets.

Therefore, two main debt-restructuring mechanisms are generally used in Russia:

- amendment of the terms and conditions of effective loans and/or payment obligations (or, alternatively, simple substitution of one loan/obligation for another); or
- a debt-to-equity swap, which has only recently been permitted by Russian corporate legislation.

Spain

Ignacio Buil
Iñigo Rubio
Jaime Ruiz Rocamora
Fedra Valencia
Cuatrecasas, Gonçalves Pereira

1. Introduction

The Insolvency Act (22/2003) regulates all material and procedural aspects of the insolvency procedure for both companies and individuals. The procedure is designed to satisfy creditors' interests and to reorganise and preserve viable companies that have become insolvent.

The act – which was last amended by Law 38/2011 – aims to convert insolvency proceedings into a fast-track mechanism to rescue viable companies, simplifying the procedure to make it faster and cheaper, and introducing new post-insolvency solutions.

Among other changes, the amended act has:

- enhanced the abbreviated procedure;
- reinforced the rules on accumulated insolvency proceedings;
- strengthened the protection of employees and eased redundancy plans;
- reduced the number of debtor trustees (from three to one, unless special circumstances apply);
- harmonised the different liability regimes during insolvency;
- strengthened distressed debt;
- eliminated the differences between early and ordinary liquidation; and
- clarified the regime of administrative expense priority claims and its order of payment.

2. Filing for insolvency

Insolvency proceedings may be initiated either by the debtor (voluntary insolvency) or by any of its creditors (mandatory insolvency). Whether proceedings are voluntary or mandatory will affect the debtor's management capacity during insolvency (ie, supervision or intervention).

Although the debtor is obliged to file a petition for a declaration of insolvency within two months of the date when it becomes aware or should have become aware of its insolvency, there is an exception to that general rule.

Pursuant to Section 5bis of the Insolvency Act – the so-called 'pre-insolvency' or Section 5bis petition – the debtor can assert that negotiations are being pursued with creditors either to enter into an out-of-court refinancing agreement or to obtain the necessary support from creditors to file a pre-pack or advanced composition agreement. In such case an extra four-month period applies. This comprises three months to reach a refinancing agreement or gather enough support from creditors, plus one month to file the petition for insolvency (in case negotiations are unsuccessful, the debtor must file a petition for insolvency once the four-month period has expired).

For a voluntary petition, the debtor must file the following documents, among others:

- a claim for insolvency;
- a special power of attorney to request insolvency proceedings;
- a report providing information on its most relevant legal and economic factual background, as well as information on the economic and legal transactions that it has carried out within the previous three years;
- a schedule of liabilities (ie, list of creditors);
- a schedule of its assets and rights;
- a list of employees and labour representatives; and
- financial information (annual accounts from the previous three years).

If a creditor petitions for a debtor's insolvency (mandatory), it must show evidence of the debtor's insolvency. Such evidence might include:

- generalised default on payments by the debtor;
- the existence of generalised seizures over the debtor's assets;
- hasty or loss-making liquidation of assets; or
- generalised default on certain tax, social security or employment obligations during the applicable statutory period (three months).

3.   Insolvency procedure

The abbreviated procedure applies where relatively small amounts are involved – that is, when the list submitted by the debtor includes fewer than 50 creditors, liabilities do not exceed €5 million and the value of assets and rights is less than €5 million. All three requirements must be met, although the insolvency judge has absolute discretion as to whether to apply the abbreviated procedure. Abbreviated procedures may also apply where a debtor files a composition agreement with creditors which includes the total transfer of all its assets and liabilities. However, abbreviated procedures must apply if the debtor files a liquidation plan together with the petition for insolvency which contemplates a binding offer to acquire the debtor's business unit, or indicates that the debtor has ceased its business activities and no employee contracts are currently in force.

Under the abbreviated procedure, common deadlines are considerably shortened (ie, the deadline for the debtor trustee to file an inventory of assets and a report including the list of creditors).

An insolvency judge may also rule for a proceeding to be conducted through the abbreviated procedure where the debtor files an early composition agreement with creditors or a composition agreement that includes the transfer of all the debtor's assets and liabilities, so that deadlines are shortened, insolvency proceedings speeded up and the value of viable components of the debtor's business is preserved.

Ordinary insolvency proceedings consist of a common phase (to determine assets and liabilities), which may be followed by a settlement/composition phase and/or a liquidation phase (if the debtor requests it, or if the settlement is not approved, is rejected by the court or is breached by the debtor).

Insolvency proceedings are triggered only if the debtor is in a state of insolvency (whether actual or imminent). Specifically, a debtor is deemed insolvent when it is regularly unable to meet its obligations as they become due (the so-called 'cash-flow test').

Pursuant to Section 2.2 of the Insolvency Act, insolvency shall be determined based on three general criteria:

- The debtor cannot meet its obligations. This inability is understood not strictly as assets minus liabilities, but more broadly, as the inability or impossibility of regularly meeting payment obligations. Consequently, it is irrelevant whether that inability is caused by an imbalanced situation where liabilities exceed assets or by the lack of liquidity of assets that exceed liabilities.
- The debtor is unable to comply regularly. Insolvency must involve an ongoing inability to comply with various obligations (ie, not a minor or isolated late payment or a single unpaid credit).
- The debtor's inability to comply regularly relates to due obligations. If the obligations are not due, there might not be an actual insolvency situation.

Pursuant to Section 3 of the act, the debtor (if a company, the board of directors or the liquidators – if the debtor started an out-of-court liquidation and filed for insolvency afterwards) and any of its creditors are exclusively entitled to file a petition for insolvency.

Pursuant to Section 5, the debtor is obliged to file a petition for insolvency within two months of the date on which it becomes aware or should have become aware of the state of insolvency. Further, Section 5.2 establishes a presumption, unless otherwise proved, that the directors became aware of the company's state of insolvency when any of the following circumstances provided for in Section 2.4 take place:

- The debtor defaults generally on its current payment obligations;
- Attachments due to pending enforcements affect the debtor's equity overall;
- The debtor removes assets or liquidates them hastily or at a loss; and/or
- There is a general breach of certain obligations (eg, non-payment of taxes due during the three months before the petition for insolvency, social security contributions, wages, indemnities or other remunerations payable due to employment relationships).

4. Effects on the debtor

As previously indicated, the effects of a declaration of insolvency on the debtor generally depend on whether insolvency is filed voluntarily and/or declared mandatorily.

If the insolvency is voluntary, the debtor usually retains the power to manage and dispose of its business, albeit under the supervision of the debtor trustee. All actions carried out by the debtor in breach of the required supervision of the debtor trustee may be declared null and void.

Where the insolvency is mandatory, the debtor is removed from office (suspension) and assets are managed by the debtor trustee.

Notwithstanding this, the regime of supervision or intervention of the debtor trustee may be modified by the insolvency judge at any time.

As a precautionary measure, where the debtor is a company and insolvency proceedings have been declared, the insolvency judge may grant injunctive relief over the assets and liabilities of its directors (*de jure* or *de facto*), or liquidators and attorneys with general powers (including all who have held these positions in the preceding two years) when there are sufficient grounds to believe that any of these parties might be obliged to cover the insolvency deficit arising out of the proceedings. Such injunctive measures serve to secure the eventual personal liability of directors, imposing liability on them to assume and pay part or all of the insolvency debt remaining after the debtor is liquidated.

5.   Insolvency judge and debtor trustee

The insolvency procedure is conducted by the commercial court with jurisdiction (ie, the court in the jurisdiction where the debtor has its centre of main interests). For companies, a legal presumption arises that this is the debtor's registered office; attempts to move the debtor's registered office within the six months preceding the declaration of insolvency are deemed to be null and void and managed by a debtor trustee (an attorney, auditor or economist with expertise in insolvency – no specific qualifications apply, although debtor trustees should generally have at least five years' expertise in insolvency and a postgraduate or relevant qualification in insolvency).

The insolvency judge has sole and exclusive jurisdiction in specific matters, in particular over:

- matters of civil jurisdiction affecting the debtor's assets;
- actions to amend, terminate or collectively suspend employment agreements and suspend or terminate senior management agreements;
- liability actions against directors, liquidators and auditors; and
- generally, all executory and injunctive relief that affects the debtor's assets.

In broad terms, the debtor trustee shall fulfil the debtor's capacity (if the debtor is under an intervention regime – for example, by expressly authorising any acts carried out by it which may affect its estate) or run its business (if the debtor is under a suspension or substitution regime). In addition, it will draft the debtor trustee report, which must be accompanied by:

- an inventory of assets;
- a list of creditors; and
- as necessary, the assessment of any proposals for composition/ liquidation.

Pursuant to Section 48*bis* of the Insolvency Act, which was introduced by the amendments, the debtor trustee is exclusively empowered to bring corporate liability actions during insolvency proceedings.

The debtor trustee's fees are calculated on the basis of specific criteria described in

Royal Decree 1860/2004 (applying a different percentage, which ranges from between 0.6% and 0.003% of the debtor's net assets and liabilities, disregarding equity).

6. Effects on creditors

Creditors have a duty to file their claims in a timely manner. Indeed, creditors shall communicate to the debtor trustee (either in writing or electronically) their identification details and the origin, amount, nature, acquisition and due dates of the debt owed by the debtor, plus the requested classification, within one month of the day following publication of the declaration of insolvency in the Spanish *Official Journal*.

Where the claim communicating the debt is given late, the claim may, in certain circumstances, be classified as subordinated debt (ie, junior to all other classes of claim). All creditors shall be classified as privileged, ordinary or subordinated. Privileged are senior to ordinary, which in turn are senior to subordinated.

Creditors' ranking determines not only the order of payment, but eventually their mandatory subjection to a composition agreement with creditors. Specifically, privileged creditors are bound by a composition agreement only if they accept it voluntarily, and then only insofar as it concerns the write-off and/or grace period agreed, without losing their right to preferential payment.

There is a special and prioritised category of debts – so-called 'administrative expense priority claims'. These are debts that arise after the declaration of insolvency (eg, expenses generated by the procedure itself). These expenses are not subject to ranking and shall be paid as they fall due. The debtor trustee may alter the order of payment for expenses if this is in the best interests of the insolvency proceedings, where there are sufficient assets to cover them all and the reordering does not affect employee, public tax and social security claims.

Privileged debts can have a special or general privilege, depending on whether the security is created over a specific asset (special privilege) or over all of the debtor's assets (general privilege). Special privilege debts generally include those in which collateral consists of specific property or rights (eg, mortgages or pledges) or equivalent rights (eg, a financial lease agreement for the leased property).

Debts with general privilege consist of:

- debts relating to salaries (subject to a limit) and indemnities for termination of employment agreements, and occupational health and safety claims, provided that these were incurred before the insolvency;
- tax and social security withholdings;
- debts for individual work by independent contractors and those corresponding to authors for the assignment of licensing rights over intellectual property accrued during the six months before the declaration of insolvency;
- tax debts, other debts of public entities and social security debts – up to 50% of their value;
- debts arising from tort liability;
- 50% of debts involving cash injections that have been granted as part of a refinancing agreement; and

- 50% of debts held by the creditor requesting a mandatory declaration of insolvency.

Subordinated debts include those where notice is given late, contractual covenants, surcharges and/or interest (except those with *in rem* guarantees), penalties, fines and those held by related parties to the debtor, or parties that have executed bad-faith actions that are detrimental to the insolvency proceedings or that obstruct the regular process of such proceedings.

Where the debtor is a company, a related party may:
- be any partner with unlimited personal liability for corporate debts;
- hold a significant stake in the debtor's share capital at the time the debt is created (at least 5% if the company has securities admitted to trading on an official secondary market and 10% if the company does not have securities or other instruments admitted to trading);
- be a *de facto* or registered administrator or receiver; or
- be a company belonging to the debtor's group and its common shareholders (if they fulfil requirements provided in the second point above).

The declaration of insolvency also has the following effects on debts:
- Interest – the declaration suspends the accrual of interest on debts, whether legal or contractual, except those corresponding to debts with *in rem* guarantees, which will continue accruing up to the amount of the guarantee. Although the accrual of interest is a controversial issue among commercial courts, most regional courts (hierarchically superior to commercial courts) indicate that pursuant to Section 59.1 of the Insolvency Act, the continued accrual of interest corresponding to privileged credits (with *in rem* guarantees) affects only remuneration interests, according to the interest rate agreed between the parties, but not moratorium interests.[1] Notwithstanding this, recent rulings stipulate that privileged claims enjoy special treatment within insolvency proceedings, similar to that regarding separate enforcement, and thus accrual of remuneration interest shall continue once the insolvency is declared and, where the facilities agreement is terminated and the credit falls due, moratorium interest shall also continue accruing. Remuneration and moratorium interest shall not accrue contemporaneously, but both are covered by the guarantee and shall be classified as part of the privileged credit up to the amount of the guarantee.[2]
- Offset – the debtor's credits and debts before the declaration cannot be offset against the debts and credits entered into afterwards. Offset is possible only where the legislation governing the main obligation, other than Spanish law, allows it.
- Guarantees – creditors holding joint additional guarantees granted by third

---

[1] Among others, rulings from the Salamanca Regional Court, November 25 2008, JUR 2009/104066; and the Zaragoza Regional Court, December 4 2008, JUR 2009/144439.

[2] Among others, the Cordoba Regional Court, February 16 2009, JUR 2009/323048; and the Madrid Commercial Court 6, September 30 2010, JUR 2011/37196.

parties that have not voted in favour of a composition agreement with creditors are not affected by the agreement in their right to claim against the guarantor, which means that they may claim 100% of their debt from the guarantor.

- Foreclosure of *in rem* guarantees – actions involving the enforcement of assets belonging to the debtor's estate, including mortgages and pledges, will be suspended until a settlement is approved, liquidation has commenced or one year has elapsed from the date of the declaration of insolvency (except if the insolvency judge rules that certain assets are not necessary for the debtor to run its business or a given production unit).

7.   Effects on contracts

Pursuant to Section 61.3 of the Insolvency Act, all clauses that entitle a party to terminate an agreement based solely on the other party's declaration of insolvency are deemed void (although it is still usual practice to use so-called '*ipso facto*' clauses), with a few exceptions (ie, agency contracts).

As a general rule, the declaration of insolvency does not affect executory contracts – that is, agreements with reciprocal obligations where either the debtor or the other party has not yet performed its obligations.

However, the debtor trustee may request that the insolvency judge terminate a contract on grounds of convenience for the insolvency proceedings and for the best interests of creditors.

8.   Composition agreement with creditors/settlement phase

The Insolvency Act encourages creditors to settle on a composition agreement. This may be proposed either by the debtor or by creditors (depending on the stage of insolvency proceedings), and sets forth how and when creditors are to be paid. Once executed, these agreements must be honoured by the debtor and respected by all creditors.

From the filing of the petition for insolvency until the creditors' deadline to communicate debts elapses, the debtor is exclusively entitled to file a proposal for an anticipated composition agreement. This must be presented with the support of creditors whose aggregate claims represent over one-fifth of the liabilities declared by the debtor at the start of the proceedings (or one-tenth if the proposal is filed together with the insolvency petition). Once the proposal is filed, the debtor must seek the support of the remaining creditors in order to obtain the necessary support to approve the proposal: half of the unsecured or ordinary claims, including those secured creditors that specifically supported the composition. If the support is insufficient, the debtor may maintain the proposal for composition during the settlement phase or apply for liquidation. However, no amendment to the initial composition proposal can be performed by the debtor.

A proposal for an anticipated composition agreement may be beneficial for the debtor:

- in terms of time, as it may be submitted along with the petition for voluntary insolvency or before conclusion of the term for giving notice of debts, allowing for it to be accepted before the settlement phase, and may be approved by the court upon conclusion of the common phase; and

- in terms of content, as if the proposed settlement requires a write-off or grace period in excess of that allowed by law, the court may allow these limits to be exceeded. However, the proposal must be submitted with the prior support of at least 10% or 20% of the total debt, depending on the timing of its filing, and may be submitted only by diligent debtors (ie, not those affected by legal prohibitions).

From the expiration of the creditors' deadline to communicate debts until the expiration of the deadline to file objections to the debtor trustee report (or, if objections are filed, up to the date when the final report is filed), the debtor and/or creditors whose claims represent at least one-fifth of the total claims listed on the final creditors' list (which is included in the debtor trustee report) may submit proposals for a composition agreement.

Finally, the debtor and creditors whose claims represent at least one-fifth of the total claims listed on the final creditors' list may also propose a composition agreement from the date that the creditors' meeting is called until 40 days before the date scheduled for the meeting of creditors (in the event that no proposal for an anticipated composition agreement has been filed and liquidation has not been requested).

As noted above, composition agreements should contain proposals for a write-off, grace period and payment schedule. With regard to ordinary credits, the write-off may not exceed 50% and the grace period may not exceed five years.

It may also contain alternative proposals for all or any of the creditors, including conversion of the debt into shares or into profit-sharing debts. It may also include proposals for the allocation of all assets or certain assets to a specific person, with a commitment from the acquirer to continue the activity and to pay off the debt as set out in the composition agreement.

The agreement must be approved by creditors representing at least one-half of the insolvent debtor's ordinary debts. If the agreement proposes payment in full of ordinary claims within a maximum term of three years or a write-off of less than 20%, the favourable vote of a simple majority will suffice (privileged creditors voting in favour of the settlement will be also counted).

The holders of subordinated debts and creditors that are not financial entities subject to supervision which have acquired their debts by means of *inter vivos* transactions subsequent to the declaration of insolvency are not entitled to vote.

9. Liquidation

Liquidation is an alternative outcome to the insolvency procedure. It takes place where no composition is reached or when it is decided upon by the debtor. The latter is also obliged to file a petition for liquidation if, during the period when the effects of the settlement are still in force, it becomes aware that it will be unable to meet the payment commitments and obligations undertaken after it was approved.

If this is the case, the debtor trustee must prepare a liquidation plan that is then approved by the court considering the aim of the Insolvency Act, which is to preserve companies or production units through their allocation as a single business unit, unless it is in the best interests of the proceedings to divide them up or sell some or all of the elements separately. Preference is given to alternatives that allow the business to continue.

If the debtor is a company, its dissolution will be declared, as well as the lay-off of its directors and liquidators (the debtor trustee will usually act as the liquidator and will be obliged to report quarterly on this).

The main effect of liquidation is that deferred compulsory debts fall due and debts consisting of other benefits are converted into cash debts.

The amended Insolvency Act updated certain sections on liquidation, eliminating the former Section 142*bis* (which governed the proposal for an early liquidation). Pursuant to the new Section 142, the debtor may request liquidation at any time during insolvency proceedings.

As previously mentioned, pursuant to Section 190.3, the insolvency judge must apply the rules governing the abbreviated insolvency proceedings if the debtor files a liquidation proposal together with the petition for insolvency. The proposal must include a binding purchase offer over the debtor's business unit in writing from a third party. Further, a liquidation proposal may also be filed where the debtor can show, and the insolvency judge confirms that its business has ceased and no employee contracts are in force.

As previously indicated, deadlines are shortened in abbreviated proceedings, even more so when a liquidation proposal is filed together with the petition for insolvency. Under this new regime, the possibility of selling part of the business as a going concern becomes more realistic, considering the usual length of insolvency proceedings and the loss of value of the assets during the process.

If the insolvency judge approves the liquidation proposal, he or she can also approve the resolution of all contracts where both parties are yet to perform their respective obligations, except those that may affect the binding offer in writing to purchase the debtor's business submitted along with the insolvency petition.

The Insolvency Act grants a greater degree of discretion regarding the rules and content of liquidation plans than those that apply to composition agreements.

However, although the liquidation plan can be adapted to maximise the value of the estate and to provide maximum recovery for creditors, the overriding principle is to preserve companies or business units as single business units, except where it is in the best interests of the insolvency proceedings to divide them up or sell some or all of the business elements separately, with preference given to alternatives that would allow for the continuity of the debtor's business and that would maintain as many jobs as possible.

10.   Claw-back period

During insolvency proceedings, it is possible to challenge only those actions deemed detrimental to the debtor's assets that took place before the declaration of insolvency. Such challenges should be made in the following terms:

- Actions carried out in the two years preceding the declaration of insolvency may be rescinded, even in the absence of fraudulent intent.

- The actions must be 'to the detriment of assets', which is presumed:
  - without admission of evidence to the contrary, for acts of disposal for no consideration or payments or other acts cancelling obligations with a due date after the declaration of insolvency (except those having an *in rem* guarantee); and
  - with admission of evidence to the contrary, for acts of disposal for valuable consideration carried out in favour of any related party, the granting of security covering pre-existing debts or new debts incurred to cancel pre-existing debts, or payments or other actions cancelling obligations that are secured by an *in rem* guarantee and with a due date after the declaration of insolvency.
- Otherwise, the damage must be proved by the person seeking rescission.
- Under no circumstances can actions carried out in the debtor's ordinary course of business and under general and acceptable market conditions be challenged.
- Certain refinancing agreements – as well as any transactions, acts, payments and guarantees entered into pursuant to such agreements – will not be subject to rescission, provided that:
  - the agreement has been entered into with creditors whose debts represent at least three-fifths of the debtor's liabilities as of the date of the agreement;
  - it is accompanied by a report submitted by an independent expert appointed by the commercial registry of the place where the debtor has its registered office, confirming the sufficiency of the information provided by the debtor, the reasonableness of the viability plan and the proportionality of the guarantees undertaken in keeping with market conditions; and
  - the refinancing agreement and the documents substantiating performance of the previous two conditions are executed before a notary and in a notarised public deed.
- Good-faith third-party acquirers of the debtor's assets will enjoy the protection and immunity provided by the registry regulations.

Where rescission occurs, both parties must return or exchange the asset or service provided (if possible) and the price or consideration paid for it. If, pursuant to that return, the debtor owes a debt, this shall be deemed a claim with administrative expense priority. In the event that bad faith on the part of the creditor is presumed, its debt shall be considered subordinated.

11. Classification of insolvency proceedings

Qualification is an optional process within insolvency proceedings. It allows for the imposition of civil liability on directors who have contributed to the negligent or culpable creation or aggravation of the situation which led to the initiation of insolvency proceedings. The effects are strictly civil and are not binding for the purposes of criminal jurisdiction.

The qualification process is not mandatory and depends upon the final outcome of the insolvency proceedings:

- Where the debtor ends up in liquidation, insolvency proceedings must be qualified when the liquidation phase is declared open.
- Where a composition agreement with creditors is reached, insolvency shall be classified only if the composition agreement is particularly onerous. In particular, qualification will proceed when write-off exceeds one-third of the amount of debts or when a grace period of more than three years is agreed for all creditors. In cases where the composition agreement is not particularly onerous, qualification will not start unless the composition is breached.

The aim of the rules governing commencement of the qualification process is to encourage directors of insolvent companies to petition for insolvency proceedings while there is still a reasonable possibility of paying off creditors. Insolvency proceedings may be qualified as fortuitous (non-liable) or culpable (liable).

Pursuant to the Insolvency Act, three elements are required to qualify insolvency proceedings as culpable:

- There was wilful misconduct or gross negligence on the part of the formal or *de facto* directors, or any person who had that status in the two years before the declaration of insolvency;
- The insolvency situation was created or aggravated; and
- There is a causal link between the first and second points.

The act stipulates certain assumptions upon which insolvency proceedings will be automatically (no evidence to the contrary is admitted) or eventually (evidence to the contrary admitted) qualified as culpable.

11.1 Non-rebuttable presumptions

The following circumstances constitute non-rebuttable presumptions:

- a material breach of accounting duties, keeping two sets of books or substantial irregularities in accounts;
- falsity or serious inaccuracy in any of the documents submitted with the insolvency petition or presented during the proceedings;
- the *ex officio* commencement of liquidation due to breach of the composition agreement, attributable to the insolvent party;
- the removal of some or all assets, which damages the creditors, or the delay or obstruction to the effectiveness of the attachment of any enforcement that has been commenced or is likely to be commenced;
- the fraudulent removal of assets or rights from the debtor's estate during the two years before the declaration of insolvency; and
- the carrying out of any legal transaction simulating a fictitious positive-equity balanced situation, before the declaration of insolvency.

11.2 Rebuttable presumptions

Likewise, the rebuttable presumptions consist of wilful misconduct or gross negligence that aggravates the insolvency situation, unless proved otherwise, by breaching any of the following duties imposed by the Insolvency Act:

- the duty to file a petition for insolvency in due time;
- the duty to cooperate with the insolvency judge and the debtor trustee to supply the necessary information and/or documentation to carry out insolvency proceedings, and to attend (whether in person or through an attorney) the creditors' meeting; and
- the duty to draft annual accounts, submit them for audit (if necessary) and, once approved, deliver them to the commercial registry in the three years before the declaration of insolvency.

The ruling that qualifies insolvency proceedings as culpable gives rise to important effects for both directors and persons (potentially) affected by the qualification. The ruling must specify the reasons for the culpable qualification, the identity of the affected directors and its effects.

The first effect for directors is a ban from:

- administrating assets for between two and 15 years;
- acting on behalf of or being empowered by any person for the same term;
- operating any business activity; and
- holding a stake in any trading company.

Directors of an entity affected by such a ban are dismissed automatically from office. If their dismissal hinders the functioning of the governing body, the debtor trustee might call a general shareholders' meeting to appoint replacement officers.

In the scenario of a composition agreement, the qualification ruling might, as an exception, authorise a banned director to remain in control of the business or as director of the debtor if the debtor trustee so requests.

The second effect for directors is the loss of any rights that they might hold as creditors in the insolvency proceedings or against the insolvency estate, and the return of any assets or rights that they may have obtained unduly from the debtor's assets or received from the insolvency estate, as well as the obligation to provide indemnity for the damage caused.

Pursuant to the amended Insolvency Act, where the qualification procedure has been started or reopened due to the start of the liquidation phase, the insolvency judge may order all or some of the directors or liquidators – whether formal or *de facto* – or those with general powers of attorney for the debtor who have been declared affected by the qualification to cover all or part of the debtor's deficit.

Where several persons have been found culpable, the insolvency judge shall specify the amount to be paid by each person affected, in accordance with their contribution to the culpable acts.

This third effect is also known as the 'liability insolvency action', through which the legislature has offered creditors the directors' assets (as a further guarantee in addition to the debtor's assets) to ensure that, under certain circumstances, those assets will be used to pay the amount of their debts not covered by the liquidation of the estate.

Pursuant to the Insolvency Act, three circumstances must be met for the liability insolvency action to apply:

- The qualification procedure must have started due to the liquidation phase being started or reopened. This means that an order for payment cannot be given if the insolvency ends with a composition agreement, even if the qualification procedure has begun and the insolvency is found to be culpable. However, an order for payment may be given if the composition agreement is subsequently breached, as this would lead to the start of liquidation and the reopening of the qualification procedure.

- The insolvency must have been qualified as culpable (ie, where the situation of insolvency has been caused or aggravated by wilful misconduct or gross negligence by the company's formal or *de facto* directors, as described above, including, as potentially liable parties, directors that held that office during the two years before the date of the declaration of insolvency).
- The insolvency estate's inability to pay the debts held by creditors must have been substantiated.

In these circumstances, the court may order all or some of the directors to be declared affected by the qualification to cover all or part of the debtor's deficit (ie, assets minus liabilities). The legislature drafted the provision concerning the court ruling with a wide margin of discretion regarding not only the order itself, but also the amount of the order, which may cover all or part of the amount of the debts.

If several people are affected by the qualification, the ruling shall specify the amount payable by each director, depending on his or her contribution to the acts that resulted in the insolvency being qualified as culpable. This is an interesting and practical aspect relating to the defence of directors, because it may avoid the joint (and insufficiently reasoned) orders for payment often found in some rulings.

Otherwise, the reforms fail to resolve the controversial question of whether the qualification procedure is designed to repair the damages caused or to punish certain conduct by the debtor's directors. However, they do resolve the issue of the beneficiary of such liability, by providing that all amounts obtained by enforcing the qualification ruling will be added to the insolvency estate.

12. *De facto* directors

The legal concept of a '*de facto* director' is not defined in the rules on corporations, the Insolvency Act or any other laws. According to the prevailing doctrine, the definition might include:

- directors whose appointment has elapsed;
- directors whose appointment is in force, but null (ie, because it contravenes some legal provision);
- those who appear as directors before third parties and who control the management and the administration of a company, despite not having been formally appointed to that role; and
- those who do not appear as directors before third parties, but who actually control the management and administration of a company by exercising a decisive influence upon the actual directors (ie, hidden or indirect directors).

Notwithstanding the above, the concept of a *de facto* director is well rooted in the

Spanish legal system and is commonly treated in civil cases, although most precedents correspond to first instance civil courts and there are relatively few precedents within insolvency case law.

The liability of a *de facto* director depends on verification that he or she has systematically interfered in the disposition and management of the debtor in such a way as to distort the company's usual corporate governance.

This should not be confused with the normal influence that a majority or controlling shareholder may exercise within its legitimate rights (non-*de facto* directors). Such influence is usually less penetrating than that exercised by a *de facto* director. Joint management is commonly exercised in cases of flexible corporate governance, so that the financial and managerial autonomy of the subsidiaries is respected. Therefore, the figure of a *de facto* director applies solely to clear cases where the dominant or controlling shareholder regularly interferes with the company's management.

In conclusion, *de facto* directors are those who systematically and permanently give express and binding instructions (ie, not mere opinions, recommendations or general criteria about the management of the whole group) to the debtor's own directors. These instructions are not only binding, they also impede the directors' autonomous exercise of their duties of loyal and diligent management, as well as giving proper attention to the debtor's corporate interest.

13. Refinancing agreements: substantive regulation and court sanction

The Insolvency Act offers legal protection from claw-back to certain refinancing agreements, as described above.

Additionally – and in connection with agreements that meet such requirements and that are entered into by creditors representing at least 75% of the liabilities held by financial institutions at the time of the agreement – the act allows the debtor to seek the approval of the refinancing agreement from the insolvency judge (scheme of arrangement) pursuant to which the term of the moratorium agreed in the refinancing agreement will be extended to financial creditors if:

- their claims are not secured with their *in rem* security, such as pledges or mortgages (in which case its contractual position is not affected by this sanction); and
- the agreement does not represent a "disproportionate sacrifice" for dissident financial entities. In the same petition, the debtor may request the stay for up to three years of all enforcement actions that the creditor financial entities could initiate during this period.

The reform also imposes time limits for court permissions for refinancing agreements, so a debtor cannot request this more than once a year.

If the financing agreement is breached, it will be necessary to obtain a judicial declaration of this from the court that originally approved the agreement. This must be obtained before any enforcement actions can be initiated or the debtor's mandatory bankruptcy can be petitioned. The decision declaring that a breach has taken place cannot be appealed.

The Insolvency Act further promotes out-of-court restructuring by introducing the privilege granted to fresh money provided through the ring-fenced restructuring framework. Thus, it prioritises the claims of entities that were party to refinancing agreements meeting the requirements of Section 71.6, resulting from cash injections made available to the debtor through those agreements, so that:

- 50% of the pre-petition claim will be allowed as an administrative expense (with a super-priority over any other pre-petition claim); and
- 50% will be allowed as a general secured claim (junior to administrative expenses and *in rem* securities, but senior to general ordinary unsecured creditors).

However, the 'fresh money' classification does not apply when cash injections were made available by the debtor or by a related party (former Section 93 of the act), through a share capital increase transaction, credit facilities or acts or transactions with similar purposes.

To improve the financing of financially distressed companies, the Insolvency Act provides that in the event of liquidation, post-petition claims resulting from a composition agreement will be treated as an administrative expense, with a super-priority over any other pre-petition claim. This is expected to promote exit financings within in-court reorganisation proceedings.

Workouts of structured vehicles

Phil Bowers
David Soden
Ian Wormleighton
Deloitte LLP

1. Introduction

Without the 2007 credit crunch, it is unlikely that structured investment vehicles (SIVs), commercial mortgage-backed securities (CMBS) and collateralised loan obligations (CLOs) would have made it out of a backwater within specialised structured finance into mainstream insolvency and restructuring.

However, with the rise – and, more importantly, the fall – of sub-prime asset-backed securities and the resultant collapse of the commercial paper market, structured finance enforcements and restructurings have become a fixture in the United Kingdom, Europe and the United States.

Since this chapter was originally drafted in 2009, the financial world has been through a prolonged period of extreme distress. It is apparent now that SIV failures were just the tip of the iceberg – an early indicator of the global financial crisis that was to follow.

While SIV restructurings are now largely complete, lessons remain to be learned and significant volumes of assets, in particular real estate assets and leveraged loans, continue to be held in structured vehicles. As asset prices have declined or assets have not performed at forecast levels, those vehicles have come under pressure to restructure. This chapter considers some of the key issues that these vehicles and their stakeholders have faced in the current environment, particularly as regards CMBS structures.

Before looking in more detail at a SIV restructuring, it is worth briefly explaining some of the acronyms used and recapping on the build-up and key events that resulted in the 2007 global credit crisis, the effects of which continue to be felt.

Table 1: Key terminology

ABS	Asset-backed security
Administrator	Administration, often outsourced to an independent party, involves providing statements to investors and all documentation associated with new investors.

continued overleaf

CDO	Collateralised debt obligation
CLO	Collateralised loan obligation
CMBS	Commercial mortgage-backed security
CP	Commercial paper
Custodian	Bank, agent or other party responsible for safeguarding the financial assets. Role involves safekeeping assets and collecting/providing information on underlying securities
Investment manager	Responsible for investing in bonds (predominantly ABS by an SIV) to meet specified investment goals for the benefit of investors
MBS	Mortgage-backed security
MTN	Medium-term note
NAV	Net asset value
Repo	Repurchase agreement or buyback
RMBS	Residential mortgage-backed security
Security trustee	Holds title to the ABS. There are relatively few institutions offering trustee services
SIV	Structured investment vehicle
Synthetic	A financial instrument that is created artificially by simulating another instrument with the combined features of a collection of other assets
SIV-lite	Combines aspects of CDO and SIV
SPV	Special purpose vehicle

2. Snapshot picture

- The period from 2002 to 2007 was dominated by significant growth in the structured finance market and in particular sub-prime RMBS and CMBS, which had grown thanks to a combination of low interest rates, a relaxation of lending standards and a strong appetite for stable yield in the worldwide investment market – be that from residential and commercial property, student loans, auto loans and so forth. These loans were packaged up into groups and sold through securitisation vehicles.

- There were then steep rises in US interest rates, combined with an end to low 'teaser' rates and a continued fall in US house prices. This was the starting point for a global meltdown, giving rise to dramatic increases in foreclosures and ultimately the failure of Fannie Mae and Freddie Mac, and the bailout of AIG, among others. The loans most at risk were those originated specifically to provide collateral for a structured vehicle, typically in the sub-prime category.

- Similarly, in the leveraged loan market, the rescue facilities put in place by the central banks, the ability to repo significant leveraged loan holdings to the central banks if appropriately structured and the subsequent failure of Lehman, led to the European Central Bank being the holder of a significant volume of distressed CLO paper.

- In the CMBS market, no stress tests in place at the time of issuance envisaged a property market that would decline by 40% combined with the illiquidity of markets. While many of the early CMBS deals concentrated on prime real estate assets, later deals included secondary and tertiary property which exacerbated the problem.

- The uncertainty of where losses would ultimately crystallise spread panic through the banking community and prompted financial institutions to stockpile cash and reserves. This led to global credit markets becoming illiquid and in particular the CP market, which was critical to the ability of structured finance vehicles, and SIVs in particular, to continue to redeem senior liabilities.

- At the same time, the 'mark-to-market' values of the underlying assets plummeted, leading to reduced net asset values triggering enforcement and insolvency provisions within a number of SIVs. The subsequent failure of the SIV model was then inevitable and six vehicles (Cheyne Finance plc, Rhinebridge plc, Whistlejacket Capital Limited, Golden Key Limited, Mainsail II Limited and Sigma Finance Corporation) ultimately entered a UK receivership process.

In late 2007 and the first half of 2008 a number of SIVs went through restructuring processes. This chapter explores the background and key issues of these SIV restructurings, with a particular focus on the practical points. It excludes those bank-backed SIVs that were subsequently taken back 'on balance sheet' by the respective sponsor bank. We then consider the implications of the SIV restructurings and subsequent developments in the structured finance restructuring marketplace.

3.   SIVs

3.1   What are SIVs?
SIVs were funds designed to profit from borrowing 'cheaply', issuing highly rated short-term debt and investing those funds in longer-term, higher-interest bearing 'high grade' assets. At their peak, total assets held by the 29 SIVs were some $400

billion, with the largest single SIV holding in excess of $50 billion in investments.

A typical SIV will be launched by a financial institution that also usually invests in the most junior or capital notes. It may also contract with the SIV to provide liquidity; otherwise there is often little or no continuing nexus to the original sponsor.

The vehicles themselves are structured as bankruptcy-remote SPVs, have limited recourse provisions throughout the structure and are usually registered in tax-efficient jurisdictions. They are generally governed by English or New York law, although jurisdiction can vary even within the legal documentation of a single SIV.

The SIV will issue multiple tranches of debt including junior, mezzanine and senior capital notes, all of which are subordinated to the equally ranking short-term (three to six month) and medium-term (six to 13 month) senior debt, otherwise known as CP and MTN. Gearing (as between the junior and senior debt) is high, usually in the region of 10 to 15 times. Unlike many structured finance models including CMBS and CLOs, SIVs are open ended, intending to stay in business indefinitely by replacing maturing assets with new assets and continually refinancing the CP and MTN as they fall due.

On the asset side, an investment manager will be permitted to invest only in high grade assets (AAA or AA), and investments are typically a combination of bank debt or structured finance securities including RMBS, CDOs, CLOs, CMBS, student/auto loans or other ABS, with some being insured or 'wrapped' by monoline insurers.

3.2 Key stakeholders

There are numerous stakeholders, including:

- sponsor banks;
- senior noteholder and capital noteholder investors;
- liquidity providers;
- derivative and repo counterparties;
- rating agencies;
- an administrator (to perform day-to-day valuations, covenant tests and rating agency reports);
- a security trustee;
- an investment manager;
- corporate service providers; and
- directors.

All are bound by detailed legal documentation that sets out how the SIV and certain of the stakeholders are to operate in its various operating states.

Investors include financial institutions, money market funds, government bodies, corporate treasurers and others with substantial cash to invest.

The rating agencies were crucial to the successful launch and ongoing operations of the SIVs. Without AAA ratings for their senior debt and high ratings for their mezzanine and even junior notes, SIVs could not obtain sufficiently cheap financing to make the model viable. In return for their high ratings, the agencies imposed certain conditions and covenants, including the NAV test (ie, the amount by which the market value of assets exceeds the senior debt, divided by the capital). This test has been a key factor in the difficulties faced by SIVs, as it has primarily been this trigger that has caused SIVs to move through the operating states to enforcement.

There are broadly four SIV states – each one indicating that the vehicle is facing additional risk factors and therefore restricts what the SIV can do. These operating states are:

- normal;
- restricted investment;
- restricted funding; and
- enforcement.

In addition, certain enforcement events may lead to an insolvency acceleration event.

A number of SIVs reached both enforcement and insolvency acceleration events. The remainder of this chapter looks at how these SIVs are restructured, with the main focus on the English law SIVs and some remarks on New York law SIVs.

3.3 English law SIV restructuring

(a) Summary restructuring framework

Following the appointment of receivers by the security trustees on the six SIVs detailed above, an English law receivership sale was used to provide a framework restructuring process for these vehicles.

Figure 1: Overall steps taken for English law SIV restructurings.

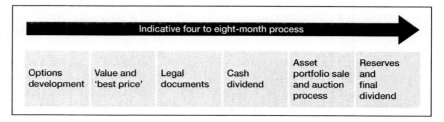

The restructuring process can be split into a number of steps:

- value and 'best price';
- options development;
- cash dividend;
- asset portfolio sale and auction process; and
- reserves and final dividend.

Each of the above steps has its own complexities, which are discussed in more detail below.

(b) Value and 'best price'

All of the English law SIVs included a combination of cash (eg, 10%) and anywhere between 60 to 400 structured finance securities (the portfolio assets) – the individual securities may have been at a notional value of between, say, $5 million and $100 million.

A key issue for any receiver is gaining comfort that the portfolio assets are being sold at the best price reasonably obtainable in the circumstances. Under a normal operating state, the assets would be valued on a mark-to-market basis using a methodology set out in the investment manager's compliance documentation. Under normal liquid market conditions, these 'marks' would be close to what would likely be received from a firm market bid for particular assets. However, following the dislocation and lack of liquidity in the markets, actual market bids on the assets were generally significantly lower than those provided by the marks.

In order to gain sufficient comfort on value, English receivers considered both the best method of sale and the timing of such sale. In terms of method of sale, an auction process of a *pro rata* share of all assets (a 'vertical strip') was adopted, whereby a number of alternative bidders were provided with an opportunity to bid on the vertical strip on a certain day; this was also used in some cases as a price to reference the whole portfolio asset sale. To ensure that the receiver had control over timing, mechanisms were also in place to halt the auction at the last minute if, for example, there was particular market disruption on that day. As is typically the case, clarity around the process and certainty of execution was a fundamental element of achieving the best price in challenging circumstances.

Options for stakeholders: During any restructuring process, clear lines of communication with all stakeholders is critical – subject to ensuring that confidentiality undertakings exist where such stakeholders are to receive non-public information. The most important communications are with informal, *ad hoc* senior creditors' committees and, where applicable, junior creditors' committees. These can include a high percentage of senior and junior creditor claims, and act as sounding boards for the receiver to provide robust input and direction in respect of key aspects, such as options formulation.

A key part within the restructuring is the provision of options to cater for the differing objectives of the respective investors. A precursor to such options is understanding where value 'breaks' and ensuring that subordinated creditors have at least some option to take out the senior creditors, by way of either a 'whole book' junior creditor solution or a part-vertical strip offer at a price that provides par to the senior investors.

A further new element of SIV restructuring was the introduction of new investors, unfamiliar to workout situations, to the table. This included pension funds, municipalities, government authorities and other parties that had invested in a SIV as 'risk free' investments with a higher yield than similarly rated options. Accordingly, there were divergent views among the senior creditors as to the objective of any restructuring, and in the absence of any consensus the receivers had to offer a wide range of options. These included:

- the ability to obtain cash following a sale of the assets ('cash out'), whereby the investor receives a cash dividend against its claim and leaves behind a stub claim for the outstanding amount;
- the ability either to obtain cash and then use it to reinvest in a zero coupon note (ZCN) or to elect to exchange the old SIV note for a ZCN, such that the ZCN pays par to the investor at a future date;
- the ability to exchange the old SIV note entitlement to subscribe for a pass-through note (PTN) in a Newco vehicle, which has purchased the remaining portfolio assets and continues to have exposure to the portfolio assets; and
- for those taking a PTN, the option immediately to convert that interest into a distribution of their *pro rata* strip of the portfolio assets in specie or some other option to be implemented at the Newco level during the months after the portfolio asset sale and after the initial restructuring has taken place.

The key prerequisite for providing the above is to have two simultaneous sales:
- a sale of a *pro rata* strip of the assets reflecting sufficient cash to pay those wishing to cash out or take a ZCN and to set the market price on an asset by asset basis (the 'auction strip'); and
- a sale of the remaining portfolio assets to a Newco. In order to achieve the sale to a Newco, an investment bank is used as arranger to implement the Newco options and to facilitate the sale of assets and exchange of the senior creditor obligations at the date of restructuring.

Taking all of this into account, Figure 3 shows schematically how the SIV restructuring options may be achieved.

Simply put, each senior creditor will fix its percentage entitlement to the assets at a certain date, on or slightly before the restructuring, and will be entitled to a percentage 'vertical' slice of, first, the portfolio assets and, second, any cash/cash reserves in or held back in the vehicle. Each creditor will then have the ability to:
- monetise its portion of the portfolio assets (cash out or ZCN, paid for by the strip auctioned to third parties);
- have exposure to them in a Newco (through a PTN); or
- seek to take its *pro rata* percentage of the portfolio assets back on to its own balance sheet through a vertical slice, subject to certain minimum denomination issues discussed below.

Cash dividend: In the normal operating state, SIV creditors were paid as their debts became due in the relevant currency and in full, plus any interest entitlement. Insolvency and the mandatory acceleration of the respective senior obligations created a number of difficulties in both the calculation of the claim and the actual payment of the dividend. Although the issues are broadly the same across the SIVs, the potential implications differ due to each SIV having slightly different provisions within its own legal documentation.

In terms of calculation, the following issues generally need to be overcome before any dividend can be made:

- Redemption price: the respective notes will have redemption price provisions that indicate the amount at which the respective note is to be redeemed. Often this requires a leading investment bank to determine the redemption price in accordance with the documentation of the SIV, which generally needs interpreting and may lead to different assumptions providing different results.
- Interest rates: different senior notes are likely to have different interest rates. Some may be fixed by LIBOR or EURIBOR, but other notes may carry interest rates that are not specified in the respective note documentation. Senior liquidity providers or repo and derivative counterparties are also likely to have differing rates, which further complicates the claim calculation process.
- Foreign currencies: where SIVs have multi-currency noteholders and multi-currency assets, the documentation should set out how claims may be converted on, for example, the insolvency acceleration event date for claim purposes. This may provide, for instance, that claims be converted into US dollars on the insolvency acceleration event date, and that a senior creditor claim then be referenced in US dollars on the redemption date (ie, the date of any dividend or the restructuring date). However, during the receivership this will give rise to hedging issues. This must be carefully communicated to investors and action be taken by the receiver where appropriate.

In relation to the actual dividend distribution, the notes are ordinarily held in global form by the clearing systems, which then pass on payment through paying agent intermediaries to the respective ultimate beneficiaries of the notes. Therefore, unless the receiver takes the decision to take the note out of global form, dividends must be paid through the US clearing system or one of the two European clearing systems. At present, a part-dividend is not a normal request and therefore requires considerable pre-planning, and new agreements may need to be put in place with third parties assisting in the process.

As shown above, a number of complications need to be overcome before an initial cash dividend can be made. These will require the receiver either to perform all actions in accordance with the noteholder documentation or to obtain agreement from noteholders (which may require 100% approval for each note issue) to change the documentation. For example, the redemption price provisions may be altered if consent is obtained from all noteholders, rating agencies, the security trustee, the investment manager and certain other parties. In most SIVs this is difficult to achieve, given the wide creditor base and potentially differing views of the respective creditors. However, where there is a small number of creditors agreeing a simple redemption price calculation, it is possible to achieve cost savings and is worthy of consideration.

(c)   *Asset portfolio sale and auction process*
Once the options and structure have been agreed and incorporated into legal documentation, the exact timing and detail of the auction process and settlement mechanics should be discussed and considered in light of all practical difficulties that

may be encountered during the countdown period before trade date ('T') and the short period of, say, three to four days between T and actual settlement, when the restructuring is finalised.

The types of event that need to take place during this period are legally and logistically complex, but in summary may include the following:

- Communication of the options to all investors: once the options and restructuring framework have been agreed, each option needs to be carefully and appropriately communicated to all investors to ensure that they understand the process, the implications of each option and what each creditor must do to ensure that it can choose an option.

- Preparation for a public auction process: the receiver needs to obtain the best price in the circumstances for the sale of the assets. Key issues to be determined are:
  - number of alternative bidders;
  - best method of marketing the assets prior to the auction date;
  - timing of sale;
  - amount of time to be allowed for alternative bids; and
  - an assessment of whether the amount of assets in the auction strip will deliver a different price from, say, a sale of the whole of the portfolio assets.

- Elections by senior creditors: senior creditors will elect which option they prefer. The process may provide an opportunity to put in a non-binding election first (eg, based on receiving indicative bids prior to the auction process) and then a binding election shortly thereafter. The binding election stage will provide certainty on who is a cash-out or ZCN creditor and therefore will finalise the amounts being sold as part of the auction strip.

- Resolution of minimum denomination and minimum increment issues: as a result of minimum denominations and increments in relation to the ability to trade individual securities, the theoretical split of the portfolio assets is unlikely to be able to be practically implemented.

- Trade and settlement: settlement of the respective asset sales as part of the auction strip sale and that of the remaining portfolio assets into a Newco are effected through settlement platforms. Cash movements then take place such that the auction strip proceeds and Newco sale proceeds are received by the SIV and distributed *pari passu* to creditors. Those cashing out will receive a cash dividend and those exchanging into a ZCN or PTN will receive a new note.

(d)   *Reserves and final dividend*

The final part of the restructuring process is to repay any excess cash that remains in the SIV. Under the documentation, a number of indemnities are provided to various third parties, as well as certain cash-backed indemnities that may have been required to be given to third parties as part of the restructuring process. In addition, since all of the assets will have been distributed, the security trustee and the receiver will need to maintain some form of cash reserve for any receivership costs, future costs and other contingencies, such as potential litigation by third parties. This amount may be significant and is likely to be retained for a period of up to six years to ensure that no claims can legally be made against the receiver.

3.5 New York law SIV restructuring

This chapter has focused on English SIV restructurings. A number of the New York-based SIVs – Axon Financial Funding, Victoria Finance Ltd and Orion Finance Corp – have also moved into enforcement. The main difference between the English law SIVs and the New York law SIVs is that a receiver was not appointed over the New York SIVs. Instead, under provisions within the respective SIV documentation, the security trustees appointed investment managers to adopt the role of enforcement manager. In addition, other financial advisers were appointed to assist the restructuring efforts and *ad hoc* senior creditors' committees were formed to assist the security trustee in implementing restructuring solutions.

The specific issues that have been encountered are similar to those prevalent in English receivership SIV restructurings. However, the New York law restructurings have been hampered by the lack of powers entrusted to the enforcement managers compared with an English law receiver, which can, for example, implement a restructuring as described above – using the receiver's power of sale – without requiring the formal consent or vote of creditors.

4. CMBS

As mentioned above and indeed since the onset of the credit crunch, market commentators have noted the imminent refinancing requirement for the commercial real estate market and CMBS in particular. Yet the restructuring that was expected to follow the SIV restructuring did not materialise until more recently. This can be partially explained by the following factors:

- 18 months to 2 years of delay between the trough of the recession and the trough of defaults in commercial real estate in past crises;
- government intervention;
- documentation and timing of origination – the 'troubled' loans were issued between 2005 and 2007, typically with five-year or longer loan maturities; and
- the potentially significant out-of-the-money hedge liabilities that could crystallise on appointment.

Refinancing difficulties were experienced from 2011 onwards, as loans matured and government intervention unwound. In 2011 it was estimated that issued European CMBS totalled $195 billion with $30 billion falling due before 2013, and within this period there were sizeable individual loan volumes maturing.

It remains difficult to see how all of these will either refinance or repay their respective investors – the value of the assets has likely fallen, there have been many rating downgrades, underlying tenants may have defaulted leading to less favourable income streams and changes in the financial markets has led to increased risk premiums. The probability of refinancing also decreases the later the issuance, as loans were increasingly interest-only, with increased subordination and more relaxed credit standards.

We now concentrate on five key 'learning points' to date, looking at how any lessons learned can assist in future restructurings and in future structured finance documentation.

4.1 Documentation – no easy answer

All CMBS structures are governed by complex documentation. However, particularly for those issued between 2005 and 2007 when demand was at its peak, documents were arguably subject to limited negotiation and diligence. As a result, loan documentation can have issues ranging from unusual covenants to basic drafting errors. For example, instances where the intercreditor agreement does not allow subordinated guarantees to be released on enforcement of the security, which has subsequently caused an issue in mainstream restructurings such as European Directories, first came to light in CMBS documentation – seriously inhibiting any restructuring and leading to potentially costly and lengthy conflicts between the respective noteholders.

Furthermore, the risk in Europe is spread across numerous jurisdictions. In 2009 it was estimated that the European CMBS market was dominated by issuances in the United Kingdom and Ireland, with over 70% of issuances in those jurisdictions. It was also estimated that of the loans at the highest risk – where the underlying properties are poor quality and the LTV was high – nearly 80% were issued in the United Kingdom and Germany. In each case, local insolvency laws will apply and local courts will interpret the documentation as they see fit, with differing implications in each jurisdiction.

In the United Kingdom, the restructuring regime is relatively creditor friendly and, without financial support from the borrower, enforcement may be preferred to an extension, at note maturity especially where the collateral is good quality. By contrast, in Germany the restructuring regime is more borrower friendly with lower recoveries compounded by higher costs of insolvency and loss of control. Accordingly an extension is more likely unless there is a fundamental breakdown in the relationship with the borrower, though whether the impact of new insolvency legislation in Germany changes this dynamic remains to be seen.

Thus, the idiosyncratic nature of European CMBS documentation, coupled with jurisdictional interpretations of underlying documentation, will more than likely drive bespoke restructuring options in each case.

4.2 Complexity – clarity is critical

CMBS structures are complex. Properties tend to be held by SPV companies based in the United Kingdom or offshore, owned by either a large corporate structure or a series of general and limited partnerships, providing management control and equity ownership respectively. These structural complexities may have provided tax efficiency at inception, but they inhibit a standardised restructuring solution.

However, not only are the structures themselves likely to be complex, but there is a raft of stakeholders whose position will be affected by any restructuring. These range from tenants in the underlying properties, special servicers, noteholders and trustees, to rating agencies reviewing and rating the notes.

Even relatively simple documentation issues were made more complicated. Class X bonds were used as a mechanism through which CMBS arrangers were remunerated in some deals, capturing excess interest after the interest on the bonds and certain expenses were paid. The problem highlighted by the recent crisis is that Class X noteholders can continue to collect interest payments even after a deal has become distressed. Investors in other parts of the capital structure, whose own bonds were out of the money, are understandably unwilling to see leakage from the structure to these bondholders, but are powerless to stop it in a pre-enforcement scenario.

To make matters worse, we have seen a lack of clarity and understanding among CMBS stakeholders. One of the keys to unlocking the SIV restructurings that can equally be applied to CMBS was to increase the transparency of the deal to allow investors to make informed decisions. Each stakeholder needs to be considered in the context of each individual restructuring, and a consensual solution will have to be acceptable to all parties; forcing a solution on a subordinated creditors or third-party stakeholders is not always achievable. This necessitates a thorough understanding of the structure to clarify where interests of stakeholders are aligned and where they diverge in order to articulate and negotiate an acceptable position for all.

4.3 Hedging – the hidden stakeholder

Within the complex structure, the CMBS issuer is likely to be required to hedge its liabilities, such that the floating-rate CMBS notes can be converted into a fixed obligation for the issuer. There are numerous significant out of the money exposures on CMBS issuances where the hedging counterparty ranks *pari passu* with the senior creditors and, in some instances, super senior. Although the hedge counterparty would not typically enjoy enforcement powers, this will limit the possibility to, for example, arrange a debt-for-equity swap because this may require the hedge to be terminated and a break cost to be paid. Equally, even if the Senior A notes of the CMBS structure are in theory covered by the valuation of the assets, they could still suffer a loss if the hedge is terminated.

4.4 Tax

Unlike SIVs where tax was, unusually, not important in the ultimate restructuring, CMBS structures were put in place to be as tax efficient as possible, leading to SPVs located in Jersey, Luxembourg, the Cayman Islands and so on. It is critical to understand the tax implications of all the consensual and non-consensual options as tax will be an important value driver. With maturity extensions or refinancing, this is less likely to be an issue as the underlying structure is unlikely to change. However, if any form of restructuring is considered, tax will be a key issue in the form of residency, degrouping charges and stamp duty land tax, among others.

4.5 External factors

While each CMBS loan and its associated documentation will involve unique facts that drive a restructuring, a number of external factors will also have a bearing on the solution. Central banks and regulators will have a key role to play as rules are changed in respect of how these loans are recognised in financial statements and as asset purchase programmes unwind. The availability and cost of debt and equity capital will also be paramount, with borrowers likely needing to speak with existing lenders or sponsors injecting further equity.

5. Conclusions

The credit crunch had a dramatic impact on the financial markets and brought structured finance products to the forefront of the insolvency profession. Although SIV restructurings are complex and time consuming, due to the specialist nature of the assets and the securities law issues involved, English receivership principles have been used to achieve successful restructurings of SIVs with many billions of dollars as assets and liabilities. However, the extent to which these strategies can be used by other structures remains unclear. We are yet to see auctions of a similar scale by a receiver, although they have been used to liquidate assets in CDOs via liquidation agents, albeit at much lower values.

With CLOs, a more active management is required as the underlying assets – the corporate loans themselves – are often low quality and in workout. As with mainstream restructuring, understanding of each exposure and the relative leverage of both lender and borrower is fundamental to realising value in each scenario.

A significant number of difficulties remain to be faced by the CMBS market. The current trend is still to extend the loan maturity where possible and wait for the market to return: the so-called 'extend and pretend' strategy. While we can see this working in certain instances, the bespoke nature of European CMBS deals will mean there are many cases for which this will not be appropriate. As CMBS matures and pressure by senior noteholders for repayment increases, we have seen (and expect to see further) combinations of:

- complex restructurings;
- consensual rewriting of documentation/extensions in return for new equity, better yield, and/or frequency of amortisations;
- unpicking of structures; and
- asset sales, potentially through enforcement.

As with traditional restructuring, the appropriate strategy will depend on the unique features of the deal in question, an understanding of the stakeholders and their relative positions; the existing external financing environment will be crucial in arriving at the optimal solution. However, as note maturities (as opposed to loan maturities) pass, there will be limited opportunity to extend the notes absent a fundamental re-write of the documentation, and we expect to see enforcement becoming more widely used to realise value in the properties and return funds to the investors.

And what of the key lessons learned throughout this process for restructuring in both structured finance situations and in general? We believe that further attention will be paid to restructuring clauses in key documentation, and that increased protection will be afforded to lenders. This may take the form of less reliance on:

- market value triggers in the underlying documents;
- increased equity capital in the SPV;
- more stringent reporting requirements;
- external liquidity support; and
- assurance and/or jurisdictional differences in the documentation.

From a stakeholder perspective, we are already observing a marked change in the levels of communication and information offered to investors by servicers and special servicers, with that increased level of transparency allowing for informed decisions by noteholders and more acceptable solutions for both borrowers and noteholders alike.

The role of trustees in restructuring

Tom Church
Judge, First Tier Tribunal (Social Entitlement Chamber), UK Ministry of Justice
Hugh Mildred
Berwin Leighton Paisner LLP

1. Introduction

The bond holder trustee's role in the restructuring process has never been more important as parties' appetite for information, direction and interaction has increased in the current uncertain economic climate. At the same time, trustees have been forced to adapt their roles in the light of complex capital market structures and the increasingly activist attitudes of investors. The exact nature of the role of the trustee and the scope of the liability for which it is exposed was the subject of intense judicial analysis across three high-profile cases that remind us of the difficulties encountered by trustees in protecting their own position, while at the same time representing the interests of the bond holders in the face of pressure from other transaction parties (including, in some cases, groups of bond holders with conflicting interests).

Concord Trust v Law Debenture Trust Corporation plc [2005] UKHL 27 ('*Elektrim*') was decided in the United Kingsom House of Lords and clarified, among other things, the scope of liability of the trustee and the extent to which it is entitled to indemnification. A subsequent first instance decision in *The Law Debenture Trust Corporation plc v Concord Trust* [2007] EWHC 1380 (Ch) provides further clarity for the trustee, even if the decisions were not entirely in the trustee's favour. *Whistlejacket Capital Ltd (In Receivership)* [2008] EWCA Civ 575 was decided by the UK Court of Appeal and provided welcome support for the proposition that the discretion of the trustee or other distributor of assets as to how it applies the money that it receives continues in a post-enforcement or insolvency scenario.

This chapter describes the evolution of the English law trustee:

- looking at its role in a capital markets transaction (particularly in the context of securitisation), examining the trustee's role in the restructuring process;
- analysing the impact of *Elektrim*, *Concord* and *Whistlejacket* on the trustee's actions; and
- reviewing some of the key incremental challenges facing the trustee in the aftermath of the 2007 to 2008 'credit-crunch'.

We will refer to the trustee in its generic sense covering two main roles: first, that of the bond holder trustee which holds, among other things, the benefit of the bond issuer's covenant to pay principal and interest when due on behalf of its beneficiaries, the bond holders; and second, that of the security trustee which holds the benefit of the security, granted by the bond issuer in its favour, on behalf of its beneficiaries, the secured creditors (typically, the bond holders and the other transaction agents or financial enhancement providers).

2.   The trustee

The concept of a trust was developed in common law jurisdictions and has become invaluable in creating flexibility in legal relations between parties. In the 1980s some of the major investment banks began to establish professional trustee businesses, usually as separate companies from the main bank group, in order to separate the banks from any potential liabilities arising from their trustee operations. Currently, the market for professional trustee providers is dominated by a mix of standalone trustee companies and trustee companies associated with investment banks.

There are many advantages to appointing a trustee for the bond holders in a capital markets transaction, such as:

- permitting the bond issuer to negotiate and deal with one static, identifiable party as opposed to a changing group of (often anonymous) bond holders;
- the presence of a 'middleman' that will act in the interests of the bond holders as a class (as opposed to rogue individual bond holders that might wish to accelerate all of the bonds to further their own particular agenda (perhaps as a more substantial investor in a different class of bonds); and
- the increased bargaining power of a trustee that will act on behalf of all (or at least a pre-determined majority) of the bond holders.

It is important to understand that while the trustee is appointed and paid by the bond issuer, it is not an agent of the bond issuer; instead, it owes its fiduciary duties to, and represents, the bond holders. This apparent conflict of interest is well known and, in the vast majority of deals that have come to market, has not prevented the trustee from discharging its duties to the bond holders to the satisfaction of all parties to the transaction. However, recent case law has provided a timely reminder that the trustee remains exposed to parties motivated to upset the status quo.

A trustee appointed under English law is appointed under the terms of a trust deed that will state that the trustee owes its duties to the bond holders of each class of bond as a class, (ie, it does not consider the interests of individual bond holders within that class but rather looks to the interests of the class as a whole) and will set out the basis on which the trustee must conduct itself in the case of a conflict of interest arising between the interests of differing classes of bond holders, and whose interests take precedence in particular situations. The trust deed will also set out the terms of the trustee's remuneration, the limitations on its liability and the trustee's entitlement to have further expenses paid for by the bond issuer. In addition to the powers provided by statute, the trust deed grants the trustee a wide range of powers. Despite these powers, the English law trustee would assert that the intention has always been that it should remain as passive as possible during the life of the transaction prior to any event of default, instead relying on the various negative covenants given to the trustee by the bond issuer. To this end, the trust deed may provide that the trustee can assume that absent any actual notice or knowledge to the contrary, there is no event of default in existence at any time. The trust deed will also provide that following the occurrence of an event of default, the trustee may (at its own discretion), or shall (at the direction of a pre-determined percentage – usually 25% – of bond holders), deliver an acceleration notice to the bond issuer declaring the bonds (and interest accrued but unpaid on them) to be immediately due and payable, and that the trustee may enforce its rights over the secured assets. The trustee will not be obliged to take any such steps, however, until it has been indemnified, secured and/or prefunded to its satisfaction against any costs or losses that it might incur as a result of taking such steps. The scope of such indemnity-type protection is discussed at greater length below.

In contrast to an English law trustee that is granted discretion prior to the occurrence of an event of default, a trustee appointed under a New York law indenture has extremely limited discretion (if any at all). A New York law trustee instead acts rather as another agent, discharging its contractual obligations (in contrast to the broader fiduciary duties placed upon an English law trustee). The New York law trustee also typically provides transactional services such as reporting financial information in respect of the transaction to investors.

2.1   The trustee's role in the restructuring process

One of the trustee's most commonly received requests from issuers and sponsors is for it to exercise its discretion to amend or waive provisions of the transaction documents without obtaining the consent of the bond holders. The trustee is granted the power, under the terms of the trust deed, to give such waivers or agree to such amendments as it sees fit in circumstances where, in its sole opinion, the amendment is to correct a manifest error or is of a formal, minor or technical nature, or where it is of the opinion that such waiver or amendment is not "materially prejudicial to the interests of the bond holders". Arrangers and sponsors of transactions are often very keen to persuade the trustee to exercise this discretion as it provides them with the opportunity not only to tidy up errors in the agreed documents, but also – should the trustee accede to such a request – to restructure the non-fundamental terms of the transaction without incurring the considerable expense and delay that any consultation with the bond holders would entail. However, as we shall see later, the increasing ambitiousness of the requests made in respect of amendments that are claimed not to be 'materially prejudicial', combined with increasingly litigious bond holders is forcing the trustee onto the defensive, with the result that the trustee is now more and more often refusing to permit amendments under this discretionary power and instead insisting that such amendments be referred to the bond holders to be voted upon in extraordinary meetings.

In order to restructure a fundamental term of the transaction (such as reducing the amount of, or changing the date or currency of any scheduled payment, usually referred to as 'basic terms modifications' or 'reserved matters') or to restructure a term of the transaction in a manner that could be considered to be prejudicial to the interests of bond holders, the party wishing to effect the restructuring will need to obtain the consent of the requisite majority of bond holders. The trustee has a central role to play in this process as it will act as a conduit for the communication of the proposed amendments to the bond holders. The exact percentage of bond holders required to agree to amendments that are of fundamental terms or of a materially prejudicial nature varies from transaction to transaction, but in most cases the approval of at least a majority of the most senior class of bond holders will be required, and frequently the approval of at least a majority of the note holders of each class will be required.

The party proposing the restructuring would typically first approach the trustee with:

- an outline of the proposed changes;
- an indication of where the trustee's power to agree to the proposed changes arises under the transaction documents; and
- the basis on which it asks the trustee to agree to the changes.

The trustee will then be able to advise as to the procedures and documentation required to bring the proposal to the attention of the bond holders in the most effective manner. In respect of fixed note bonds, if the proposal is complicated or likely to receive a mixed response from bond holders, the trustee may suggest an approach to the Association of British Insurers (ABI). The ABI will undertake a survey to see which of its members are holders of the bonds in question and will attempt to form a steering committee comprising bond holders holding a significant percentage of the relevant bonds to provide some input into proposals and to indicate whether they would be willing to recommend the proposed restructuring to bond holders. If the feedback from the bond holder committee indicates that the bond holders will all agree to the proposals, it may be possible to avoid holding a meeting (which can be costly and time consuming) by executing a written resolution (which typically requires certification that it is being signed by 100% of the relevant bond holders) approving the requested amendments. If, however, the reaction from bond holders to the proposal remains mixed, then if the party nevertheless wishes to proceed with proposing the restructuring to the bond holders as a whole, a meeting of the bond holders will need to be called.

Once the ABI consultation process is complete, the trustee will provide input into the final form of the necessary documentation in anticipation of it being sent to the bond holders as a formal proposal and will agree a timetable for the process, including setting the date and venue to convene a meeting to approve or reject the proposal. The trustee (or its counsel) will also prepare the necessary voting documentation and send out any necessary notices. The trustee will attend the bond holder meeting and will oversee matters, including determining whether the meeting is quorate and therefore whether it can proceed. The trustee will distribute any necessary voting forms at the meeting and will count and record the number of votes cast, whether by attendees or by those bond holders voting by proxy. In practice, the vast majority of voting is usually by way of the provision of block voting instructions to the principal paying agent. The trustee will record the outcome of the meeting and will notify all the bond holders (whether or not they attended the meeting) accordingly.

If the proposed restructuring is approved, then the trustee is likely to be involved on a practical level, mainly in its role as security trustee. It is possible that security will need to be released in full or in part, and that further security will need to be taken following the completion of the restructuring steps. The trustee's role will be to review the draft documentation intended to effect the amendments and it will need to be satisfied that the various steps, notifications and registrations have been completed appropriately. Once the restructuring is complete, the trustee's role should become more passive again, prior to the occurrence of any event of default.

2.2   **Impact of *Elektrim* and *Concord* on the trustee's liability and indemnity**
In *Elektrim*, the House of Lords was asked to consider, among other things, the potential scope of the trustee's liability and the extent of its ability to require that it be indemnified to its satisfaction before taking action. In *Concord*, the English High Court dealt with the issue of whether the trustee was entitled to make distributions conditional upon certain factors, including the provision of further indemnities, despite the earlier House of Lords ruling on the matter.

Elektrim BV issued bonds in 1999 that were due to be redeemed in 2005. In 2002 the company encountered financial difficulties and agreed to a restructuring of its bond financing. As part of the restructuring the bond holders were entitled to nominate a director to Elektrim's management board; Elektrim was obliged to accept the bond holders' nominee and was not entitled to remove the nominee without complying with various conditions. The bond holder appointed a nominee, but – in breach of the restructuring terms – Elektrim removed the bond holders' nominee from the management board without the bond holders' consent. The bond holders then requested the trustee to certify that an event of default had occurred on the basis that Elektrim had breached its obligations in a manner that was materially prejudicial to the interests of the bond holders. The trustee was unsure whether Elektrim's actions were in fact materially prejudicial to the interests of the bond holders and sought directions on the matter from the Chancery Division of the High Court.

The High Court judge (Morritt VC) ruled that Elektrim's actions were materially prejudicial to the interests of the bond holders. On the basis of this decision, the trustee proceeded to certify that an event of default had occurred. A group of bond holders requested that the trustee then proceed to issue an acceleration notice, but the trustee refused to do so on the grounds that it had not yet been indemnified to its satisfaction (as it was entitled to be under the terms of the transaction documents). While the trustee and the bond holders were discussing a mutually acceptable level of indemnity, Elektrim put the trustee on notice that acceleration would cause Elektrim to incur substantial losses. Now on notice of the potential scope of losses that might be caused by its actions, the trustee sought indemnification for those losses from the bond holders. A deadlock was reached and the bond holders issued proceedings against the trustee to oblige it to give the notice of acceleration. The case was heard in the Court of Appeal, where the bond holders failed to obtain the relief sought. Both the trustee and bond holders appealed to the House of Lords. The House of Lords largely disagreed with the Court of Appeal's judgment and stated that while the trustee was clearly entitled to be indemnified against the cost of any court proceedings in which the notice of acceleration was considered to be invalid or otherwise, there were no grounds for Elektrim to pursue an action against the trustee for the consequential losses Elektrim might incur as regards third parties if the notice were served and, therefore, the trustee should not need to be indemnified against such remote and fanciful claims. Once the trustee had been indemnified to its satisfaction against the losses of litigation that might reasonably be expected in respect of the serving of the notice of acceleration, then it was obliged – under the terms of the transaction documents – to serve the notice of acceleration.

This decision highlights a few points of great interest regarding the trustee's role in the restructuring process. First, it demonstrates the increasing tendency of trustees to look to the courts for directions in respect of contentious issues (eg, whether or not an action is 'materially prejudicial' to the interests of a party). Trustees are becoming more and more reluctant to resolve such issues absent judicial guidance in light of the increasingly litigious nature of parties to restructurings. Second, it provides useful guidance as to the grounds (or lack thereof) under which the trustee could be liable for serving notices under the terms of the transaction documents absent bad faith or clear negligence on its part. Lastly, it clearly establishes that trustees are not entitled to demand to be indemnified against remote or 'fanciful' risks of loss.

In *Concord*, over two years later, although the trustee had served the notice of enforcement and received €525 million from Elektrim, it had still not distributed the funds to the bond holders or released the security for Elektrim's liability. This was because the trustee considered that there was still a shortfall of approximately €17 million owing to it (on behalf of itself and the bond holders), and that it would not pay the bond holders until, among other things, it had been determined whether it was entitled to retain funds available for distribution to cover its indemnified losses. Meanwhile, the trustee had not released the security for the original debt and therefore Elektrim issued proceedings to require the trustee to release some, if not all, of the security as the value of the security greatly exceeded the €17 million claimed by the trustee.

The High Court handed down its verdict in June 2007 and again the decision raised points of great importance to the trustee's role in a restructuring. First, it stated that the trustee did not have to release any of the security at present and would not have to do so until the bonds had been redeemed in full. The judge went on to say that the bonds would not be considered 'redeemed in full' until the trustee had distributed all realisable proceeds (save for any amounts that it was entitled to retain in respect of indemnities) to the bond holders. This was hugely significant because interest was accruing at the default rate on the full amount outstanding of the bonds and would continue to do so until they were redeemed in full. The judge then considered the issue of distributions and decided that the trustee was obliged to pay out to the bond holders all sums that it currently held. The trustee was not entitled to attach any conditionality to such payments (eg, the trustee requiring the bond holders to identify themselves in order that it could pursue them under the indemnity in the future). However it was entitled to hold back an amount effectively as collateral against its potential losses under extant indemnities given to it by bond holders, qualified by reference to its reasonable but worst-case assumptions about expected losses. This decision has gone a long way to clarify the position of the trustee with regards to retention of sums to cover indemnifiable losses that will allow quantum of recovery on future restructurings to be calculated with greater certainty.

2.3 Impact of *Whistlejacket* on the trustee's discretion to determine payments

In *Whistlejacket*, the Court of Appeal provided some welcome clarification as to the proper construction of clauses setting out priorities of payments and whether or not a receiver has a discretion in respect of the making of distributions in circumstances in which a company is in receivership and its assets are inadequate to meet its liabilities.

Whistlejacket Capital Ltd was a type of company known as a 'structured investment vehicle' (SIV), a vehicle which raises short-term money to finance the purchase of longer-term assets. The growing unease with developments in the US sub-prime mortgage market and their consequences for the capital markets as a whole led to a decrease in asset values in the second half of 2007. In addition, the sub-prime fears triggered a dramatic reduction in short-term liquidity available to vehicles such as SIVs. The combination of these factors led to Whistlejacket breaching certain financial ratios designed to maintain the adequacy of its assets in relation to its liabilities. This breach constituted an enforcement event under the terms of the transaction documents and led to the trustee appointing receivers on February 12 2008. Three days after the appointment, one class of senior notes owed by the SIV (in this case in the form of dollar-denominated medium-term notes (US MTNs)) fell due for payment and the transaction's investment manager notified the trustee that it considered that an insolvency-based acceleration event had occurred because it appeared likely that the SIV would no longer be able to meet its payment obligations to the holders of its senior debt in full. The trustee forwarded the notice to the company, thereby accelerating the senior debt, which had the effect of bringing forward the date on which all outstanding classes of senior debt were to be redeemed to March 16 2008, even though some of the classes of senior debt were originally due to have been repaid at a later date.

The holders of the US MTNs due on February 12 2008 (Party A) claimed that they were due to be paid in full in priority to the other classes of senior debt (including other US MTNs falling due for payment at later dates) as their debt had already fallen due for payment (ie, on February 12 2008), and that they therefore enjoyed a priority in time over the other holders of senior debt instruments whose debt fell due for payment at a date after February 12 2008 (Party B). Party B, unsurprisingly, disagreed with Party A's interpretation of the construction of the documented priority of payments and a dispute arose. The receiver applied to court for directions. The first instance decision was appealed and the case came before the Court of Appeal where judgment was handed down on May 22 2008.

The question raised in the appeal of greatest relevance to a trustee (often faced with decisions similar to the receiver in this case) was whether it should be forced to pay moneys as soon as they were received to meet obligations as they arose or whether the trustee has the discretion to hold onto the funds and apply them at a time of its choosing taking into account the requirements of all the holders of the same class of debt – even if those debts were due to mature at differing times. The Court of Appeal found in favour of the receiver's interpretation of the priority clause in agreeing that the priority of payments applied to the time at which the receiver decided to make distributions, but did not oblige the receiver to make a distribution at a specific time. Therefore, Party A would not be able to claim payment in priority to Party B. The receiver of a SIV, as with other companies, will be able to "exercise its discretion … as to how to realise the assets, what reserves of retentions they should make, and what they can properly pay out".

The ability of the trustee to make distributions at its own discretion during enforcement and receivership is crucial in allowing the trustee to negotiate restructurings with interested parties with a degree of certainty. In addition, the clarity that the judgment has provided will allow future investors to purchase structured products, issued by SIVs or otherwise, with a greater understanding of the insolvency process and the effect that it will have on the likelihood that they will recoup their investment in a default scenario.

3. Challenges facing trustees post-credit crunch

The credit crunch has brought home – to those who had not already realised – the fact that financial structures have become significantly more complex in recent years and, consequently, the role of the trustee in relation to such structures has also become more difficult. One of the reasons that the impact of the credit crunch on the financial markets was so great is that many investors began to realise, as the transactions in which they had invested started to be downgraded by the rating agencies or to default, that they did not understand the products that they had bought. This was especially the case in the world of collateralised debt obligations and SIVs where the underlying assets generating the money to be used for repayment of the debt securities were often hard to identify as they formed part of dynamic pools of assets that were being bought and sold, and that were often themselves debt securities of other underlying assets. The difficulty of identifying the assets underpinning the repayments increased investors' fears about the level of their exposure to the defaulting US sub-prime mortgage market.

The increase in the level of downgraded or defaulting transactions, which has been a symptom of the credit crunch, has led to an increase in the level of restructuring activity as arrangers and sponsors of such transactions try to avoid imminent or actual breaches of financial covenants or other market value-based tests. However, in the same way that transactions have become more complex, restructurings are also now becoming more complex and this is creating fresh challenges for the trustee, as bond holders want more active involvement from trustees in the restructuring process. Restructuring proposals are no longer single options, merely to redeem assets and distribute what is left. More and more proposals now contain multiple options including repackaging certain assets, auctioning other assets and redeeming some bonds (often significantly below par value), but also offering the opportunity to exchange old securities for new ones and participate in a new, restructured transaction (eg, the restructuring of the Opera Uni Invest transaction). The restructuring of the Whistlejacket transaction is a good example of the level of complexity that bond holders and trustees are faced with in the current market. The trustee's role in the restructuring is further complicated by the fact that during the credit crunch a significant amount of bonds were bought by speculative investors significantly below par value and therefore a trustee, when acting for bond holders that are considering whether a proposed restructuring is in their interest, may find itself having to steer the correct course between bond holders in the same class which have greatly different views on the merits of the restructuring options offered.

4. Conclusion

It is clear that the role of the trustee in a restructuring is becoming more complex and burdensome as a result of more complicated transaction structures and the increasingly diverging interests of various groups of the bond holders that it represents. This increased complexity will have a significant commercial and practical impact on the trustees' business model, which will no doubt present them with challenges in the years to come. However, continued clarification from the courts as to the exact scope of the trustees' role and its potential exposure to liability should go some way to alleviate some of the trustees' concerns and provide a more stable platform from which to negotiate and restructure transactions in the future.

The publishers and authors gratefully acknowledge the assistance of Tamara Box as a co-author for the version of this chapter that appeared in the first edition of this book.

Stakeholder management

Glen Fietta
AlixPartners

This chapter offers an alternative perspective on the restructuring process. It looks at the financial restructuring process from the viewpoint of a company seeking to proactively lead and drive the process toward a consensual solution for the benefit of the company and its stakeholders.

Whilst all restructuring deals are subject to different institutional constraints, market conditions and stakeholder dynamics, the chapter sets out an illustrative restructuring process in order to explain the process as a whole and show how the company itself can seek to drive and influence the process at each stage, in the hope of reaching a solution which provides stability for the company going forward and preserves value for stakeholders.

From the company's perspective, a restructuring should be designed to transition the company from unsustainable overleverage and financial distress to a position of stability and control, with an adjusted package of debt facilities structured specifically to fit with an achievable business plan and associated financial forecasts.

In order to manage the process as a whole, the company and its advisers must take time to understand the approach and negotiating positions that various stakeholders are likely to adopt through the process, and their individual requirements and priorities in relation to the restructuring deal. The company's desire to stabilise its financial position and gain access to the level of liquidity necessary to implement its business plan is likely to be shared by its financial stakeholders. However, each stakeholder is likely to have different specific requirements and constraints regarding terms that it can agree to, either because of its appetite for a specific company or sector, or because of specific institutional requirements or a strategy to manage down exposures to high risk credits. For example, certain stakeholders such as those purchasing distressed debt on a 'loan-to-own' strategy may seek to create uncertainty in order to strengthen their own position. Such aggressive action might be intended to reinforce legal rights under loan documentation, or to generate a liquidity crunch in order to create an opportunity to provide additional funding in exchange for an improvement in their own position. By contrast, other stakeholders may have no interest in supporting the company further, preferring to observe the process passively while finding a buyer for their credit, or may simply act disruptively until offered an acceptable exit.

The above examples represent a few of many potential scenarios. The key point is that many variables influence the behaviour of stakeholders during a restructuring. If the company is to drive the process successfully it must understand these different behaviours and the reasons behind them, and work with all stakeholders individually to find sufficient common ground so a solution can be found. As an illustration of how difficult it can be to find common ground between stakeholders with conflicting agendas, the optimal solution is often one which leaves a number of stakeholders slightly (or even, very) unhappy with the outcome, but still prepared to support the deal based on their assessment of the alternatives and understanding of the constraints upon other parties in the process combined with the underlying desire to preserve value for all stakeholders and provide the stability needed in order to turn around the business.

When it comes to executing a restructuring deal, numerous tools and techniques are at the disposal of legal and financial restructuring practitioners to get the deal done as quickly as possible and with maximum value preservation. Analysing the various options available to a company in a given situation and selecting the most appropriate restructuring tool is often absolutely critical to maintaining value in difficult circumstances. While the company may (and in the personal view of the author definitely should) exhaust all opportunities to find a consensual solution, it is a fact of life that this will not always be possible and in order to preserve value it may be necessary to force a solution on one or more stakeholder group against their wishes. Under these circumstances the company's legal and financial advisers should assess the various restructuring tools (including companies act and insolvency processes) in order to find a mechanism through which to execute a deal which is not supported by all stakeholders.

These tools and techniques are invaluable and often implemented by companies in order to preserve value; however, the main focus of this chapter is on how underperforming companies can help guide their lenders and other stakeholders to a consensual restructuring solution where possible, thereby reducing the risk of value loss often suffered when lenders' rights are prematurely exercised via an unnecessary insolvency process.

One of the fascinating features of restructuring work is that the dynamics of every case is different. There is therefore no single process which can be relied upon to result in a successful outcome. Not only are the hard facts of each case different, but the restructuring solution in any given case will be influenced heavily by the financial institutions involved, any internal pressures and institutional restrictions affecting decision making within these organisations, as well as the personalities involved. The unique combination of these factors within any single case will affect not only the solution necessary to achieve consent of all parties, but also to some extent the speed and nature of the process itself.

Notwithstanding the fact that negotiating a restructuring is an art, with science employed as appropriate in order to sculpt the finished product, this chapter seeks to present a simplified view of the sequential stages that a company must navigate in order to achieve a consensual restructuring.

1. Objective of a restructuring

For the purpose of this discussion, a restructuring refers to situations where a deal is struck between the company and its various debt and equity holders, the result of which is to provide stability and the return of normal relations between the company and its stakeholders. This may be executed either via a consensual or non-consensual process. The company should be more concerned with the terms of the restructuring than with battles between stakeholders regarding the apportionment of value – however, the following process will maximise the chance of achieving a consensual deal.

2. Restructuring process

From the perspective of the company, the restructuring process can be described as a more or less sequential (but overlapping) process as follows:

- Phase 1: Stabilisation –
  - acknowledge and diagnose the problem;
  - take control of liquidity; and
  - prepare management team for restructuring process.
- Phase 2: Stakeholder engagement –
  - initial information provision and introductory discussions; and
  - initial discussions with each major stakeholder regarding restructuring options.
- Phase 3: Develop business plan –
  - suggested content of business plan; and
  - valuation and capital structure implications.
- Phase 4: Business plan implementation –
  - building credibility of the plan.
- Phase 5: Structure and execute the deal –
  - understand institutional constraints; and
  - ensure headroom between debt facilities and company business plan.

We will explore some of the major issues arising at each of the above stages, making reference to challenges for companies or restructuring professionals in seeking to manage and control the process.

3. Phase 1: Stabilisation

Stabilisation is a critical first step before a company can address the causes of its underperformance and restructure.

3.1 Acknowledge and diagnose the problem

Most restructurings start with a business problem. Sometimes a single event derails the business, but more often than not a series of commercial and operational issues impact on financial performance and raise questions of the company's ability to serve its capital structure, and hence its viability as an ongoing business.

At the point of detecting a decline in financial performance, it is not unusual for a management team to explain (hope) that these issues are a temporary blip, following which the company will eventually get back on track and perform in line with expectations. In some cases, management will cling to this story for an extended period, while employing ever more creative strategies to conceal the extent of the decline in performance, or to distance themselves from the perceived underlying cause of decline.

Sooner or later the company's stakeholders will start to view the underperformance as permanent, and pressure upon banking covenants or other measures of financial performance will force the company to acknowledge the reality of the situation.

The initial problem diagnosis may not have a major impact on the final shape of the restructuring, but it is the start of a new chapter in the company's relationship with its stakeholders, whereby issues will need to be raised sooner and discussed in more detail than is usual for a business which is performing against its own projections. A savvy management team will take sufficient time and effort to make sure that a full and open investigation into the causes of underperformance are shared with stakeholders in an appropriate way – that is, openly and frankly but in a measured and controlled fashion. It is important to the ongoing credibility of the management team themselves that they demonstrate both a sound understanding of the underlying drivers to underperformance and also an ability to engage in constructive dialogue with stakeholders as to the issues faced by the business and their implications.

Management should also be aware that, in the likely event that the company's performance does not bounce back immediately, the company will be engaging very closely with stakeholders and advisers through a restructuring process which could last for some time. During this period, stakeholders and their advisers will be reviewing company plans and forecasts, and forming views as to whether management changes will be needed as part of the restructuring solution. The nature of the dialogue between the parties, starting at the problem diagnosis phase, will influence views on these matters and the likelihood that they will survive through and beyond the restructuring. The level of trust earned at this early stage will also determine how influential that management team will be over the restructuring process.

3.2   Take control of liquidity

The management of liquidity is widely acknowledged as important, especially within distressed businesses, but is often given surprisingly little senior management attention, and therefore the effectiveness of cash forecasting and management is very variable, even within large corporates.

In a restructuring, the spotlight naturally turns to how much liquidity the business has and how it is managed in order to minimise additional funding needs, and if possible maximise the amount of cash available to service interest and debt repayments.

Stricter control over liquidity will be demanded by the board of directors, which will need regular forecast reports highlighting cash headroom or any shortfall for immediate discussion with stakeholders. Restructuring bankers and their advisers will also seek regular update discussions with management to be sure that the business does not unexpectedly run out of cash while the restructuring is still being discussed!

One of the benefits of detailed cash forecasting during a restr[...] to identify in advance whether the company is able to fund interest a[...] payments due in the short term, or whether additional liquidity is n[...] trading during the restructuring period. Whereas many creditors may [...] appetite to put new money into a struggling company, especially while th[...] any restructuring are yet to be agreed, new money can still be available if t[...] sound financial rationale and acceptable terms. Good communication fro[...] company can significantly increase the chances of new money being made availa[...] and an understanding of the strategy and perspective of each stakeholder is help[...] in order to know the most likely sources of liquidity, if needed, and the likely terms requested.

In the event that stakeholders are not able to make additional funding available, it is important that the company has well-developed contingency plans, including plans to generate cash from working capital sources, sale of non-core assets or other internal sources, and that these plans together with any impact on trading performance are clearly communicated to stakeholders.

3.3 Prepare management team for restructuring process

Once there is broad acknowledgement among stakeholders that a restructuring is required, the magnitude of the task facing the management team will start to become apparent. Active leadership of the process by the company, though potentially very helpful, can also inevitably put enormous pressure on the management team – and the CEO and CFO in particular.

The restructuring is likely to demand the creation of a detailed bottom-up business plan, and operational improvements to be rolled out across the business. All of this fundamental operational change will need to be implemented at a time when cash and liquidity are scarce and under tight management. Stakeholders and their advisers will be taking up a significant amount of senior management time and attention and this activity will filter down through the organisation, in the finance and legal functions in particular.

At this time the board of directors should consider whether the company has the right team in place to address the business challenges that it faces, and also deal with all of the additional legal, financial and operational workload associated with a restructuring. In many cases a capable management team can be augmented with a small team of experienced corporate turnaround practitioners who can lead the more technical areas of the restructuring and support the company in developing its business plan and external communications. In cases with a complex multi-layered capital structure, or where there are more significant gaps in the management team, the board should consider an interim management solution or hire a chief restructuring officer to help lead the company through its restructuring and represent it in negotiations.

The restructuring process can be very unsettling for the management team for a number of reasons, including lack of certainty as to whether there will be a role for them after the restructuring and how the outcome will affect any equity or other incentive programmes in place. Stakeholders dealing with the consequences of an

...may not wish to address these items until after a ...ability within the management team is nonetheless ...ocess, and therefore the final phase of preparing ...an appropriate short-term retention programme in ...nagement until such time as it is appropriate to

...ent

...rformance dips below acceptable levels, stakeholders will ...mselves behind the scenes to deal with a possible restructuring. ..., banks will shift the credit into specialist restructuring teams, and many ...ors will organise themselves into committees in order to facilitate communication and leverage their negotiating position. In cases where the capital structure is more complex, various layers of committees may exist, each with separate legal and financial advisers hired to build a case which can best leverage their client's position and influence the process accordingly.

4.1 Initial information provision and introductory discussions

While all this is going on and new teams are getting up to speed on the situation, there is an opportunity for the company to take the initiative and prepare a story for their stakeholder group, setting out:

- the company's analysis of the causes of decline;
- its most recent liquidity forecasts; and
- its proposal for regular reporting over the coming period, including a timetable for the preparation of an updated business plan on which a restructuring can be based.

The company should also consider, in the context of the company's performance versus its banking covenants, whether a standstill or similar arrangement should be requested at this stage. Such an arrangement has the benefit of providing time and stability for the business while it works with its stakeholders on a consensual solution. During this period, the company typically agrees to certain terms such as information provision and minimum liquidity headroom in exchange for a suspension of the banks' rights in respect of any actual or anticipated breaches of terms.

4.2 Initial discussions with each major stakeholder regarding restructuring options

During this initial period of getting up to speed, there is also an opportunity for the company and its advisers to engage with major stakeholders individually in order to establish communication lines and to start the process of socialising views regarding business performance, restructuring options and the preference of each stakeholder regarding the forthcoming restructuring. The purpose of these discussions is:

- to identify areas of consensus and difference in approach;
- to identify and start to manage any unrealistic expectations; and
- to get an early indication of which stakeholder-specific issues are likely to be

key to determining whether a consensual deal is achievable, or alternatively the agreements necessary in order to execute a transaction via another route.

These stakeholder discussions will continue through the process, and it is unlikely that any firm conclusions can be drawn at this early stage, but it is very helpful to understand the landscape before developing the business plan on which the restructuring will be based.

5.   Phase 3: Develop business plan

The creation of a robust and credible business plan is arguably the most important single document to drive the restructuring process. It influences discussions as to debt capacity, funding needs, valuation and capital structure options.

The business plan will be scrutinised in detail by all stakeholders and their advisers. Each separate group of stakeholders will approach the plan with a different perspective and agenda, depending on where they fit within the existing capital structure, and their preferred outcome from the restructuring. For example, secured senior lenders may argue that the business has reached a 'new reality', and is therefore unlikely to recover in line with prior expectations. This approach implies that, while the company's cash flow and valuation is able to support the senior debt being in the money, other subordinated lenders may no longer have an economic interest in the business at all. Conversely, junior creditors and equity holders are likely to take a more optimistic view of the company's near-term future, thereby indicating ongoing value within subordinated layers of debt and equity.

The importance of credibility of the plan cannot be underestimated. By the time a restructuring plan is developed, it is likely that prior plans for the business will have proven to be unrealistic. Because it is of course critical to the success of the process that the new plan is viewed as credible and achievable by all stakeholders, it will be highly advisable for the company to work alongside professional advisers in the creation of their business plan. Advisers used to restructuring situations can ensure that the plan is generated in a way that facilitates the detailed stakeholder review to follow. The support of company-side advisers will also add credibility to the key plan assumptions and outputs themselves and the way that the outputs are presented. In particular, the company's adviser can help the company present not just the plan itself and the underlying assumptions and funding requirements, but also an analysis of the implications of the plan for funding needs and debt capacity, and therefore the optimal shape of the company's restructured facilities.

Another role which advisers can play during the business plan generation process is to act as a link between the stakeholders and company during the period that the business plan is being generated. The advantage of this is to ensure that the company develops a plan which recognises the appetite of the lenders to offer additional support, and as appropriate develops different planning scenarios based on the availability of support for discretionary items including capital investment, M&A activity and so on.

In the context of a restructuring, management should also be aware that the process is best served by creating a prudent but realistic base case plan, rather than the more aggressive forecasts which might be developed as part of a standard disposal process. This is a balancing act for the company, and the decision as to what level to pitch the business plan and how to deal with risks and upsides will certainly influence the restructuring discussions and the perception of the management team themselves. However, future financial covenants will be set based on the plan, and therefore managers and their advisers should ensure that sufficient headroom exists to ensure that the company does not risk future covenant breaches and excessive pressure on the capital structure.

To an extent the format of the business plan to be generated will depend on the situation, but as a guide the plan should be prepared in a detailed presentation format with supporting models, and should include the following content:

- situation assessment;
- company description;
- market and competitive analysis;
- historic financial results;
- business plan assumptions;
- summary business plan outputs, (P&L, balance sheet, cash flow);
- valuation;
- capital structure implications;
- options analysis; and
- restructuring process and timeline.

Ultimately, it is helpful to the restructuring process if all stakeholders have confidence in both the company's business plan and the management's ability to deliver upon it. Once the plan is created, it is critical for the company that stakeholders and their advisers are engaged in constructive discussions regarding the capital structure implications of the plan, rather than discussions as to the credibility of the plan itself, and by extension the credibility of the management.

5.1 Valuation and capital structure implications

The ultimate purpose of producing a restructuring business plan is to facilitate an informed discussion of enterprise value, while stakeholders retain an economic interest in the organisation and appropriate options in terms of capital structure. Although a technical area best addressed with appropriate professional support, value and capital structure implications should be addressed as part of the company's formal business plan. This will be subject to detailed review by stakeholders and their advisers, but it acts to set out the potential options and to frame the next stage of negotiations necessary in order to achieve consensus.

6. Phase 4: Business plan implementation

Implementation of the base case business plan should commence as soon as the plan is approved by the company's board of directors, although of course implementation of any initiatives requiring capital investment or cash restructuring costs will need to be deferred beyond the restructuring period, and should be phased accordingly in any version of the plan containing significant capital investment.

While implementation continues beyond the financial restructuring, finalising the plan in the first few months is particularly important, not least because during this period restructuring negotiations will be ongoing and the credibility of the plan will be reinforced by consistent performance against plan.

During this period, management should be focussing on hitting underlying trading forecasts and ensuring that the company maintains sufficient liquidity throughout. Even at the cost of additional resources to support implementation, the critical line item is trading earnings before interest, taxes, depreciation and amortisation (EBITDA) and the conversion of EBITDA to trading cash flow. With appropriate explanation, creditors will understand the value of investing in implementation support to help deliver improved trading performance, and will understand that related costs and advisory fees will be reduced once the restructuring is completed, with enduring benefits.

As well as building credibility at a critical time, demonstrating an ability to meet the new business plan can also help stakeholders reach a consensus on the forecasts, helping to shift the debate away from a discussion of what the base case forecast should be toward more valuable discussions regarding the appropriate capital structure for the business and how future capital investments should be supported.

7.   Phase 5: Structure and execute the deal

In order to agree on a restructuring deal, it is not enough merely to provide information and explanations about the business and forecasted performance so that stakeholders understand the capital structure needs of the business.

It is also necessary to understand the workings of each of the institutions involved, and any internal restrictions on their ongoing support of the company. Since the crisis in 2008, the growing influences of institutional restrictions on what type of structure can and cannot be supported should not be underestimated. These restrictions can manifest themselves in a variety of ways, and range from not being able to offer any additional support to businesses in certain non-core sectors, through to being unable to extend any facilities beyond a fixed date. Such restrictions can make certain structures either impossible or more complex to agree, but at the time of writing there are no signs that these restrictions are going to be lifted anytime soon. It is therefore critical to understand the unique position of each of the stakeholders, and their requirements for the restructuring deal in order to determine the key conditions necessary to obtain the support of each individual lender and the points of difference which will need to be discussed further and negotiated in order to attempt to find a solution.

This book sets out many of the techniques available to the restructuring practitioner for the execution of a restructuring. Many of these techniques help to maintain value and it is therefore in the interest of the company that its advisers investigate whether these various tools could be used to preserve value in the specific case in hand. However, in this chapter we focus on the features of a restructuring that are of most value to the company itself.

To an extent, the company should rise above disputes between stakeholders over relative shares of the value (even if managers themselves may have their own interests to fight for), and should focus on influencing the overall shape of the restructuring to support the company's pursuit of value for all stakeholders. As part of this, while stakeholders turn their attention to how the detailed structure and terms of the restructuring deal affects their own value, the company should focus on ensuring that the restructuring leaves the company with an appropriate amount of debt facilities in total, and with a repayment profile which fits with the expected shape of financial performance over the medium term.

The company should also run its own financial model of the business post restructuring, illustrating the interaction of the new capital structure and financial covenants with the business plan, in order to ensure a level of headroom appropriate to the situation given a degree of uncertainty over the amounts and timing of trading cash flows. For example, how much flexibility is there in the capital structure to accommodate a range of possible sensitivities to the company's business plan? And what rights would creditors be afforded in the event that the company was to miss its own financial projections temporarily?

8.   Use of advisers

The company and its advisers have a key role in a restructuring, and if played to its full potential this role can help drive the process to a swift conclusion, providing stability for the company, as well as appropriate access to capital in order to execute an agreed strategy and business plan.

If a company is neither resourced nor experienced in restructuring matters, it is likely to feel subjected to an externally driven process, rather than in a position to influence the process to the benefit of the stakeholder group as a whole. A well selected adviser can help the company to exert a positive influence on the restructuring process, taking the lead in a number of restructuring related matters and leaving the executive management team with sufficient time to continue running the business and delivering on trading expectations.

Chief restructuring officers: In some cases, especially for large companies or those with complex capital structures involving large banking syndicates, creditors will require the company to hire a chief restructuring officer to guide the company through the restructuring process. This individual, who will join the executive management team until the restructuring is complete, generally takes responsibility for the following matters, working alongside the company's permanent management team:

- liaising with debt and equity holders on matters relating to the restructuring, and providing updates and information as necessary in order to support discussions and stakeholder decision making;
- supporting the company in the development of a credible business plan, and the presentation of the plan to stakeholders;
- representing the company in restructuring negotiations, including – as necessary – negotiating standstill agreements, covenant default waivers, deferral of debt repayment obligations, etc;
- forecasting liquidity and liaising with stakeholders regarding short-term funding needs;

- coordinating other advisers, including agreeing scope of advisers to other parties; and
- structuring and negotiating the restructuring on behalf of the company.

Due to the focused nature of the role, the chief restructuring officer can either step away from the business once the financial restructuring is completed, or as appropriate stay involved for a period of time after the restructuring in order to drive the implementation of operational restructuring activities.

9. Concluding comments

Experience suggests that restructurings in which the company and their advisers take an active role in shaping the outcome tend to lead to more sustainable restructuring solutions.

However, leading a restructuring is a specialist job, and one which is extremely time consuming and fraught with risk. Juggling these unfamiliar responsibilities together with effectively managing a company in distress is a task few management teams succeed at without external professional support.

This chapter sets out an illustrative restructuring process, which is broadly sequential and highlights the key issues for the company at each stage of the process. The common themes throughout are to maintain financial control of the company through tight management of liquidity, and to keep in close dialogue with all stakeholders in order to maintain stability and to understand the key issues and constraints for each party and any points of consensus or difference.

Clearly each case will be very different, and consensus is not always possible or even necessarily desirable. However, following the above steps puts the company in a strong position to influence the situation positively regardless of the restructuring tools that may be appropriate or necessary to get a deal done.

Restructuring (and enforcing) in a development context

Barry Gross
Ben Jones
Berwin Leighton Paisner LLP

1. Introduction

The principal factor that differentiates real estate restructurings from corporate restructurings is that the assets are 'bricks and mortar' and this is where their value resides: you can literally touch them.

For the most part, this simplifies matters. A lender will usually have the benefit of a fixed security package over the real estate asset against which it has advanced moneys, and thus the ability to exert significant control over the restructuring process and the asset itself. Moreover, unlike in the corporate restructuring space, enforcement by a lender is generally a much less risky, less value destructive and, therefore, less unpalatable option, with fewer of the complexities that frequently arise when dealing with living, breathing businesses (eg, employee, customer and supplier issues), and the risk of rapid value evaporation. For this reason, a lender's decision as to whether to restructure or enforce can be approached on a simple cost/benefit basis: the costs of preserving the status quo versus the cost of enforcement. Enforcement will often win, especially if the lender does not believe that the existing management will deliver value.

2. Developments

Whereas enforcement against an investment property or a bare piece of land involves a relatively limited number of moving parts, where the asset is a development the decision as to whether to enforce requires a significant amount of pre-planning due to the greater number of potential stakeholders. These may include:

- the borrower;
- the developer (assuming that this is not the borrower);
- the main building contractor;
- the professional team (eg, employers agent, quantity surveyors and architect);
- subcontractors;
- suppliers of materials;
- potential tenants which have entered into agreements for lease;
- local authority and non-contractual stakeholders; and
- second charge holders or unsecured lenders to the borrower.

An enforcement will not affect all of those parties in the same way. Most stakeholders will have some ability to make decisions following enforcement which could affect the successful outcome of the development in a material way. Therefore, the most fundamental question that any lender must consider is whether to enforce.

3. To enforce or not?

In deciding whether to enforce, a lender must take numerous factors into account. The following will play an important role in this decision.

3.1 Relationship with the borrower

Enforcement can lead to value erosion. Enforcing mid-development can result in even greater value loss due to the potential for delays and the increased risk of other stakeholders taking actions to protect their own positions – a particular risk if there are significant arrears where the borrower has been stretching its creditors. If the lender still has faith in the borrower and its ability to deliver the project, it may make more sense to avoid enforcement at this stage and enable the development to be completed before agreeing on a consensual exit (eg, a refinancing or a disposal) or enforcing. This is a difficult balance to achieve, especially since once the borrower becomes aware that it is likely not to realise a profit from the development, it may be tempted to leverage its position by threatening to down tools. While some incentivising may be necessary, the lender needs to seek careful independent financial advice to consider the likely negative impact on value of enforcing against the cost of incentivising the borrower to complete the development.

3.2 Stage of development

The point in the development at which the need to enforce arises plays an important part in the decision-making process. Where enforcement is required early on, it may be easier to bring on board a new development team which can deliver the project more efficiently. Further, there is more time to make up any delays caused by the enforcement. By contrast, enforcing when a building is nearing completion by keeping on the existing development team can minimise delays and reduce risks in terms of delivering the finished product with less room for additional cost overruns. In reality, enforcement can be necessary and made to work at any stage in the development process. The key is to ensure that enforcement will deal with whatever issues are likely to arise – it should not be avoided simply because of the project's stage of development.

3.3 Relationship with building contractor

Quite apart from the developer/borrower, a key party in any development is the building contractor; while the developer is responsible for delivering the finished development, the building contractor physically constructs it. Depending on the type of procurement route used, the building contractor could also have significant design input and may provide a solution to many of the issues and risks that enforcement raises. Where the borrower and the building contractor are related entities, careful consideration needs to be given to the risk that enforcement against the borrower could result in the building contractor become obstructive. This could happen either where the borrower is a building contractor by trade or – as is becoming more common – where the development is a joint venture between land owners and developers. In those circumstances, it may be necessary to consider a joint enforcement against both the borrower and the building contractor. Of course, this is possible only where the lender has enforcement powers over the building contractor.

4. The legal framework

4.1 Which enforcement route?

There are really only two potential routes for enforcement in the context of a development scenario: administration and fixed-charge receivership.

4.2 The fixed-charge receiver

Fixed-charge receivership is a relatively simple process for a secured lender to initiate. The receiver is appointed by the lender under the lender's security over the property; all that is necessary is for the lender to execute a simple deed of appointment, following the security becoming enforceable. The receiver is 'the lender's man' – its duties are owed primarily to the appointor (ie, the secured lender) and its job is to get it repaid. Unlike administrators – who must be licensed insolvency practitioners – receivers tend to be property specialists (often surveyors) who have spent their careers dealing with real estate. Receiverships also often tend to be less expensive than administrations. For most plain vanilla enforcements over real estate, therefore, receiverships are a good choice.

However, in a development scenario, the limitations of receivership are more apparent. The receiver can deal with the property over which it has been appointed, as well as its income – these powers are typically widely drawn and contained in the security documentation. However, the receiver has no powers over the property-owning vehicle itself (eg, the power to take possession of information, books and records) or over assets which are not contained within the lender's fixed security package (eg, building materials). There is also a perennial debate over the ability of receivers to offset input value added tax (VAT) incurred against output VAT on the property, which can have significant cash-flow implications for an ongoing development, which will have to be funded by the lender.

Most significantly, unlike administration, the appointment of a receiver brings no moratorium on claims being made or continued against the borrower. This means that there is no stable basis from which a development can be continued. There will always be a risk of interference and disruption by creditors who are owed money and take action to recover it.

4.3 Administration

Administration is a much more powerful tool in the development context. An administrator can be appointed relatively quickly and easily by a lender that holds, as part of its security package, a qualifying floating charge (ie, a floating charge over the whole – or substantially the whole – of the borrower's assets and undertaking). Administrators must be qualified insolvency practitioners, typically from an accountancy firm; many have experience of real estate and the larger firms have specialist teams comprising surveyors and other real estate experts.

Administration is a collective insolvency procedure, which means that the administrator acts in the interests of all creditors generally, not just the lender which appointed it. However, in practice, the administrator will work closely with the lender and the relationship is generally consensual. As is often the case, the lender will be first in line for any proceeds of realisation of the asset by virtue of its priority as a secured lender. As a result, the administrator will be careful to ensure that the lender's loss is minimised and will adopt a consensual approach to strategy to mitigate any subsequent criticism should it not go according to plan. Moreover, the administrator will need funding to complete the development, which is usually available only from one source: the lender. Administration offers an advantage over receivership when it comes to funding, because the administrator has the power to borrow; when it does so, its repayment obligation ranks with super priority.

Unlike a receiver, whose powers start and stop with the property over which it has been appointed, an administrator is appointed over the corporate and will collect into its custody and control all of the borrower's assets. For all intents and purposes, it is as if the directors have been replaced by the administrator. The wider scope of the administrator's role – coupled with the increased compliance and reporting obligations imposed on administrators by statute – means that administration is generally more expensive than receivership.

The fact that the administrator will control the company in all of its actions, as opposed merely to controlling it in respect of the property, means that no questions can arise as to its ability to manage all aspects of the development's completion. The administrator also has statutory powers to require the directors and other parties to hand over documents, and to provide assistance and explanations, which can be very useful if the enforcement is hostile.

As mentioned previously, the commencement of administration triggers a moratorium. As soon as the borrower becomes insolvent, it is at risk of potential claims – both legitimate and opportunistic. The moratorium will deter the more opportunistic claims and provide sufficient time in respect of more legitimate claims to enable a more sensible behind-the-scenes discussion to take place. Receivers have no such tools in their armoury.

5. Identify the impact

As with any enforcement, a detailed review of important relationships is important, but perhaps even more so in the development context. As already mentioned, an ongoing development has many stakeholders. It is not simply that stakeholders can lose out as a result of enforcement; they have the ability to influence the ultimate outcome.

5.1 The building contract

The ability to keep the building contractor in place is often critical. First, the process of appointing a new building contractor would take a long time to have any substantial impact on the project's delivery. However, just as crucial is the recognition that it is often the building contractor that holds the various subcontracts together. Losing the building contractor could create a domino effect, making successful delivery of the project virtually impossible. A detailed understanding of the building contract and all subcontracts identifying the key risk areas is necessary to mitigate this risk. As with all commercial contracts, the prime concern of the building contractor will be payment and, therefore, showing a clear commitment to build out the project and make payments in accordance with the contract will help.

The funding of these payments is an important element of contingency planning for enforcement. The lender will need to understand, and have approval for, the project's cash-flow requirements. Legal input will be needed to ensure that the funding is properly secured and ranks senior. As a general principle, post-appointment funding should rank senior to other debts. Unlike in some jurisdictions which the legal regime facilitates this (eg, Chapter 11 in the United States), in the United Kingdom the super priority accorded to liabilities incurred by an administrator (referred to as 'administration expenses') ranks behind debt secured by fixed charge. This can be problematic if – as is often the case – the debt secured against the property is underwater. Analysis will have to be done to determine how to graft the administration funding onto the existing facilities. Where the lending is not bilateral or there is hedging, this can be a relatively complicated exercise.

5.2   The tenants

Delivering the completed project may require keeping the building contractor onside, but there is little point in completing it if the original tenants have all used this opportunity to walk away.

Save in the context of a completely speculative development – which lenders largely steered clear of even during the boom period in the United Kingdom – there are likely to be various agreements for leases in respect of the development. In a mixed-use development, there will be different forms of agreement for the different types of letting. Commercial lease agreements will contain longstop dates, liquidated damages and *force majeure* provisions. Enforcement will cause delay in delivery of the completed property. Therefore, before deciding to enforce, consideration must be given to the timetable and the ability to meet it, taking into account likely delays.

Further, in the retail sphere agreements tend to provide that the tenant does not have to take the lease at certain times of the year to avoid opening during a traditionally poor trading period. Therefore, even if the delay will not result in a termination right due to the longstop date arising, it may result in a significant delay in being able to complete the lease and commence income generation. A similar concern applies in the student accommodation sphere where there is a very limited window (ie, tied to college term times) by which the development must be fully completed to avoid a full year of voids.

Further, there are often cases where a delay may not be significant enough to enable a tenant to terminate its agreement for lease, but might give rise to significant liquidated damages. The purpose of these damages is to provide a fixed amount of compensation to the tenant for the scheme's late delivery. They are meant to be a genuine estimate of the likely loss that would be suffered by the tenant in the event of delay. For example, where the development is intended to be the new head office for a large company, the liquidated damages will reflect the cost of alternative accommodation during the overrun period, as well as other expected costs. However, these costs will have been considered at a different time, so may not reflect the actual cost and could be higher (or lower); this does not affect the tenants' right to receive them. As administrators, there may be an argument that those damages could become administration expenses (not a direct issue for lenders holding fixed charge security, as their claim will rank ahead, but an indirect issue because the administration expense liability will be payable ahead of the costs, expenses and remuneration of the administrator) and so rank behind, especially where the administrators have given strong positive signs to the tenant that they wish the agreement to remain in place.

In the residential context, lease agreements tend to be much more favourable to developers – largely because solicitors acting for buyers do not spend time negotiating the terms. As a result, any longstop dates tend to be generous. Where residential buyers can pose an issue is where their agreements have been protected on the title to the property. While any claims for their original deposits will be unsecured claims against the borrower, their notices on the title protecting their agreements will prove disruptive to any attempt at a future sale. Therefore, the cost and negative public relations that can result from difficulties with residential buyers should be factored in to the decision-making process.

5.3   *Force majeure*

Developers and building contractors have long concerned themselves with the risk of factors outside their control causing a delay to the development. The concept of *force majeure* is intended to manage this risk by allowing additional time in the programme where delay is caused by a matter outside the control of the relevant party. Issues can arise when different contracts contain different *force majeure* provisions. Commercially, this is to be expected, since a building contractor should not be liable if the developer becomes insolvent, but should take responsibility for picking and managing its subcontractors carefully to avoid the risk of insolvency. Well-advised tenants will seek to limit the *force majeure* options open to the developer, so its own insolvency will not give rise to a right of termination. However, sometimes the main building contractor's insolvency is 'snuck in' – if this happens, then putting the building contractor into an insolvency process can provide some additional time.

5.4   Lender step-in rights

When advising on financing a development, much emphasis is placed on the lender's ability to step into the shoes of the developer with regard to the building contractor and sometimes certain key agreements for lease as well. The difficulty that arises is that the lender will rarely, if ever, take over the development literally. By taking out of the borrower's hands the power and duty of managing and controlling the property, the lender may become a mortgagee in possession, which is deeply unappealing. A mortgagee in possession is liable:

- for the burden of freehold/leasehold covenants;
- to account (for rents/profits);
- to repair/maintain the property;
- for deliberate and negligent damage to the property; and
- potentially, for rates (the act of taking possession may constitute a change in the rateable occupier for rating purposes).

Well-drafted step-in rights enable the lender to provide a nominee to take over the obligations. This may work well where it is the developer that has become insolvent and not the land owner, since it is merely a case of novating the development agreement and other contracts to the new nominee developer. However, where the developer and the landowner are the same person (as is often the case), it becomes necessary to transfer the ownership of the land. Transferring the property at its full value is difficult to achieve. Valuing a development mid-build with the myriad of interrelated contractual arrangements and risks is not an easy task, even for a seasoned valuer. Further, the need to consider in depth the interests of second charge holders and unsecured creditors complicates the decision-making process. The most attractive route in dealing with this scenario is the hive-down, discussed later in this chapter.

5.5   The exit strategy

When taking enforcement action, it is important to consider the ultimate exit strategy. This will affect both the initial enforcement route and further decisions along the way. While some asset management may be necessary in the case of a completed development, the strategy will be a sale of the asset as a whole. In the development context, and especially in a mixed-use development, a sale of the whole is unlikely to produce the best returns once complete, even assuming that a buyer can be found. Due to the complexity of the investor market, marketing a fully completed mixed-use development which is unlet in significant parts will limit the market considerably; many investors will only consider or be able to invest in specific asset classes, such as retail or offices. Therefore seeking to complete the letting of the development will help to increase the exit value and the lender's recovery. However, achieving this is not straightforward.

5.6   Meeting existing obligations

As already highlighted, the first step in achieving a let development is to keep hold of all tenants already committed to the development. There are three aspects to this. First is ensuring that all required deadlines are met. This aspect has already been discussed: delays caused by enforcement must be controlled carefully through detailed planning. Second is dealing with scenarios where tenants are entitled to terminate their agreements on the developer's insolvency. Third is the ability to comply with obligations regarding the actual grant of the lease on completion of the development and any agreement becoming unconditional. This is not always straightforward. The agreement, in addition to financial obligations regarding contributions to tenant fit-out works, will often require certain legal requirements to be met – in particular, the obligation to grant any lease with full-title guarantee. Administrators will not be prepared to grant any lease or enter into any contract with full-title guarantee. In fact, even limited title guarantee may not be given, since the administrators will be concerned about any encumbrances that the borrower may have granted of which they are unaware – the effect of even limited title guarantee is to guarantee that such encumbrances do not exist. Any claims under such a contract could be an administration expense.

5.7 Achieving further disposals

Unless a development is fully let or forward sold, the ability to let it further can add significant value to the property and increase realisations for the lender – perhaps even returning value to other stakeholders. However, an insolvent property owner does not present a particularly attractive landlord/counterparty. Further, the requirements of administrators in relation to the avoidance of incurring any liability in order to reduce the risk of administration expenses results in bulky documentation, which focuses on the protection of administrators and can leave holes in the future management of the completed development, thus itself impacting on value.

5.8 Second charges

The existence on the title of charges in favour of third parties (quite often shareholders that have provided equity by way of shareholder loans) can also impair the maximisation of value from the development. While the lender should have priority and thus be able to overreach charges ranking junior to it, this is generally used only in the context of a sale when the lender sells by exercise of its power of sale. It is not a route utilised for granting leases and – where there are junior charges – those charge holders can have hold-out value as a consequence.

Often, some thought would have been given to these issues when the deal was first put together, with an intercreditor agreement or deed of priority put in place to regulate the relationship between the senior and junior positions. However, many of these arrangements are unfortunately lacking when tested – pre-2008 documentation in particular. Careful legal analysis must therefore be undertaken to ensure that any junior charge holder opportunities for hold-out are identified in advance and a workaround found or consent obtained.

5.9 Title insurance

Forms of insurance designed to replace the full title guarantee that an administrator cannot give are available on the market. Although these are not a solution for all of the issues that arise when considering the exit strategy, they can be useful for offering additional comfort to potential tenants/buyers. Alternatively, a sufficiently confident administrator could rely on the policy itself to give the full title guarantee and use the insurance in the event that a claim arose. Bearing in mind the more limited risk where a lender has taken a full security package and has been involved throughout, this is a viable option. What such a policy does not deal with is the unwillingness of an administrator to take on more detailed obligations regarding – for example, the provision of services. Further, such insurance will not remedy the termination right arising in favour of a tenant if the developer becomes insolvent. A more radical solution is required to resolve these issues.

5.10 The hive-down

When faced with the risk of tenants exercising termination rights in agreements for lease on insolvency of the developer where the lender has got step-in rights, the only solution is to move the development out of the insolvent entity and into a new solvent entity. While the property can always be sold to a third party, as already discussed, doing so partway through a development is likely to result in a very poor financial result and may not achieve the best possible outcome for the lender. From the lender's perspective, taking the property onto its balance sheet may not always be attractive and partially defeats the purpose of appointing a third party to run the development.

In certain circumstances, it is possible to achieve a result which removes the second charges, enables a solvent nominee to enter into unfettered agreements and take novations of agreements for leases, while at the same time retaining control within the original borrower entity now in administration.

The process is as follows:

- The administrators set up a new entity, which is normally a wholly owned subsidiary of the original borrower (NewCo).
- NewCo acquires the insolvent entity from the property; the sale is a transaction by way of the lender exercising its power of sale and overreaching any obstructive second charges on the title.
- The acquisition of the property is financed by a new loan to NewCo from the lender in respect of which new security is granted.
- The sale proceeds are used by the original borrower to repay part of the outstanding debt.
- NewCo takes a novation of the building contract and any other relevant contracts.
- NewCo is the nominee which enters into required deeds of covenants with those tenants benefiting from a termination right.
- NewCo can now deal with the property subject only to the bank's new security, while the administrators retain control via the shareholding in NewCo.

While this is an attractive solution, it is not without its problems, including the following:

- Second charge holders – by utilising its power of sale to transfer the property, the lender can disenfranchise second charge holders. Therefore, the value at which the property is transferred for is highly relevant, as is the level of debt in the original borrower. The closer the level of original debt to the valuation, the greater the risk. Further, it is advisable to provide sufficient opportunity to second charge holders to be involved in the process and consider alternative ways of replicating their security. While granting them a second charge over the property once hived down would be counterproductive, providing second charges over, for example, the shares in NewCo is an option that can be considered. Alternatively, equity in the NewCo could be considered where the ultimate value may be sufficient to create a surplus.

- Reality as opposed to perception – while NewCo is not in insolvency proceedings, it is totally dependent on the lender to provide the necessary funding to complete the development. Both the building contractor and other stakeholders may seek additional assurance that the lender will continue to provide funding before being convinced that NewCo will be able to fulfil its obligations.
- NewCo compliance – where NewCo is a company, it will require a real person to act as director. While there are individuals who will take directorships in entities of this nature, they tend to be expensive due to the potential risks involved and will insist on comprehensive insurance to cover their liabilities.
- Tax leakage – as a separate corporate entity the tax consequences need to be considered carefully. One variation on the hive-down option is to utilise a limited liability partnership which is transparent for tax purposes. However, this introduces additional issues, due to the need for the partnership to have at least two members. Further, there can be grouping issues if further intra-group transfers or leases are required (eg, in the context of residential lease structuring).

6.   Conclusion

Every development scenario is different and we have sought to identify some themes common to many mixed-use developments. The aim must always be to analyse carefully and prepare in detail. Identifying the key contractual relationships and issues that will need to be dealt with on enforcement will help avoid unpredicted value destruction. However, to maximise value, it is important to map out the process from enforcement right through to the ultimate final disposal. This way, it is possible to structure steps that will help to ensure that despite having to take the unattractive measure of stepping in on a partially completed development, the ultimate outcome will be as positive as possible – not only for the secured lender, but for the other stakeholders as well.

How UK-defined benefit pension schemes affect a workout situation

Michael Bushnell
Alex Hutton-Mills
Lincoln International

The impact of UK-defined benefit pension schemes on the nature and process of corporate restructuring has continued to increase since the passing into law of the Pensions Act 2004. With the addition of the Pensions Act 2008, guidance from the UK Pensions Regulator (TPR) and significant case law, the area is increasingly important to restructuring professionals yet increasingly opaque.

The changes in UK legislation since 2004 have strengthened defined benefit pension scheme protection significantly. Simultaneously, a general increase in pension scheme deficits (and therefore claims in restructuring) has occurred, driven by the financial crisis that began in 2007 and the government's response.

This chapter considers the main stakeholders in the restructuring process where a defined benefit pension scheme exists and the manner in which they can impact on the process.

1. Major stakeholders

The Pensions Act 2004, which came into force in April 2005, brought a number of additional stakeholders into the restructuring process:

- scheme trustees;
- the Pension Protection Fund (PPF); and
- the TPR.

1.1 Trustees

The trustees are custodians of the scheme and its assets on behalf of the scheme members. They may be individuals, companies or a combination of both. It is not unusual to find directors of the principal group company, which may or may not be the sponsoring company of the scheme, on the trustee board (eg, the finance director) – notwithstanding possible conflict issues. An independent trustee may also be appointed to balance or provide particular expertise to the trustee board. In addition, there are rules requiring that at least one-third of the board is nominated by scheme members. Broadly, the role involves paying the correct benefits to members, investing scheme assets appropriately and acting in the best interests of scheme members. Extensive duties are imposed on trustees by both trust law and current legislation.

1.2   PPF

The PPF came into being in April 2005 under the Pensions Act 2004. It was established to pay compensation to members of eligible defined benefit pension schemes following a "qualifying insolvency event" in relation to the sponsoring employer – in effect, a form of statutory insurance. The PPF is a statutory fund, managed by the board of the PPF. Schemes pay the board of the PPF annual levies calculated on various bases (including the risk of the relevant scheme).[1]

1.3   TPR

The Pensions Act 2004 also created the TPR in April 2005. This is the regulatory and supervisory body for work-based pension schemes, including defined benefit occupational pension schemes. Its statutory aims are set out in the Pensions Act 2004, the most relevant (for this chapter) being:

- protecting members' benefits; and
- reducing the risk of schemes needing recourse to the PPF.

In the Budget 2013, the chancellor of the exchequer confirmed that a new objective will be introduced for the TPR to support scheme-specific funding arrangements that "are compatible with sustainable growth for the sponsoring employer" and are fully consistent with the Pensions Act 2004 scheme funding legislation. The new objective will be set out in legislation whose implementation will be subject to review after six months. The TPR's code of practice on scheme-specific funding will be updated accordingly. This new objective may have an important impact on restructuring situations relative to the existing statutory objectives highlighted above.

The TPR has been given wide-ranging powers affecting employers (ie, corporates supporting pension schemes) and trustees, including its 'moral hazard' powers.

These moral hazard powers are designed to reduce the risk of pension liabilities being transferred to the PPF. These provisions permit the TPR to issue either financial support directions (FSDs) or contribution notices (CNs) to persons in circumstances where it believes that an employer is deliberately avoiding its pension obligations. Contribution notices can be issued against any "associated or connected"[2] person of any employer who has been involved in a deliberate act or failure to act, the main purpose of which is to avoid pension liabilities. A financial support direction can be issued against any associated or connected person requiring an employer to put in place arrangements to guarantee the pension liability of an employer which is insufficiently resourced[3] or which is a service company.[4]

---

1   For more information on the PPF, see the PPF's website at www.pensionprotectionfund.org.uk.
2   The Insolvency Act 1986 provides the definitions for 'associated' and 'connected' persons broadly to include directors, shadow directors and all companies in a corporate group (including shareholders holding at least one-third of the voting rights). However, FSDs cannot currently be issued against individual directors or shadow directors.
3   An employer is insufficiently resourced if the value of its resources is less than 50% of the estimated Section 75 (or buyout) liability of the scheme and the value of the resources of a connected or associated person when added to the employer's resources would be 50% or more of the estimated Section 75 liability.
4   A company is a service company if its revenues are mainly derived from providing services to other companies within the same corporate group.

These powers can potentially require substantial contributions from companies if, as a result of their action (or inaction) with respect to a particular transaction, they are perceived to have weakened the security of the scheme. Although one of the principal purposes of a workout may be to permit a particular business to continue trading in some shape or form, or to preserve employment, the scope of the TPR's powers may mean that a workout solution may be caught within the TPR net. This may be because the ability of a sponsoring company to support a scheme is adversely affected by the proposed restructuring. This raises the possibility of the TPR seeking to use its enforcement powers against a potentially broad range of parties involved in a workout.

Accordingly, companies may wish to seek clearance from the TPR to avoid the risk of having to make substantial additional contributions or provide other forms of support to a scheme. This is considered further below.

The TPR also produces guidance and codes of practice setting out what it expects employers' and trustees' behaviour to be to facilitate demonstration of compliance with parties' legal and regulatory obligations. For example, guidance has been issued relating to scheme abandonment, clearance of corporate transactions and conflicts of interest.[5]

2. Solvent restructuring – impact of the TPR's powers

Solvent restructurings/refinancings can be as simple as negotiating covenant resets or terming out maturity dates on certain facilities. Alternatively, there may be a more complicated balance-sheet restructuring involving a debt-for-equity swap with other features, such as moving assets around a group in forgiveness of indebtedness owed to certain lenders.

One would assume that the principal purpose behind these transactions would not be to avoid pension scheme liabilities; however, given the principles-based approach of the TPR, the trustees may require some form of mitigation to improve the position of the scheme to offset any possible deterioration in the support provided to the scheme (ie, the employer covenant) post-event.

Solvent, consensual balance-sheet restructurings will seek to reduce the degree of financial stress on the company by, for example, equitising debt and creating a balance sheet that can support the operations. Throughout this process, the actions taken have a direct impact on the 'covenant' of the sponsoring employer to the pension scheme. As part of discussions around balance-sheet restructuring, two main issues arise:

- events negatively impacting on the scheme; and
- the appropriate level for future payments to the scheme under the scheme-specific funding regime following any restructuring activity.

The other key point to note is that restructurings are often time critical. The TPR understands the time pressures involved in such scenarios. Moreover, it would not

---

For more information on the TPR, and for copies of the various codes of practice and guidance, see www.thepensionsregulator.gov.uk.

be consistent with one of the TPR's statutory objectives (ie, reducing the likelihood of schemes needing recourse to the PPF) if the TPR were not to be responsive to the needs of stressed/distressed employers and/or trustees of schemes associated with such employers – a failed solvent restructuring will by definition become an insolvent restructuring.

Invariably, there is significant pressure on liquidity in the run-up to either a consensual/solvent restructuring or an insolvency event. As such, the impact of the scheme-specific funding regime also implemented through the Pensions Act 2004 becomes relevant. While the initial public focus surrounding TPR concerned clearance (discussed below), the broader ongoing responsibilities of scheme-specific funding are now becoming increasingly evident.

Under scheme-specific funding, trustees are obliged to assess the covenant of the sponsoring employer and reflect this assessment in setting technical provisions (the trustees' view, with actuarial advice, on the value of the liabilities). Introducing covenant strength as a concept within the trustees' assessment of the liability, and therefore the deficit, means that the weaker or more stressed the sponsor becomes, the more prudent trustees will be regarding the assumptions behind the technical provisions; and the greater the likely view of the size of the deficit. In simple terms, if the corporate sponsor is close to insolvency, the trustees might ordinarily conclude that they should target a buyout value of the liabilities compared to a more ongoing basis – perhaps similar to International Accounting Standard 19/International Financial Reporting Standard 17 for a strong employer covenant.

The impact of scheme-specific funding is therefore to accelerate the pressure and likely funding demands of a pension scheme as the financial strength of the supporting employer weakens. Another aspect of scheme-specific funding which is sponsor friendly, however, is that the sponsor is obliged to agree on a recovery plan for any deficit to technical provisions "as fast as it can reasonably afford". What is 'reasonably affordable' when trade and secured creditors are competing for liquidity raises interesting questions – invariably, in lay terms, the trustees assess that there is a large hole in the pension scheme and the sponsor says that it does not have the means to fill it. The TPR's new statutory objective in restructuring situations will likely increase the focus on the tension between an assessment of a sponsor's realistic prospect of achieving sustainable growth[6] versus the protection of the pensions creditor in such circumstances.

A solvent restructuring that will likely de-leverage and reduce financial stress will also be expected to be covenant improving. This should reduce the level of liabilities on a technical provisions basis and lead to the company being able to agree on a suitable scheme-specific funding recovery plan. It is important that the pension scheme is treated equitably in these discussions. The restructuring activity may well be such that the parties involved consider TPR clearance to be relevant.

---

6   This will most likely be captured through an analysis of the sponsor's working capital and capital expenditure requirements and its access to external capital in light of the sponsor's turnaround plan, bearing in mind the pension scheme.

3. Solvent restructuring – TPR clearance

As noted above, to minimise the risk of the TPR making an order for immediate contributions or longer-term financial support, parties may apply for clearance – that is, confirmation that the circumstances of the workout or refinancing will not cause the TPR to use its powers against the named parties.

The principles-based guidance issued by the TPR concerns itself with events materially detrimental to the ability of the scheme to meet its pension liabilities. It categorises corporate events as either employer-related or scheme-related.

(a) 'Employer-related' events

'Employer-related' events are events affecting the employer and/or its group and, accordingly, the potential scheme funding. Clearance need normally be considered only where there is a 'relevant deficit'[7] on the scheme. However, where there is significant detriment, the TPR's guidance is clear that there is no requirement for a relevant deficit.

The guidance provides a non-exhaustive list of events that constitute employer-related events. The following are likely to be most relevant in a workout:

- change in the level of security to creditors;
- return of capital;
- change in group structure (including a change of control which may be the result of a debt-for-equity swap by lenders); or
- asset sales (eg, with sale proceeds going to lenders as a means of reducing indebtedness).

No thresholds are provided in the guidance. Instead, parties need to consider whether the event is detrimental to the scheme.

(b) 'Scheme-related' events

'Scheme-related' events are those directly affecting the scheme. Examples include compromising a debt owed to the scheme. For these events, scheme funding is irrelevant – the TPR will want to hear about them.

Clearance is voluntary. However, the TPR is keen to hear from both trustees and employers. Trustees need to ensure that the scheme receives appropriate mitigation to offset any detriment to the employer covenant caused by a restructuring. This could range from direct cash or asset contributions to the scheme, to contingent assets that would provide funding on the occurrence of specified events. Once granted, clearance ensures that no contribution notice or financial support direction will be made against those parties named in the application in relation to events specified in the clearance application.

4. Solvent restructuring – the impact of the PPF

The board of the PPF may also take part in solvent restructurings that involve a

---

7   Trustees need to look at the funding level implied by the highest of the Financial Reporting Standard 17/International Accounting Standard 19 (ie, accounting basis), the scheme-specific/ongoing funding basis and the basis used to calculate the PPF levy to determine whether there is a relevant deficit.

compromise arrangement entered into by the trustees regarding the employer statutory debt. This is because any such compromise (which will separately require TPR clearance as a scheme-related event) that takes place without the agreement of the PPF or, in any event, is below the PPF's calculated level of protected liabilities, will otherwise render the scheme ineligible for PPF protection going forward. The board of the PPF and the TPR may also be involved in discussions regarding regulated apportionment arrangements, which are one of a number of means of allowing employers in multi-employer schemes to allocate a statutory debt falling on employers among the various employers in such a way that the arrangement approved by the TPR will not render the scheme ineligible for entry into the PPF.[8]

Where it can be demonstrated that, in the short term, the employer's insolvency is inevitable, the board of the PPF will engage with other stakeholders in any attempt to restructure the business. The board of the PPF has proved itself to be reasonably commercial in its short life, but there are certain conditions to its participation. It must be satisfied that the restructuring will:

- result in a recovery for the scheme which is demonstrably better than that which would result from the otherwise inevitable insolvency of the business;
- offer a better recovery for the scheme than that which would be sacrificed because the TPR clears the transaction and thus relinquishes its ability to recover funds for the scheme by issuing a financial support direction or contribution notice;
- treat the scheme fairly in the sense that it gets an equitable share (relative to other beneficiaries) of resultant upside from the restructuring; and
- offer the scheme an equity stake in the business – one-third if the existing participants to retain ownership and one-tenth if they are non-connected or non-associated. This is really an 'anti-embarrassment' provision.

If the board of the PPF does not think that it is being treated equitably, it can and has walked away from a prospective deal, resulting in everyone losing out.

5. Insolvent restructuring – the impact of the PPF

Provided that certain conditions are met, following the insolvency of a sponsor company, the PPF will assume scheme assets from an eligible scheme and pay compensation to eligible individuals. These payments are made to members from PPF funds derived from a combination of:

- scheme assets;
- the compulsory annual levies paid by all defined benefit and hybrid (ie, part defined benefit, part defined contribution) schemes;
- investment returns; and
- dividends from the insolvencies of the employers.

The board of the PPF assumes responsibility for a pension scheme only where:

---

8   The Uniq 'deficit-for-equity' swap in 2011, for example, involved a regulated apportionment arrangement.

- a 'qualifying insolvency event'[9] has occurred with respect to an eligible scheme;
- the scheme has not been rescued (eg, by the sale of the business to a new employer that takes over the scheme's funding obligations); and
- the scheme's assets are below the PPF's calculated level of protected liabilities.

If the above conditions are not met, the board of the PPF will cease to be involved once the relevant assessment procedures have been completed. If the conditions are met, the scheme will transfer to the PPF and the scheme members will receive compensation payments in lieu of their pensions. Broadly, the level of compensation payable will depend on whether the members in question are over or under normal pension age on the date of the insolvency event. The rules for calculating compensation are complex and beyond the scope of this chapter, but can be found on the PPF's website.

The board of the PPF may have a role to play in insolvent restructurings. This is because it assumes the creditor rights of the scheme once the insolvency has occurred. In these circumstances, the board of the PPF – as an unsecured creditor in the insolvency – may be able to influence the adoption or otherwise of a restructuring plan by having a vote at any creditor meetings. That claim will be for the Section 75 (full buyout) debt of the scheme, which is usually a significant sum.

6. Insolvent restructuring – impact of the TPR

The TPR's moral hazard powers, in particular, have had a significant impact on insolvent restructuring, both in the United Kingdom and internationally. Since inception in 2005, the TPR has brought its moral hazard powers to bear in five reported cases, all in relation to insolvent restructuring. While those powers are not intended to apply exclusively in insolvency, by their nature insolvent restructurings can require extreme measures and limit the possibility of a negotiated settlement. Three instances of the execution of the TPR's powers have been financial support directions and two have been contribution notices.

The TPR's moral hazard powers are intended to pierce the corporate veil and allow pension schemes to attribute liabilities to connected or associated parties that may not have previously considered the pension scheme as a liability. In the event that the moral hazard powers are exercised after that connected or associated party is rendered insolvent, the scheme's claim will crystallise and become a liability of that entity. However, as the claim was not a liability of the connected or associated entity prior to insolvency and the exercise of the TPR's moral hazard powers, the courts have deemed the claim to rank as an expense of the insolvency against floating charge realisations. The requirement for an insolvency practitioner to meet a pension scheme's claims ahead of their fees has the potential to disrupt insolvency processes in the future or shape the asset realisation strategies adopted on insolvency.

---

9   The list of categories includes most of the usual types of insolvency, including administration, voluntary arrangements, administrative receivership and most types of liquidation. However, voluntary liquidations, where the directors of the employer have signed a declaration of solvency, are excluded. In addition, it must be the first insolvency event to have occurred to that employer on or after April 6 2005.

Legislative change will likely be needed to settle the position – probably to the insolvency legislation, in our view.

There has been considerable uncertainty in the restructuring profession regarding the TPR's powers and how they may be exercised in cases such as 'pre-pack' insolvencies. The circumstances surrounding the five issued moral hazard powers are particularly extreme and there have been many more cases where either the TPR's powers were not applicable or a negotiated settlement was reached.

Any use of the TPR's moral hazard powers must be deemed 'reasonable', a test which is often determined with reference to the distribution of financial benefit around a corporate group. All five of the successful uses of the TPR's powers have been in situations where some measure of value was transferred from the sponsoring employers (and therefore the pension schemes) to the wider group. Restructuring professionals and corporate groups can limit the potential for unanticipated uses of the TPR's powers through close consideration of the following:

- Historic value movements – to what extent could financial value be deemed to have moved from the employers to the group, for example, through under-value asset transfers or special dividends?
- Reasons for insolvency process – the reasoning behind an employer entering insolvency may have a bearing on whether a use of the TPR's powers is reasonable, for example, where the main driver of insolvency was to limit exposure to a pension scheme.
- Due process and marketing in insolvency – where fair value is obtained and fairly distributed, there is likely to be little additional justification for TPR involvement, even where the business and assets of an employer are returned to a group via a pre-pack.

7.   Outlook

The United Kingdom's low growth period will likely persist for some years. However, the limited volatility has minimised the often-mentioned 'wave' of insolvent restructurings that many were expecting. In particular, the low interest rate environment that existed in 2012, together with lenders' willingness to extend financing, ensured that insolvency rates remained relatively low despite ongoing weakness in many markets.

However, the impact of UK-defined benefit pension schemes in solvent restructuring processes continues to grow, especially where new money or a business sale may be rendered difficult or impossible by a lack of certainty over the use of the TPR's powers. As time goes on, those powers are being used more widely, and as the market becomes more knowledgeable about pension issues, it is likely that there will be less concern from potential investors. This greater flexibility may even arrive in time to buffer any future rise in interest rates and the associated cost of financing.

In general, we expect that transactions involving the PPF and the TPR will become more numerous and complex in nature. We also expect new market providers of financial solutions and advice to emerge and prosper as corporate, lenders and trustees need incremental specialist help. One thing is clear: defined benefit pension issues are firmly on the restructuring agenda and the trend is for them to assume greater importance as key stakeholders in any restructuring.

We hope that this overview of the backdrop, consequence and options available is of benefit to practitioners through what could well continue to be choppy waters.

About the authors

Alan Augustin
Director, PwC
alan.augustin@uk.pwc.com

Alan Augustin is a director in PwC's business recovery services practice.

Mr Augustin spends much of his time in the financial services and wider corporate space providing restructuring and advisory services, and has a particular specialism in the innovative use of schemes of arrangement and similar restructuring mechanisms to deal with contingent liability issues, delivering value for stakeholders in both solvent and distressed arenas.

Mr Augustin's experience in this sector extends worldwide: he has advised on the implementation of scheme and restructuring solutions for multinational organisations in territories including the United Kingdom, Ireland, Bermuda, New Zealand and the Middle East to deal with a range of corporate obligations and long-tail liabilities.

Matthieu Barthélemy
De Pardieu Brocas Maffei
barthelemy@de-pardieu.com

Matthieu Barthélemy has been a member of the Paris Bar since 1999. He holds a master's degree in management from the *Université de Paris – Dauphine*, a master's degree in business law from the *Université de Paris X – Nanterre* and an advanced degree (DESS/Master 2) in business tax law from the *Université de Paris – Dauphine*.

Mr Barthélemy specialises in debt restructuring, distressed companies and insolvency proceedings, particularly in the context of international transactions. He regularly handles financial and commercial litigation matters.

Mr Barthélemy advises French and foreign financial institutions, investment funds as well as French and foreign industrial groups and service providers.

Mr Barthélemy is a member of the Society of Turnaround Professionals (*Association pour le Retournement des Entreprises*).

Mark Batten
Partner, PwC
mark.c.batten@uk.pwc.com

Mark Batten is a partner in PwC's business recovery services practice

Mr Batten has over 25 years' experience of restructuring, particularly within the financial services and real estate sectors.

He has advised on many solvent restructuring cases undertaken for capital, regulatory and tax reasons. He has also acted as scheme adviser for a number of schemes of arrangement for addressing long-tail insurance and other liabilities, in respect of both UK and European books of insurance business.

Mr Batten has also acted as the licensed insolvency practitioner in relation to a number of insolvent insurance companies, many of which have exited from insolvency through schemes of arrangement.

Alastair Beveridge

Partner, Zolfo Cooper

abeveridge@zolfocooper.eu

Alastair Beveridge is a partner in the corporate recovery department at Zolfo Cooper, a leading advisory and restructuring practice. Mr Beveridge is based in London and focuses on business reviews, restructuring and corporate recovery for companies of all sizes and complexities, many with cross-border elements. He is an appointment-taking insolvency practitioner who has been assisting companies in financial difficulty since 1987. He qualified as a chartered accountant with a large international accountancy firm in 1991.

Phil Bowers

Partner, Deloitte LLP

pbowers@deloitte.co.uk

Phil Bowers is a partner in the London office, having worked in restructuring services since 1993. During that time he has worked on formal insolvency assignments and performed complex security/option reviews and asset-based insolvency valuations for lenders and other stakeholders. Mr Bowers has also been involved in advising and assisting directors in respect of solvency issues generally.

Recently Mr Bowers has focused on complex contingency planning and insolvency appointments for various sectors, including structured finance (mainly collateralised mortgage-backed securities (CMBS) transactions and structured investment vehicle restructurings), property, hotel and retail insolvencies.

Ignacio Buil

Senior associate, Cuatrecasas, Gonçalves Pereira

ignacio.buil@cuatrecasas.com

Mr Buil Aldana is a senior associate at Cuatrecasas, Gonçalves Pereira and a member of the finance group in the Madrid office.

Ignacio has extensive experience in financing transactions and debt restructuring operations (both judicial and out-of-court) and negotiation of financing and refinancing agreements with respect to a wide range of capital structures including the refinancing of leveraged buyout financings, project finance, real estate finance and corporate finance. He represents both borrowers and lenders and advises financial institutions, hedge funds and private equity funds in financing and refinancing transactions and distressed investing strategies. He has also participated in several national and multi-jurisdictional financing transactions.

Mr Buil Aldana was a regular associate in the New York office of a major US law, where he represented several debtors and creditor in chapter 11 reorganisations, including advising on 363 sales and debtor-in-possession financings.

Michael Bushnell

Associate, Lincoln International

mbushnell@lincolninternational.com

Michael Bushnell is an associate in the pensions advisory team of Lincoln International in London. He has spent the last six years advising sponsors and trustees on the financial aspects of restructuring and insolvency.

Mr Bushnell has advised clients in a broad range of circumstances and industries, including industrial manufacturing, pharmaceuticals, retail and consumer products, financial services and technology.

In particular, he has advised clients in relation to pursuing and defending financial support directions and contribution notices. He also has extensive experience of solvent corporate restructurings, the use of regulated apportionment arrangements and the negotiation of clearance for pension scheme contribution holidays.

Christine L Childers
Partner, Jenner & Block LLP
cchilders@jenner.com

Christine L Childers is a partner in the bankruptcy, workout and corporate reorganisation, bankruptcy litigation and commercial law and Uniform Commercial Code practice groups of Jenner & Block in Chicago. She graduated *magna cum laude* from the Valparaiso University School of Law. Ms Childers focuses her practice on corporate reorganisation and bankruptcy litigation.

Ms Childers represents a broad range of clients, including Chapter 7 and 11 trustees and creditors, debtors, creditors' committees and lenders in a wide variety of bankruptcy-related matters. In particular, she represented Covanta Energy Corporation and its affiliated entities in their reorganisation and liquidation proceedings, and represented the Chapter 11 trustee of Sentinel Management Group, Inc in liquidation proceedings. She currently represents the liquidation trustee of the Sentinel Liquidation Trust in avoidance actions and other litigation.

Tom Church
Judge, First Tier Tribunal (Social Entitlement Chamber), UK Ministry of Justice

Until recently, Tom Church was a partner in the banking and capital markets team of Berwin Leighton Paisner LLP, based in the firm's London office. His practice covered securitisation, structured finance and other capital markets transactions. Mr Church acted for all constituents in the capital markets, but had a particular focus on advising trustees and agents both on new issues and on post-issue events, including advising in relation to restructurings.

Mr Church has advised on many domestic and cross-border securitisations in relation to assets located in the United Kingdom, France, the Netherlands, Germany, Luxembourg, Italy, Spain, Portugal, Denmark, Sweden and Russia. His practice has covered all major securitisation asset classes, including CMBS, residential mortgage-backed securities, whole businesses, credit cards, real estate, energy offtake receivables and IP and media rights.

Mr Church has been heavily involved in securitisation restructurings, including related consent solicitations, tenders, exchange offers and new issues.

Mr Church now sits as a judge hearing social security cases.

Karl Clowry
Partner, Paul Hastings LLP
karlclowry@paulhastings.com

Karl Clowry is a partner in the finance department of Paul Hastings LLP. His practice focuses on debt finance and restructuring, acting for lenders, special situation investors, bond holders, distressed investors, financial sponsors, loan services, insolvency practitioners and corporate debtors, particularly on large cross-border transactions involving complex capital structures, advising on some of the most high-profile restructurings in leverage financing, real estate finance, commercial mortgage-backed securitisations and sovereign credits.

Mr Clowry has degrees and higher degrees in science and law, and formerly practised as a barrister in London. He regularly speaks at restructuring and banking conferences, and contributes to various financial and restructuring publications.

Philippe Dubois
De Pardieu Brocas Maffei
dubois@de-pardieu.com

Philippe Dubois has been a member of the Paris Bar since 1994 and holds a doctorate in law. He teaches business law at *Université de Paris X – Nanterre*.

Mr Dubois's practice focuses on restructuring and on litigation and arbitration in diverse areas such as shareholder disputes, indemnification agreements and liabilities. He also has considerable experience in real estate financing. He advises banking and financial institutions and large French and foreign industrial groups in a wide range of economic sectors.

Glen Fietta
Director, AlixPartners
gfietta@alixpartners.com

Glen Fietta is a director at AlixPartners, a global restructuring, consultancy and financial advisory firm.

Mr Fietta has worked on a number of high-profile restructurings, including MFI plc, Jarvis plc, Viking Moorings and Readers Digest.

He is accustomed to working as a hands-on adviser or serving in an interim executive capacity to lead the restructuring of a business and its capital structure. In particular, he has deep experience of serving in chief financial officer and board positions within highly leveraged and underperforming businesses. In this context, he has led successful international turnaround plans, public capital raisings and debt restructurings, and has also worked closely with private equity shareholders in order to secure additional equity funding.

Prior to joining AlixPartners as a founding member of the London practice in 2003, Mr Fietta worked in the restructuring and M&A groups of Arthur Andersen. He holds a first-class degree in business administration and is a qualified chartered accountant.

Barry Gross
Partner, Berwin Leighton Paisner LLP
barry.gross@blplaw.com

Barry Gross is a partner in the London real estate department at Berwin Leighton Paisner LLP (BLP), which is consistently ranked as the leading real estate team in England and Wales. He holds a degree in accounting and law and has broad sector

experience acting for lenders, investors and occupiers.

Mr Gross leads the real estate restructuring practice at BLP, working with the restructuring and insolvency team, and acts for lenders, special servicers and debt funds advising on the acquisition, restructuring and enforcement against a variety of properties and structures from buy-to-let portfolios to commercial mortgage-backed security defaults.

Mr Gross has been involved in a number of innovative approaches to restructuring and enforcement, including the creation of asset management platforms for a leading UK lender, enforcement over The Cube in Birmingham and the sale of the White Tower portfolio.

He is a recognised market commentator, appearing on television and radio in relation to market developments. He is also an avid tweeter (@uklegaleagle) and sporadically blogs under the same name.

Martin R Gudgeon
Senior managing director, Blackstone
gudgeon@blackstone.com

Martin Gudgeon is a senior managing director at Blackstone and head of its European restructuring advisory practice. Prior to joining Blackstone, Mr Gudgeon was the chief executive and head of European special situations advisory at Close Brothers Corporate Finance in London. Mr Gudgeon has represented debtor and creditor stakeholders in a broad range of European transactions, including the private sector creditors of Greece, Punch Taverns, Deutsche Annington, Viridian, Northern Rock, British Energy and Eurotunnel.

Paul Hemming
Partner, Zolfo Cooper
phemming@zolfocooper.eu

Paul Hemming is a partner in the corporate finance department at Zolfo Cooper, a leading advisory and restructuring practice. Mr Hemming was recruited in 2002 to develop the firm's corporate finance operations, which focus on complex mandates and distressed M&A. As lead corporate finance adviser for over 20 years, Mr Hemming has worked with a wide range of clients, from entrepreneurial private businesses to major multinational corporations. He has extensive private equity experience working with many of the leading mid-market private equity houses on opportunities across the United Kingdom and Europe.

Jacques Henrot
De Pardieu Brocas Maffei
henrot@de-pardieu.com

Jacques Henrot was admitted to the Paris Bar in 1979. He holds a master's degree from the European School of Management, a *maîtrise* in civil law from the University of Paris II and an LLM from Harvard Law School. He started his career with Sullivan & Cromwell in New York. Mr Henrot specialises in real estate financing matters, leasing, credit insurance, debt restructuring, restructuring of troubled companies and bankruptcy proceedings, both advising clients and representing them in court. He has represented banks, corporations, insurance companies and real estate companies, both in France and abroad.

Alex Hutton-Mills
Managing director, Lincoln International
ahuttonmills@lincolninternational.com

Alex Hutton-Mills is a managing director in the pensions advisory team of Lincoln International in London. Previously at Citigroup, he was part of the global special situations and insurance and pensions structured solutions groups that successfully completed the non-insured buy-out of the Thomson Regional Newspapers Pension Scheme. Since 2008, he has specialised in advising UK pension schemes and sponsors on the financial aspects of corporate transactions.

Recently, Mr Hutton-Mills has led teams advising on the disposal of a major division by a FTSE 100 insurer and on the restructuring of a global packaging business. He also provides advice on regulatory matters to trustees, lending banks and sponsors, including negotiations around Pension Protection Fund entry and clearance procedures.

His broad experience includes transactions in industries including retail and consumer products, financial services, mining, energy and oil and gas, infrastructure and infrastructure services, debt servicing, healthcare, media and telecoms, information services and real estate.

Marina Ivanova
Associate, Goltsblat BLP
Marina.Ivanova@gblplaw.com

Marina Ivanova specialises in commercial disputes, including disputes involving real property or deriving from construction activity, disputes related to the protection of IP rights, bankruptcy and international arbitration.

She has significant experience of representing Russian and foreign clients in international commercial arbitration, as well as in domestic litigation, including bankruptcy proceedings and federal antitrust proceedings.

Ms Ivanova's recent experience in insolvency proceedings has included successful representation of a large sportswear distributor and a large automobile producer in their roles as creditors in respective bankruptcy proceedings.

Ben Jones
Partner, Berwin Leighton Paisner LLP
ben.jones@blplaw.com

Ben Jones is a partner in the restructuring and insolvency team of Berwin Leighton Paisner LLP in London. He specialises in corporate restructuring and insolvency, with experience primarily in financial restructurings. He acts for sponsors, corporates, boards, banks, secondary investors and hedge funds on all aspects of corporate insolvency, restructuring and distress.

Shirish A Joshi
Vice president, Blackstone
joshis@Blackstone.com

Shirish Joshi is a vice president at Blackstone and a member of the European restructuring practice in London. Before joining Blackstone in 2007, Mr Joshi assisted in advising on a variety of restructuring transactions in the European special situations group of Houlihan, Lokey, Howard & Zukin. Selected restructuring transactions include Tus Group, Skeie Drilling & Production, Corral/Preem Petroleum, Profine, Nybron, Basis Capital, Polestar and Gate Gourmet.

Ben Larkin
Berwin Leighton Paisner LLP
Ben.Larkin@blplaw.com

Ben Larkin is head of the restructuring and insolvency department of Berwin Leighton Paisner LLP. He has specialised in restructuring and insolvency since qualifying as a solicitor in 1993 and has a significant reputation as an expert in workouts related to structured finance and real estate.

Notable recent assignments include advising the administrators of the White Tower conduit, one of the largest UK securitisation administrations to date; the administration of the Readers Digest group of companies; the restructuring of Marken Limited; the restructuring of the Q Hotels group; advising the Robert Dyas group on the sale of the group's parent company; the restructuring of the European Directories group; and the real estate restructuring of Westferry Circus.

Mr Larkin is recognised as a leader in his field in both *Chambers* and *Legal 500* and is a regular speaker at industry events.

Andres F Martinez
Private sector development specialist, World Bank
AMartinez3@ifc.org

Andres F Martinez is a private sector development specialist for the World Bank Group's Investment Climate Debt Resolution and Insolvency Technical Assistance Programme, providing technical assistance to governments around the world. He advises governments on insolvency reforms focusing on Eastern Europe and the Middle East and North Africa, and is currently working on insolvency reform projects in eight different countries. Prior to this, he led the "Resolving Insolvency" chapter of the World Bank-International Finance Corporation *Doing Business* report, which captures insolvency reforms around the world, at the same time leading the dialogue with insolvency practitioners, judges and policy makers.

Mr Martinez is an Argentine lawyer (2000) admitted to the Buenos Aires Bar. Prior to joining the World Bank Group in 2008, he practised for several years as a senior associate in the area of insolvency and creditors' rights at a leading Argentine firm, based in Buenos Aires.

Antonia Menezes
Private sector development specialist,
World Bank Group
AMenezes1@ifc.org

Antonia Menezes is a private sector development specialist in the World Bank Group's investment climate debt resolution and insolvency team. She primarily works in Africa, the Middle East and South Asia, advising governments on strengthening creditor rights and insolvency systems. She has lectured and published in this field. Prior to this, Ms Menezes was a lawyer at Shearman & Sterling LLP in Paris and Linklaters in London, where she worked in international arbitration and alternative dispute resolution for a variety of private and public sector clients. She holds an LLM from McGill University, the LPC from the Oxford Institute of Legal Practice and an LLB from the London School of Economics.

Heinrich Meyer

Partner, BEITEN BURKHARDT

Heinrich.Meyer@bblaw.com

Heinrich Meyer is partner and co-head of the restructuring and insolvency practice group at BEITEN BURKHARDT's Frankfurt office. He advises on the financial aspects of restructurings, insolvency law as well as bank regulatory law. In particular, he advises national and international clients in respect of all financing issues, security agreements, banking supervisory provisions and insolvency-related matters, including contractual trust agreements.

Mr Meyer studied law at the Universities of Würzburg, Lausanne and Regensburg, and was admitted to the German Bar in 1993. After his legal studies, from 1991 until 1997, he worked at Deutsche Bank AG in the fields of financial risk management and work-outs. He subsequently joined KPMG. He has been working with BEITEN BURKHARDT since 2002 and became partner in 2004.

Hugh Mildred

Senior associate, Berwin Leighton Paisner LLP

hugh.mildred@blplaw.com

Hugh Mildred is a solicitor in the banking and capital markets team, based in the firm's London office. He specialises in acting for banks and financial institutions in relation to structured finance, collateralised debt obligations, collateralised loan obligations and derivatives transactions, and has experience in a broad range of securitisation asset classes, including CMBS, whole business and credit cards in both domestic and cross-border transactions

Recently Mr Mildred has been heavily involved in advising on the restructuring of real estate structured finance transactions.

Anton Panchenkov

Head of group, Goltsblat BLP

anton.panchenkov@gblplaw.com

Anton Panchenkov has broad experience in advising on corporate/M&A transactions, private equity, joint ventures, corporate restructuring, corporate governance and corporate finance projects. He also focuses on restructuring and insolvency. He advises a wide range of clients, from local mid-level corporates to international and Russian blue-chips.

Before joining Goltsblat BLP in 2008, Mr Panchenkov worked for five years as head of legal and corporate for a major Russian glass manufacturer, where he was responsible for the integrated debt restructuring programme, a number of corporate restructurings, various M&A projects related to industrial, merchandising and logistic assets and business units, as well as representing the company on governing bodies (boards of directors and audit commissions) of subsidiaries and affiliated entities.

Iñigo Rubio

Partner, Cuatrecasas, Gonçalves Pereira

inigo.rubio@cuatrecasas.com

Iñigo Rubio specialises in advising on the financing of infrastructure projects (public-private partnerships and private finance initiatives) and real estate projects, whether simple, syndicated or structured (eg, sale and leaseback and off-balance sheet transactions).

He also has ample experience in corporate and asset finance, and debt restructuring transactions, having participated in several of the most important and complex refinancing processes in recent years.

Since joining Cuatrecasas, Gonçalves Pereira in 2000, Mr Rubio has developed most of his career in the firm's offices in Madrid and then London, where he was managing partner between 2010 and 2013.

Jaime Ruiz Rocamora
Associate, Cuatrecasas, Gonçalves Pereira
jaime.ruiz@cuatrecasas.com

Jaime Ruiz specialises in advising on insolvency proceedings, effects on executor and non-executor contracts, claw-back actions, classification of insolvency proceedings, composition agreements negotiation and liquidation plans.

Also, he specialises in resolving corporate disputes, in both the pre-litigation and litigation phases. He has participated in several proceedings challenging directors' liability resolutions, enforcements and civil and commercial contracts.

He worked at Pérez Alati, Grondona, Benites, Arntsen & Martínez de Hoz in Buenos Aires, Argentina (2007-2008), where he advised on capital markets financings, international debt offerings to issuers and underwriters and issuance of convertible debt and exchangeable securities by the largest companies and banks in Argentina.

Mark Shaw
Partner, BDO LLP
mark.shaw@bdo.co.uk

Mark Shaw leads the London business restructuring team at BDO LLP.

He specialised in insolvency at the start of his career, moving into restructuring work following a secondment to the Royal Bank of Scotland plc. He has also undertaken corporate finance and expert witness work.

Mr Shaw has acted on a wide variety of restructuring and insolvency matters in the United Kingdom and globally over the course of his career.

Graeme Smith
Partner, Zolfo Cooper
gsmith@zolfocooper.eu

Graeme Smith is a partner in the corporate finance department at Zolfo Cooper, a leading advisory and restructuring practice. Mr Smith has worked in the corporate finance industry for around 15 years, with the past seven years being spent executing complex M&A, refinancing and restructuring transactions. These transactions have been completed across a number of European jurisdictions, with a particular focus on deals in the hotel, leisure and retail sectors. After qualifying as an accountant with PricewaterhouseCoopers, he joined the European M&A team at investment bank Dresdner Kleinwort before joining Zolfo Cooper in 2005.

David Soden
Director, Deloitte LLP
dsoden@deloitte.co.uk

David Soden specialises in all aspects of corporate recovery, with a focus on restructuring and insolvency advice and implementation. He has worked on a number of complex multi-jurisdictional cases for lenders in all tranches of the capital structure, management and equity. He joined Deloitte in 2006 and has over nine years' experience of restructuring assignments.

During the past four years he has undertaken significant financial services engagements, leading the Whistlejacket and Rhinebridge structured investment vehicle receiverships and the receivership of Clio European CLO. He has also developed significant experience in the real estate sector, following various advisory assignments for UK house builders and property development companies and special servicers to CMBS vehicles.

Mr Soden holds a BSc from the University of Warwick, and is a chartered accountant and a qualified insolvency practitioner.

Elena Trusova
Partner, Goltsblat BLP
Elena.Trusova@gblplaw.com

Elena Trusova's practice areas are commercial disputes, insolvency and bankruptcy, international arbitration, IP protection, antitrust disputes, disputes over real property and unfair competition.

Ms Trusova has accumulated vast experience in handling commercial disputes in arbitration courts, courts of general jurisdiction and international commercial arbitrations (International Commercial Arbitration Court, Stockholm Chamber of Commerce, London Court of International Arbitration).

Mr Trusova has represented major manufacturers of cosmetics, construction materials, motor and food companies and banks in insolvency proceedings.

She is an attorney at law, a member of the Moscow Region Chamber of Attorneys since 2002 and a patent attorney of the Russian Federation.

Mahesh Uttamchandani
Global product leader, World Bank
Muttamchandani@worldbank.org

Mahesh Uttamchandani is the global product leader for the World Bank Group's Investment Climate Debt Resolution and Insolvency Technical Assistance Programme, providing technical assistance to governments around the world. Previously, Mr Uttamchandani was a senior counsel in the World Bank's Legal Vice Presidency and led the World Bank's Insolvency and Creditors' Rights Report on the Observance of Standards and Codes Initiative. Prior to joining the World Bank, Mr Uttamchandani was insolvency counsel to the European Bank for Reconstruction and Development in London. He has extensive experience of advising governments of developing and transition economies on insolvency matters.

Mr Uttamchandani is a Canadian lawyer who practised for several years exclusively in the area of insolvency and creditors' rights at a leading Canadian law firm. He is a board member of International Corporate Rescue and an adjunct professor of law on the St John's University LLM in insolvency.

Fedra Valencia
Partner, Cuatrecasas, Gonçalves Pereira
fedra.valencia@cuatrecasas.com

Fedra Valencia is a renowned specialist in the legal management of bankruptcy proceedings and corporate and financial restructuring transactions. She has participated in several bankruptcy proceedings, including some of the most relevant on a national scale, as well as in debt refinancing transactions (both in and out of court) and corporate restructuring agreements, which were beneficial for her clients with respect to their creditors. She is also an expert in administrative liability.

Throughout her professional career, she has advised and represented various debtors in the preparation, presentation and follow-up of bankruptcy proceedings, including many companies in the real estate and industrial sectors, as well as participating in agreement proposals and *ad hoc* processes arising from the aforementioned proceedings (both ordinary and reintegration).

She has also represented the interests of creditors, advising financial institutions and companies in corporate bankruptcy proceedings across a wide variety of sectors.

Ian Wormleighton
Partner, Deloitte LLP
iwormleighton@deloitte.co.uk

Ian Wormleighton is a partner in the Deloitte restructuring team based in London and has over 10 years' experience in the sector specialising in contingency planning, stakeholder management and insolvency based solutions.

In recent years Mr Wormleighton has undertaken a number of significant engagements in the financial services sector, including the receivership and restructuring of a number of structured investment vehicles and other property and pub securitisations.

Mr Wormleighton is a chartered accountant and a qualified insolvency practitioner.

Index

Globe Law
and Business

Related titles

European Debt Restructuring Handbook

Leading Case Studies from the ...
Consulting Editors Kon Asimacopoulos and Justin ...

Cash Pooling and Insolvency

Cross-Border Insolvency

A Commentary on the UNCITRAL Model Law,
Third Edition
General Editor Look Chan Ho

for further details and a free sample chapter go to
www.globelawandbusiness.com